Andrew Lambert is Laughton Professor of Naval History at King's College London. His books include *Nelson: Britannia's God of War*, *Admirals: The Naval Commanders Who Made Britain Great*, *Franklin: Tragic Hero of Polar Navigation*, *The Challenge: Britain Against America in the Naval War of 1812*, for which he was awarded the Anderson Medal, and *The Crimean War: British Grand Strategy Against Russia 1853–1856*. His highly successful history of the Royal Navy, *War at Sea*, was broadcast on BBC Two.

Further praise for *Crusoe's Island*:

'In *Crusoe's Island*, naval historian Andrew Lambert traces the history of island castaways and the rich cultural history that their experiences have inspired . . . In this imaginative book, Lambert uses the history of one small group of Pacific islands to illustrate England's and Britain's break with a narrow European sense of identity as it turned into a global power, and demonstrates the role that literature played in this transition . . . a brilliant achievement that demonstrates Lambert's vast knowledge of maritime history.' A.W. Purdue, *Times Higher Education Supplement*

'Engaging . . . This is vibrant history and Lambert teases out the individual stories of treachery and opportunism among the privateers . . . Lambert traces the development of the seesaw relationship between Britain and these islands which the British never formally owned . . . His story spans five centuries and is told chronologically in nimble chapters. With so much to say, the action whips along at a pace . . . As the EU totters and our union falters, Lambert's enquiry begins to feel less like a foray into the past and more like an urgent investigation into that strange blend of qualities that bound Britain together in the first place.' Peter Moore, *Literary Review*

'[Lambert] takes the reader on a steady voyage, from the moment the uninhabited islands emerged from the gloom of geographical ignorance after the Spaniard Fernández discovered them in the sixteenth century. The tales involves piracy, the South Sea Bubble, fish "so plentiful that in less than one hour's time two men caught enough for our whole company", whaling, sealing, shifts in imperial ambition following Britain's loss of America, evolving global trade patterns and the fashion for oceanic travel books.' Sara Wheeler, *Spectator*

'Lambert, a highly respected naval historian, describes the many expeditions, as well as their military and economic contexts, with characteristic aplomb . . . a very entertaining volume.' Jonathan Wright, *National*

'Lambert, a renowned naval historian, does an excellent job at showing the power these remote islands exerted over the British imagination.' Ben Wilson, *Sunday Telegraph*

'A thought-provoking book.' Roger Lewis, *The Times*

'One of the most eminent naval historians of our age.' Amanda Foreman

---

by the same author

Trincomalee: The Last of Nelson's Frigates
War at Sea in the Age of the Sail
The Foundations of Naval History
The Crimean War: Grand Strategy Against Russia 1853–1856
Nelson: Britannia's God of War
Admirals: The Naval Commanders Who Made Britain Great
Franklin: Tragic Hero of Polar Navigation
The Challenge: Britain Against America in the Naval War of 1812

Crusoe's Island

A Rich and Curious History of Pirates,
Castaways and Madness

ANDREW LAMBERT

FABER & FABER

First published in 2016
by Faber & Faber Ltd
Bloomsbury House
74–77 Great Russell Street
London WC1B 3DA
This paperback edition first published in 2017
First published in the USA in 2017

Typeset by JS Typesetting Ltd
Printed and bound in the UK by CPI Group (UK) Ltd, Croydon CR0 4YY

A CIP record for this book is available from the British Library

ISBN 978–0–571–33024–9

FSC
www.fsc.org
MIX
Paper from
responsible sources
FSC® C020471

2 4 6 8 10 9 7 5 3 1

This book is dedicated to my fellow travellers
on the 2010 Caligari Expedition

Contents

List of Illustrations ix
Preface xi
Acknowledgements xiii

CONTENTS

List of Illustrations

—◦◦◦—

Victorian statue of Alexander Selkirk (photograph by
  Sylvia Stanley)
Daniel Defoe, creator of Robinson Crusoe
Frontispiece illustration and title page of the first edition of
  The Life and Adventures of Robinson Crusoe
  (© Bettmann / Getty Images)-
The island of Utopia from Thomas More's *Utopia*, 1516
  (© Culture Club / Getty Images)
Herman Moll's 'New and Exact Map of the Coast, Countries
  and Islands within the Limits of the South Sea Company'
Coastal perspective of the anchorage in Cumberland Bay,
  Juan Fernández (The National Archives, ref. ADM344/2256)
William Dampier, buccaneer author
George, Lord Anson
Lord Anson's encampment on Juan Fernández (courtesy of
  King's College London, Foyle Special Collections Library)
Elephant seals on Juan Fernández (courtesy of King's College
  London, Foyle Special Collections Library)
Selkirk's fabled cave, Juan Fernández (© Classic Image /
  Alamy Stock Photo)
Advertisement for 'Scientific & Sporting Cruise', 1910
  (pg. 4; Issue 39303 © Times Newspapers Ltd)
SMS *Dresden* in Cumberland Bay (© IWM, Q 46021)
View of El Yunque, Juan Fernández (Andrew Lambert)
Cumberland Bay, Juan Fernández (Andrew Lambert)

Preface

This book addresses the long, curious relationship between English identity and an island on the other side of the world, one that was never owned by Britain, and only very briefly occupied by British sailors. Despite that, Juan Fernández (now officially known as Robinson Crusoe Island) assumed a remarkable place in British naval and imaginative literature in the first half of the eighteenth century. Daniel Defoe's *Robinson Crusoe* and Commodore Anson's *Voyage*, the best-selling publications in their respective genres, set the island within a distinctive English vision, at once oceanic, global, insular and dynamic.

Both quickly escaped their intended audience, achieving striking international success. They helped to sustain British dominance of the oceans in an easily accessible and yet highly structured way. Not only did eighteenth-century Britons have the self-confidence to project themselves onto an island on the other side of the world, but these texts, and the genres they created, shaped ideas of Britishness, as Scotland, Ireland and Wales adopted a predominantly English approach to the world, and those ideas stretched around the world. Over time, these quintessentially English cultural productions would escape the distinction between fact and fiction, and were translated, copied, emulated and developed into truly international possessions.

Ultimately Juan Fernández became a mirror held up to the English, one in which they perceived themselves and their ambitions. It acquired an abiding place in the national culture because every generation found a reason to return. If their Spanish and Chilean owners ever thought about these tiny islands, they saw them as a burden, a threat or at best a navigational beacon.

There was no land to farm, there were no minerals to extract, and there seemed little reason to remain beyond denying them to English pirates. By contrast Juan Fernández played a critical role in expanding English intellectual horizons, one that is hard to estimate. Literate visitors like William Dampier, Woodes Rogers and George Anson offered the English a way of seeing the world, one that suited their insular character and seafaring focus. Those voyages opened new horizons, and this book tries to locate them.

Defoe Avenue, Kew, 2015

Acknowledgements

—◦◦◦—

A project of this scope incurs many debts, first and foremost to Jürgen Stumpfhaus and everyone at Caligari Films, for the journey that inspired the book, and the fine company they assembled on the island. A sense of place is essential to any historical enquiry, nowhere more so than that outlandish place Juan Fernández. Once again the forbearance and understanding of my family meant I could travel, and the Department of War Studies at Kings College, London allowed me to reorganise my teaching to create the necessary space. My thanks are due to staff and students for that indulgence. It was greatly appreciated. I hope this small book is at a least a record of not entirely wasted time. Once I returned, absorbed with Crusoe and the Great South Seas, I turned to those who knew far more than I, among whom Glyn Williams was, once again, an unfailing source of wisdom and insight. The Great South Sea is his domain, and I a mere interloper. I have debts to many more, Larrie Ferreiro, Jonathan Lamb, Anne Savours, Catherine Scheybeler, Carlos Corben Trombalen, and many more who indulged in conversation about an island at the end of the world. They did much to save the author from his errors and omissions, but I alone bear final responsibility for what appears.

And then there is Julian Loose, editor extraordinaire, who once again indulged a strange idea from a wild-eyed, scurvied traveller, sketched in a salt-stained journal. The production team at Faber have once again rendered the traveller's tale coherent, and delivered a book that melds the worlds of travellers, poets, scientists and artists, with war, cannibalism and madness.

Introduction

Robinson Crusoe emerged into the daylight on 1 February 1709, when an English boat crew encountered 'a Man cloath'd in Goat Skins, who looked wilder than the first Owners of them'[1] on the beach of a distant island. The goatskin-clad castaway, Alexander Selkirk (a Scot), had been marooned on Juan Fernández Island for four years and four months. When he arrived home his story, suitably garnished with captured treasure, caught the imagination of a newly forged British nation, tired of continental wars and despotic monarchs. Selkirk became an instant (if short-lived) celebrity. His tale helped promote the greatest stock market fraud of all time; it also inspired the modern novel, and ultimately came to define a peculiarly English way of seeing the world. In the process his island found a place on every map, its minuscule dimensions and long name defeating all attempts to preserve the scale of the South Pacific.

When Daniel Defoe created Crusoe he set the story on a very different island, on the other side of South America, but no one cared. Juan Fernández became Crusoe's island despite the author's intentions – and so it has remained. Defoe had other plans for Crusoe: he created this half-German hybrid hero as an exemplary Englishman, a model for George I, the incoming Hanoverian King, who Defoe hoped would become an enlightened, insular ruler, keeping his island apart from the entangling dangers of Europe, the better to prosper through expanding worlds of trade and maritime endeavour. In the two centuries that followed the vision Defoe set out in 1719, dominated British policy. George's great grandson George III became a Robinsonian leader, promoting trade, exploration and agriculture, while refusing to visit his continental dominions. In this maritime world view, an empire of islands and oceans mattered far more than European territory and subject peoples.

Focusing on the English/British engagement with this one tiny green speck amid a vast ocean will help to unravel the complex DNA of a unique world view, tracing its lineage through buccaneers and pirates, intellectuals and lunatics, explore its later development and ask if such distinctively oceanic ideas have any place amid the ever-closer homogeneity of a European Union. Meanwhile Scotland debates the dissolution of the United Kingdom, and the three hundredth anniversary of Crusoe's publication looms. It seems the British, having forgotten their past, cannot plot a course for the future. We need to remember the stories that made us, and re-examine what they mean, to be reconciled with any present, or future. Until we admit to an oceanic and insular past there can be no intelligent debate about the future, because we are the children of Crusoe.

—⌒⊙∅∅⌒—

This book is about journeys – journeys made, imagined and remade. It revolves around a very small island in the South Pacific, one that witnessed many such journeys – journeys that made it famous, and gave it the name of a fictional character.

My journey was driven by a combination of older journeys, curiosity and opportunity. On 28 November 2010 I left Defoe Avenue in Kew, heading for Robinson Crusoe's Island, Más a Tierra in the Juan Fernández group, via Heathrow and Frankfurt, where I met up with a German crew from Caligari Films, led by director Jürgen Stumpfhaus, and two German academics. After the interminable ordeal of checking in a complete arsenal of camera and lighting gear, boxes of props and a little personal luggage, we boarded a flight to Santiago de Chile via Madrid.

Having come straight from a hectic work schedule, essential to free up time for the trip, it only slowly began to register that we were heading for a quasi-mythic island, in pursuit of

Robinson Crusoe, Alexander Selkirk, Lord Anson, and even the eponymous Juan Fernández. We split up for the flight; we would be spending a lot of time together once we arrived. By the time we touched down at Madrid I had reread Defoe's classic, and begun to contemplate islands. Jürgen had been before, filming the German Juan Fernández story, the sinking of the cruiser *Dresden* in 1915. He retailed wild and strange tales, which I would come to recognise as modern-day robinsonades – tales of adventure set in a real landscape, but endlessly retold to the point of mythology.

Fourteen-hour flights are rarely a pleasure, but this one passed without undue strain. The moving map of the world ticked off well-known names in Africa and then Brazil, food arrived at intervals, and the cabin was largely lost in the silence of sleep and the curious practice of watching cinema blockbusters on a thumbnail screen, only inches away. Leg stretches and meal breaks broke the monotony. By the time we reached South America the sun was high, showing the country around the Argentine city of Cordoba in stark relief from 30,000 feet. Then we reached the Andes, top-lit by the noonday sun, a mighty range of implausibly steep, jagged peaks each one seemingly reaching up to heaven, many flecked with snow. This monstrous wall barred the path west to mere mortals, but we sailed over, serene and swift. No sooner had we crested the peaks than Santiago hove into view, a fresh sensation of sparkling light and brown smog as the descent began. Touchdown was a relief, but it heralded fresh toil. Having queued through immigration, and begun collecting and checking the mass of bags, we were relieved by the arrival of Martin Westcott, our Anglo-Chilean facilitator, who turned up just in time to explain the German invasion to a nervous customs officer. A friendly face, local expertise and colloquial Spanish was most welcome as the Chileans wanted every detail of our immense baggage train. Eventually the ordeal was over, and we moved to the domestic side of the airport.

Only now did we venture outside, into a baking hot Santiago summer afternoon. Fresh in from freezing London and dressed accordingly, the heat was a shock, but a pleasant one. After crossing the airstrip we found the Aerotransportes Araucana aircraft that would take us over to the island, a pair of twin-engine Beechcraft. Given the slightly lurid stories passing round about the short airstrip I took some comfort from the fact that the pilot was of a good vintage. Both planes were packed with gear, bags and finally bodies, every space occupied. Even so this leg of the journey contained strong elements of normality, aircraft, airports and passengers. We were just flying to another place; surely it would be much like everywhere else.

Then we landed. Everything changed. First impressions were not good. The airstrip ran from one side of the island to the other, it was metalled, but strangely quiet. There was a new airport building, but there was no one in the tower, indeed the whole building was empty. Outside a small group of passengers were waiting to board our plane, and they were going to share the journey back to Santiago with a stack of wriggling banana boxes. The second plane landed and we began the heroic task of getting all the gear out, loading it onto a battered truck and moving off. One of the outbound crew was a Chilean archaeologist who had been studying the defences, recording the artillery pieces of the Spanish era. Befuddled by the journey, I forgot to make any notes of his conversation, or his name. I lifted the lid of a banana box only to find a dozen bound crayfish, clawless crustaceans of truly gargantuan proportions. Destined for the surf and turf restaurants of Santiago, they had little more than six hours to live.

I may have been stunned by the gaunt, grim landscape, a scattering of vibrant red poppies lighting up the desiccated remains of what had once been topsoil, deep gullies evidently eroded by rain and wind, filled with rocks and other debris. There was something post-apocalyptic about these ridges of reddish/brown desert emptiness, stretching out to sea in most directions. We hurried on down the road to Horseshoe Bay, la Heradura, otherwise known as Bahía del Padre. Rounding the crest of the ridge opened a magnificent view of an almost perfectly circular bay, with a single exit, a deep wet space, packed with seals and sea lions. The steep cliffs were savagely eroded, with jumbled rocks piled up closer to the shore. Once we reached the jetty there was more loading to exercise tired, stiff muscles, filling two open boats with gear and passengers. All around the bay seals and sea lions sported and snorted.

The boats took us along the coast, past strange rock formations jutting out of the sea, so weirdly anthropomorphic that they seemed to come straight from the set of *King Kong*. Elsewhere waterfalls fell into the ocean, while valleys of lush greenery, desiccated peaks, sheer cliffs and the odd rocky ledged linked island and ocean. Wherever an opening existed seals and sea lions clustered. Dolphins sported in the free rider zone just ahead of the boat. Birds clustered above, a sure sign that far below immense cetaceans were hunting these rich waters. Almost as soon as we left the bay, the light faded and the wind picked up, hinting that rain was not far away.

The journey was long, for around each new headland another stretched into view, a landscape seemingly without end. Those who had been before offered a little guidance, but the spectacle defied easy comprehension. Our boatman and his son were amused by our surprise; for them this was the daily commute, not a voyage of wonder.

Finally we rounded the last headland, pushing into Cumberland Bay under a lowering sky and scudding clouds, the temperature already 20 degrees lower than it had been on the sunlit concrete airstrip at Santiago. Ahead a Chilean Navy landing ship, tied up alongside the prominent concrete jetty, was loading scrap metal by noisy crane-loads.

As we stepped out of the boat and began hauling our gear up weed-encrusted steps, the low cloud base, a cool breeze and the lugubrious face of our new guide left me wondering just what I had let myself in for. Pedro Niada spoke movingly of a great wave that had roared into the bay ten months before, smashing into the village, and washing his new waterfront hotel into the bay, along with his wife and children. He pointed to a platform of smooth stones, and the low cover of nasturtiums, before describing their miraculous escape. As Pedro and his wife struggled to keep the children afloat, a boat drifted past, they scrambled aboard, and reached the shore. They lost everything but their children. The hotel was reduced to matchwood; the old Land Rover became a fish trap.

There were raw gashes in the foreshore, recently turned earth, wild poppies and a striking growth of scrub. Old donkeys and broken-down horses grazed amid the chaos. On the beach bundles of twisted metal, corrugated iron sheet, smashed timber and weed-encrusted wreckage lay ready for embarkation. Just then a team of scuba divers came back to the shore, at the end of another day spent clearing the bay. As they trooped off to the container that provided a base I was transfixed by the sight of a large satellite dish, at least 30 feet across, parked amid the trees at a crazy angle. Festooned with weed, twisted out of shape and broken it looked for all the world like the paddle wheel of some long lost Mississippi steam boat, abandoned in the shallows of Louisiana bayou.

Another day would reveal much more, but first impressions linger. San Juan Bautista had been hit hard, and so had I. Before I had time to ask any more questions another boat arrived, and we began to load the gear for a short journey across the bay. The metallic clanging crash of bundled scrap hitting the deck of the landing ship punctuated the evening, the wind fell away and the boats puttered across to Bahía Pangal, the last hotel left standing. Here we resumed the routine of heavy lifting, this time up slippery, broken steps. We were tired and hungry, and the work was harder than ever as we laboured like ancient donkeys under a weight of stores that implied prolonged occupation. Finally the procession ended and we took possession of a curious hotel with all mod cons, save the two we really wanted: hot water and global communications.

The relief and release was wonderful, a fine meal of local fish and Chilean wine restored the spirits, and we had a chance to reflect on exactly what had brought us to the ends of the earth.

We had come in search of Alexander Selkirk, the Scots mariner who spent four years on the island, and his legendary alter ego Robinson Crusoe; we had also come to find Lord Anson and Juan Fernández. These ancient names still owned the island, but the reality of their occupation had long since been lost. The film crew had come to tell these stories, I was here to add some history, while the German scientists knew a great deal about the island's ecological history. The search would be long – an opportunity for an ongoing expert seminar, mixing local and imported knowledge, both unique, and largely distinct. Once again I had landed in a strange place with some engaging companions. This book is the result of that journey, as well as a longer, more fluid exploration of the subject across the myriad of sources, subjects and situations that it inspired.

It had not always been so easy to reach the island, but even in the twenty-first century it retains an other-worldly quality, a place out of time and mind, one that inspired diseased and excited mariners to fantasise about paradise. Even now it grips the post-modern imagination as the putative home of Robinson Crusoe, the ultimate castaway, a universal story of the human spirit overcoming adversity. Three hundred years later Defoe's tale still has the capacity to upset the equilibrium of otherwise sane people.

I

Of Islands and Englishmen

Juan Fernández exists in the English imagination because it is a distant, tiny island that was never English, a shimmering rocky speck, wrapped in lush vegetation, set in an azure ocean of dreams. In the fifteenth century, before America had been discovered, English writers began to emphasise that their island stood apart from Europe, emphasising the commercial and strategic advantages that flowed from controlling the sea. Such thoughts pre-dated the disastrous end of the Hundred Years War, and the shattering Wars of the Roses. Ambitious monarchs still dreamed of an English Empire in Europe, but the reality proved less glorious. Defeated in Europe and diminished by internal strife English monarchs did well to die in their beds. Their weakness invited invasion. Without control of the Channel no English King was safe against invaders bent on usurping his throne. Successful usurper Henry VII adopted a different approach, based on warships, coastal defences and the search for new markets outside Europe. Insularity became the basis of a policy, driven by weakness and fear, but it had limited economic value until New Worlds were discovered. In the meantime the English created a suitably mythic seafaring identity, an island nation at once enterprising and outward looking, tales retold so many times that they acquired a sort of truth.

Reformation, religious persecution and the French invasion attempt of 1545 emphasised differences, unifying the country against a European 'other', foreign in tongue and faith, and all too obviously hostile. The English sense of insularity, being set apart, and self-contained, kept on growing. Shakespeare's England may have been 'set in a silver sea', but it was the ability of his contemporaries to command that sea that allowed the English project to progress despite the weakness of the state, in manpower and money, when set against Habsburg Spain and Valois France. Little wonder imaginative Englishmen chose distant island settings for their imperial dreams.

As Tudor England struggled to find a place in a Europe of expanding nation states, an over-mighty Habsburg Empire that spanned the Atlantic and a Universal Church, Thomas More offered the policy-makers of the era an idealised England far from danger. More understood Continental politics only too well. His *Utopia* of 1516 was an alternative England, a place of peace and equality, beyond the menace and violence of the continent, and the threat it posed to English interests.[1] The book opened in Antwerp, the greatest commercial city of northern Europe, where Raphael Hythloday (literally Raphael Nonsense), a Portuguese traveller, brought news from Utopia, which he had visited after sailing to America with Amerigo Vespucci, the Florentine adventurer who gave his name to two continents. The imaginative way in which More read Vespucci's text reflected the realities of contemporary travel writing – a fanciful, sensationalist literature.[2] Older texts were read into the landscape, travellers expecting to experience the same sensations as their precursors. Vespucci's hyperventilated descriptions of his first encounter with America suggest the effect of scurvy, a reality that quickly unravels any attempt to assess truth and falsehood in his writings. More reworked these imaginative writings into an English vision, building on the classical learning of the Renaissance. The facility with which the Utopians learned Greek, and developed printing, emphasised More's humanist approach, as did the reference to Venetian printer Aldus Manutius. Among the Greek texts Hythloday passed to the Utopians were Aldine editions of Thucydides and Herodotus, the core texts of seapower imperialism.[3]

More placed his island in Vespucci's America. He wrote only twenty years after Columbus's first voyage, when this largely unknown land was still being read through layers of classical philosophy and geography. Vespucci's America linked the new world with Paradise. Yet behind the humanist scholarship and American discoveries, real or imagined, More recast English diplomatic and strategic policy to escape the snares of a European diplomatic system increasingly beyond English control. He advised retreating to the island and changing the economic model. To represent his policy choice More made the island an artificial construction. King Utopos had cut a fifteen-mile-wide channel and civilised the Utopians at the same time: the two processes were intimately connected. His quest for insular security created Britain's enduring preference for island bases. Far from compiling a text on an ideal political and social system, More stressed that in order to avoid the baleful influence of Europe it would be necessary to live without the advantages of external trade.

Parallels with the mature British Empire are obvious. His imagined society had strikingly English characteristics. While generations of commentators have been fascinated by communist approaches to private property and production, and the more unusual social customs of the imaginary islanders, few have troubled to ask why Utopia was an island, and an artificial one at that. More moved among the policy-making elite of Tudor England, he worked closely with the Chief Minister, and grew up in the household of his predecessor. He did not invent these policy options, he retailed ideas that were already beginning to transform the idea of Englishness, in response to a changing European power structure.

The island identity extended across the new world: Utopians, like all islanders, were curious about the outside world, and carried their exports to market in their own ships – an approach that anticipated the Navigation Laws in the mid-seventeenth century. He wrote, it should be recalled, at a time when the English had little expertise in oceanic navigation, most English exports travelled to Antwerp or the Mediterranean in foreign ships. Among the greatest achievements of Utopian science were studies of the heavenly bodies, the key to oceanic navigation.[4]

Such attainments echoed Vespucci's boasts, and appealed to the scientific mind of Francis Bacon.

The key to More's text was a woodcut illustration, with three-masted ships in the foreground. Three-masted ships made it possible for the English to choose another identity, as an island race, seeking out and trading with the rest of the world, exerting power by controlling the sea. *Utopia* helped shape the English world view, providing it with an enduringly insular character.

More opened the English mind to ideal islands, linked to Plato's Atlantis. A century later Francis Bacon, another philosophical statesman aiming to influence policy, took the concept a stage further, situating his island in a Pacific Ocean unknown to More or the ancients. Bacon's *New Atlantis* of 1627, which opened with the evocative phrase 'we sailed from Peru', constructed an insular location that melded contemporary knowledge of the 'South Sea' and the nature of scurvy, with a smattering of seaman-like terms, mostly borrowed from travel narratives. The more immediate models for such writing were the voyage narrative of Fernández de Quirós, reporting a possible *Terra Australis Incognita* in the South Seas, Will Adams's letters from Japan, and Raleigh's *Discovery of Guiana*. All three were in print in England when Bacon wrote; elements from all three appear in his text. When the planned voyage to China or Japan falters the navigators find themselves at a South Sea island state of advanced Christian peoples. After a period in Quarantine, a distinctly Mediterranean approach to sickly mariners, although in this case taken from Adams's account of his reception in Japan, the travellers joined their hosts. The islanders had long been aware of the outside world, using covert missions to collect information, while their intellectual resources included otherwise unknown ancient wisdom, including books on natural history written by King Solomon, deliberately confused and conflated with an ancient king of the island named Solamona, architect of the islanders' universal search for knowledge.[5] Bacon's link between advanced islanders, ancient learning and sea-based research methods was a classic statement of the humanism, inspired by the transmission of ancient wisdom through Byzantium and the Arab world to Europe, specifically through the print shops of Venice.

Ultimately Bacon's magical island was both a haven of peace and civilisation, and universal research centre. This imagined land reflected a personal agenda, voiced by one of the islanders: 'The end of our foundation is the knowledge of causes and secret motions of things; and the enlarging of the bounds of human empire, to the effecting of all things possible.' Nor was Bacon alone in seeking insular wonders in the distant seas. Shakespeare had already created Prospero's Island, another magical place where the wickedness and folly of men would be defeated. Bacon reinforced his biblical theme by referring to the navigational expertise of the ancients: 'The Phoenicians, and especially the Tyrians, had great fleets; so had the Carthaginians their colony, which is yet further west.'[6] As in so much of Bacon's maritime writing his dependence on Raleigh was obvious, but the westward trend he gave to Phoenician seafaring hinted the islanders were of Carthaginian descent.

Bacon's view of British expansion echoed More's equivocation: the New Atlanteans, an advanced and learned people, were not interested in colonies. Yet European expansion had been the key to their discovery. Bacon had already explicitly linked the search for colonies with the search for knowledge; the illustrated frontispiece of *The Great Instauration* featured a fully rigged galleon heading out beyond the Pillars of Hercules, the limits of the Ancient World, and the emblem of Spanish global power, on a voyage into the unknown.

While More and Bacon shaped subsequent English/British island writing, many of their subtler insights have been missed by readings that privilege universal themes over contemporary English concerns. They made the island a central focus of Englishness in the formative century that separated Henry VII from James I, and their texts lived in the libraries of all literate Englishmen, read into the mental world of statesmen, scholars, warriors and travellers, generation after generation.

While the magical qualities of these idealised islands have fascinated the English across the centuries, they can never be realised by those who live on continental land masses. Continentals must abandon their homes to find the island dream. The success of *Robinson Crusoe* in Europe, especially in Germany, spoke to a profound longing for a fresh start, a new world, and above all peace and tranquillity. After a century of bloody conflict, a succession of major wars ravaged much of Germany between 1618 and 1713, imaginary islands were the last refuge of hope and dreams. So profound was this longing that Crusoe has inspired any number of Germanic robinsonades through the three centuries that separated the age of Defoe from that of space flight.

There are other ways of reading the English connection with islands and oceans. Linda Colley has argued that Crusoe's version of Empire, occupation, control and enlightenment leading to well-earned reward should be set alongside the experience of his contemporary Gulliver, endlessly enslaved, abused and exploited by other peoples.[7] While captivity was a major theme in the British imperial project, one shared by Crusoe, most captives were taken as they voyaged for an oceanic empire because Britain was a small, weak state, incapable of exerting power on the European mainland. Recognising this inherent weakness Bacon and Raleigh laid out the philosophical basis of seapower as an alternative to the 'Roman' military might of continental empires. Ancient ideas and concepts, transmitted through Venice, the quintessential seapower state, began to have a significant influence on English thought from the first decade of the sixteenth century.[8] More, John Dee, Raleigh, Bacon and John Selden used them to evolve an English concept of seapower, linked to the development of a sea empire, a critical phase in evolution of a national identity. These works defined the parameters of seapower in an English setting. In 1607 Bacon defended the Union of England and Scotland in the House of Commons by stressing the strategic benefits of seapower:

this kingdom of England, having Scotland united, Ireland reduced, the sea provinces of the Low Countries contracted, and shipping maintained, is one of the greatest monarchies, in forces truly esteemed, that hath been in the world.[9]

Such texts, addressed to Kings and Councillors, looked to influence policy, providing historical, strategic, legal and economic arguments for an empire of islands at a time when England was perfectly incapable of attempting anything else. Later English voyagers would build on that vision, none more assiduously than that expert textual voyager Daniel Defoe.

The imperial and strategic writings of More, Raleigh, Bacon and Defoe matter because an empire, like a state, is a work of art, a cultural construction.[10] These ideas shaped the English/British response to Juan Fernández, and many another distant island. Once the Tudors had begun the 'British Empire', a phrase coined by John Dee in the 1570s, it was taken up, repeated, developed and sustained. Each generation built on the achievements of the last, and added to the stock of heroic texts, images and structures that repeated the message to the ignorant, and bolstered the fragile self-confidence of a small, weak nation situated off the coast of a great continent, and desperately vulnerable to larger states.

2

Spanish Lakes and English Dreams

———◦◦◦———

Islands are nothing without people to see them, and voyages are pointless without landfalls. Spanish conquistadores first sighted the South Pacific early in the sixteenth century. Driven by the lure of gold, a habit of conquest and an aggressive religious mission, they overthrew the Aztec and Inca empires in three decades. The resulting flow of unprecedented riches, coinciding with a fortuitous turn in the dynastic politics of Europe, transformed Spain from a tough frontier state with Mediterranean ambitions into the first world power. American wealth funded a Habsburg drive for European hegemony, and the Catholic Counter-Revolution. For Protestant England, Spanish bullion and military might posed the ultimate threat: invasion, conquest and the forced reimposition of an older religious settlement. Little wonder English seamen, politicians, merchants and geographers dreamed of the South Sea and the silver mines of Peru. Redirecting Peruvian bullion from Seville to London would restore a European balance of power, secure the English kingdom and the new religion. The original Elizabethan search for an alternative source of bullion ended in the icy fiasco of the Northwest Passage, while raiding in the Caribbean met stiff resistance. By the early 1570s the English were ready to attempt the South Sea. That they knew anything at all about the region reflected insatiable curiosity, and not a little spying.

From the mid-1530s, Spanish ships linked Peru to the Caribbean via Panama and the overland route to Nombre de Dios. Peru quickly developed a strong coasting trade to exchange local produce within a region that stretched from the centre of modern Chile to Ecuador, along the settled coastal strip to the west of the Andes. By 1600 around a hundred ships were at work, including a handful of royal galleons, taking silver from Callao to Panama; the rest, far smaller, worked the local trade. These ships proved essential to English predators. While the silver fleet attracted attention, and provided the occasional windfall, local ships offered fresh supplies and experienced pilots. The problem for Spain was simple, but insoluble. The flow of silver from Peru to Madrid was critical to the imperial project, but the remaining local trade of the west coast was of no interest. Therefore the Spanish South Seas Armada, the local naval force focused on escorting silver shipments. The defence of local ports was left to soldiers and forts; local trade defence was left to the merchants who owned the ships and cargoes. Losses were acceptable as long as the silver continued to flow. This system worked tolerably well as long as the threat was intermittent and the aggressors weak.[1] In the absence of any threat Peru became conspicuously wealthy; ships travelled without cannon, and ports were hardly fortified. This happy situation would not endure.

For English seafarers Spanish South America soon became a mythic promised land of commercial opportunity, and plunder. All they needed was a friendly port. Silver flowed from the fabled mountain mine at Potosi, where a city of 120,000 souls, the size of contemporary Amsterdam, supplied the needs of an industry that chewed up Indian labourers as quickly as the labourers chewed the narcotic coca leaves that got them through working days that combined the dangers of deep mining with an atmosphere so thin that walking was difficult, and temperature shifts of thirty degrees Celsius between the sweaty, sulphurous depths of the mine and the icy winds that ripped round the exposed mountain. Unaware of the human misery it entailed, Europeans adopted Potosi as the ultimate expression of unimaginable riches; 'the mines of Peru' fuelled the dreams of avaricious men, and the risky voyages of those who tried to make them real. The silver was shipped as bullion, or minted into pieces of eight at Lima, coins that were accepted across the world, providing liquidity for the first global economy. Without

Potosi it is unlikely English seafarers would have troubled to enter the Great South Sea.[2]

While the Spanish ruled a vast continental empire stretching from California to the Argentine pampas, and operated an extreme mercantilist economic system, designed to direct all trade through Seville, with endless opportunities to impose taxes and fees to fill the Imperial treasury, the Great South Sea would remain *mare clausum* and *mare incognita* to legitimate English trade. As foreigners, heretics and eventually enemies Elizabethan seafarers, denied access to Spanish markets, turned to piracy and privateering. After three raids into the ocean, raids that transformed the economics of the Peruvian Viceroyalty, the English finally, rather belatedly, learned that the key to this ocean would be a tiny island off the coast of Chile, discovered and abandoned by the Spanish.

Juan Fernández discovered the island that bears his name while trying to solve a problem. On the west coast of South America the powerful Humboldt current flowed northwards, while the light, contrary coastal winds meant that a voyage south from Panama to Callao, the port of Peru and hub of the regional trading system, was a three-month ordeal. The next leg, from Callao to Valparaiso (the port of Chile), was equally tedious. By contrast, the northbound return voyage was quick and easy. A silver convoy from Callao sailed every year, carrying bullion and mercury to use in the mines of Mexico, but the round trip was so demanding that each ship only sailed biennially.

While on passage south from Callao to Chile, Fernández struck out to sea to avoid the tedious coastal passage, discovering the island on 22 November 1574. His new route cut the voyage south from three months to one, transforming colonial economics by developing internal markets between tropical Ecuador and the temperate wheat fields of Chile. While Fernández went back to the island in 1575, it is not clear if he ever went ashore.[3]

Some 415 miles due west of Valparaiso, the group consists of the mountainous volcanic remnants Más a Tierra (meaning 'nearer land'), Más Afuera ('further away') and the far smaller

Santa Clara off the western end of Más a Tierra. Más a Tierra lies approximately 33°38' south, 78°50' west, it is 15 miles east to west, and less than 5 miles north to south, with a surface area of around 15,000 hectares. The highest point, El Yunque, stands at 3,000 feet above sea level. Much of the coast is vertical and inaccessible. Lying around 110 miles to the west, Más Afuera, the more recent of the two main volcanic islands, is roughly 14 miles long and 3 miles wide, almost conical, deeply scored by ravines, with very little low-lying land, and lacking anything that might serve as a harbour. It was never going to be a suitable location for significant human settlement.

Historians of Pacific exploration have lamented the 'failure' of the Spanish to push on beyond Juan Fernández, open the Southern Ocean and find new lands, but this 'failure' was entirely logical for a land empire bent on occupying and exploiting a continent. In Spain's imperial vision oceans were necessary evils, a means of communicating between the different parts of an unfeasibly vast imperial sway, rather than a theatre of dreams and discovery. Such foolishness was the province of eccentric English islanders. For Spain, expansion was a matter of soldiers and territory. Oceanic discovery was fortuitous, and risky. It was no accident that many of the men who pushed Spanish oceanic exploration – Columbus, Magellan, Cabot and Quirós – were foreigners. Once the mainland had been reduced to order offshore islands were a source of anxiety and cost. News of key discoveries was hidden.

The Spanish did not add the islands to their charts, aware that such knowledge posed a serious threat to their wafer thin grip on the ocean. The details were left in the heads of local pilots. Just how valuable silence could be was demonstrated four years after the initial discovery. Francis Drake sailed up the coast of Chile and across the Pacific without finding the islands, or any record of their existence.[4] The English began looking for a place to settle in the South Seas by the early 1570s. When Drake attacked Peru, he relied on the latest Portuguese maps, and his ability to acquire pilots and cartographic intelligence. He became only the second mariner to sail from the South Atlantic to the South

Pacific, via the Straits of Magellan. While English intelligence gathering efforts facilitated Drake's voyage, Juan Fernández's islands remained hidden. Drake refreshed his crew in southern Chile, far from Spanish towns. Coasting northwards in early 1579 he learned nothing of the new island, even at Valparaiso. Instead he took a fabulous prize – the silver galleon *Nuestra Señora de la Concepción*, which rejoiced in the altogether earthier nickname of *Cacafuego* ('shit fire') – between Callao and Panama, before heading north and then west for the spice markets of Asia. Windfall profits from his voyage paid off the national debt, and prompted the next surge of English overseas expansion, legitimate or otherwise.[5] It also excited emulation, for ever held up as the exemplary feat of English enterprise. 'The World Encompassed' put the Pacific into the English vision of identity and purpose. Every subsequent English raider was a new Drake, dreaming of similar prize and esteem. Little wonder the Spaniards did not put these islands on the map.

Although the Spanish responded to Drake's invasion with uncommon urgency, Thomas Cavendish arrived in 1586, before much could be done. Although no more successful in finding Juan Fernández, Cavendish captured a Manila galleon laden with Asian exotics, generating massive profits for his investors. The voyage of Richard Hawkins, the last Elizabethan voyager to enter the South Pacific ended in defeat, captured off the coast of Ecuador in May 1595. Imprisoned at Lima, and lucky not to be executed as a pirate and heretic, Hawkins was detained until the Anglo-Spanish war ended, to deny his local knowledge to other raiders. The first Englishman to mention the islands in print, in 1622, Hawkins noted they were 'plentiful of fish, and good for refreshing'. However he had not visited, only discovering their existence in a Dutch book after he returned to England.[6]

Hawkins had returned home after the Stuart succession brought peace with Spain, closing the South Pacific theatre of dreams. No English mariners would reach Juan Fernández for another eighty years. Not that the Spanish had any great plans for these isolated rocks: they responded to Drake's incursion with an insane scheme to build a fortified city inside the Straits of Magellan, one of the least hospitable regions on earth.

Needless to say the settlement was a disaster, most of the settlers died where they had been abandoned. Cavendish picked up a solitary survivor, and brought the story of an abandoned city of dead Spaniards deep inside the Straits of Magellan back to England, where it excited a strikingly odd response: Englishmen wished to emulate the catastrophe.

The madcap settlement had been led by Pedro de Sarmiento de Gamboa, who would later fuel Raleigh's 'dreams of El Dorado', a South American city of gold.[7] For all his vanity, ambition and duplicity it was in the brilliant mind of Raleigh that a British seapower empire moved from imagination to reality. Judged by the measure of practical results Raleigh left precious little, beyond heroic failure in Virginia, but his ideas, and above all his captivating words had the power to unsettle the complacent, and inspire the ambitious. Pursuing dreams of gold and paradise into the Orinoco River proved disastrous for the aging Raleigh, but his expansive vision of empire, treasure, profit and glory, expressed in magical Elizabethan prose, would torment the imagination of poets, empire-builders and historians for centuries to come.[8] Ultimately those dreams would collide with the very real island of Juan Fernández, turning one small corner of the South Pacific into an English paradise.

Between 1591 and 1599 the Spanish made two attempts to settle the island – without success. Spanish sailors and fishermen continued to visit, the islands provided a useful navigational mark and a rich fishery, but they failed to sustain a settlement. By 1600 a disappointed colonist had given the island to the Jesuits, but even the redoubtable Society of Jesus, a key engine of Spanish imperium, could not make a success of island life. It seems the very idea of offshore existence, living beyond the horizon, did not agree with the Spanish. During these early attempts at colonisation hardy Pyrenean goats, introduced into Chile a few decades before, arrived, along with European food crops.[9] Although the colonists soon departed their animals and plants devastated the island's unique ecosystem, largely the product of seeds and spores borne by wind, wave and visiting birds.[10] Having evolved without indigenous land mammals the vegetation remained low crowned and succulent. The only animal population was aquatic: massive breeding herds of elephant seals, sea lions and fur seals covered every inch of accessible beach. Much of this natural world would be annihilated by the two centuries of intermittent human engagement.[11]

Abandoned Spanish settlements left the islands packed with goats, turnips, cress and other European crops to supplement the astonishing richness of marine life, and the iconic cabbage trees. Finally after forty years of complete silence Spain's guilty little Pacific secret was uncovered. On 1 March 1616 a Dutch expedition led by Jacob Le Maire and Willem Schouten sighted the islands of Más a Tierra and Santa Clara, but was unable to anchor, 'to the very great pain and sorrow of the sick'. Schouten's crew were suffering from scurvy, the symptoms included loose teeth and self-absorbed nostalgia. A boat went ashore for food and water, noting the abundance of feral livestock and fish, along with evidence of occasional Spanish visits. While the Dutchmen anchored, and fished with great success, they did not manage to get ashore 'to the great grief of our sicke men, who thereby were clean out of comfort'.[12] Suitably refuelled, the expedition passed on, 'with very great pain for not being able to rest longer in so pleasant an isle'.[13] Any 'pain' was relative; the sickly crew finally made an insular landfall to the northwest forty distressing days later, but not one man died before the ship reached Djakarta in the Indonesian archipelago several months later.[14] Willem Schouten's narrative appeared in English in 1625, combining a seaman's guide to the anchorages with an estimate of the vital food and water supplies, and 'a faire green valley, full of greene trees, pleasant to behold', which lifted the spirits of the sick.

Schouten's report of a green and fruitful island, with fresh water, goats, pigs and an immensity of fish, attracted predatory mariners and anxious Spanish officials alike.[15] The Dutch mariners needed the islands because they were at war with

Spain. The curative powers of fresh food and water for scorbutic mariners, exhausted by the demanding voyage from Europe, had already given the islands a quasi-miraculous identity. Englishmen would reuse Schouten's language for centuries, demonstrating the enduring utility of Samuel Purchas's voyage collection. The narrative became common property; men more familiar with ship-handling than literary craft were only too willing to adopt Schouten's opinions, and even the very words he had used to convey them. Once consigned to print, such descriptions persisted in the seafaring imagination, seamlessly sliding into other narratives. Voyagers arrived expecting to find what they had read and, unless profoundly disappointed, tended to repeat the language of their precursors.[16] It also cloaked predatory ambition in curiously repetitive lyrical prose, the pirates unwilling to waste a good line.

Two published accounts of the Dutch voyage transformed European views of the South Sea, putting the island onto the world map; 'it became thereafter a sought after haven for navigators of all flags who entered the Pacific, but most particularly for those who would not find a welcome in the ports of Spanish America'.[17] While Schouten's text had been read and quoted by Richard Hawkins it was put to more obvious use by another Dutch expedition. The expedition led by Jacques l'Hermite set off to conquer Peru, using Juan Fernández as the fleet rendezvous. Between 5 and 13 April 1624, eleven Dutch ships, carrying 2,600 men (including 1,000 soldiers), assembled in what would become Cumberland Bay. They came for fresh water, fish, meat, fruit and vegetables. Once ashore, discipline began to fragment, the voyage had not been as healthy as Le Maire's, largely a factor of overcrowding, and now free of the ship the men looked to their own interests. Five were convicted of stealing wine, and sentenced to hang, only to be pardoned. Six sick Dutchmen begged to be left, they were never heard of again. Despite a Dutch naval victory the Spanish had improved their local defences and the expedition achieved little, other than reinforcing the idea of Juan Fernández as the ideal refreshment stop.[18]

This argument struck a chord with Abel Tasman, the first European to reveal the continental scale of Australia and find New Zealand. In 1642 Tasman recommended establishing a settlement, linked to his other discoveries to secure Dutch control of the South Pacific, expand trade and increase the national pool of ships and seamen, 'which are the true and natural strength of this country'. It would also 'extend our naval power, and raise the reputation of this nation; the most distant prospect of which is enough to warm the soul of any man who has the least regard for his country'.[19] Ultimately the islands were too small to be economically attractive, and too far from the Dutch Asian settlements to be sustained. The Dutch had problems nearer home, knocked off their naval perch by the fatal combination of a French invasion and an English alliance.

Seventeenth-century Dutch voyagers described the island's attractions for scorbutic mariners, and mapped their location for the English, who were drawn to a veritable flood of information highlighting the Achilles heel of Habsburg Spain. The maritime culture of the Dutch Republic was at once a subject of envy and admiration; much was borrowed or stolen from Dutch sources in the last forty years of the century.[20] Tasman's spirited prospectus, like the other Dutch voyage narratives, was soon available in English. It reappeared in John Campbell's great 1744 compendium, where it served to emphasise that eighteenth century England was following in the well-marked track of heroic maritime precursors.

These geographical and piratical borrowings collided with the emergence of a vibrant print culture: the Dutch-led Glorious Revolution of 1688 significantly reduced the impact of government censorship. A growing literate audience existed, and by the 1690s voyage literature had become a major genre, combining travelogue, shipwreck, piracy and wilder flights of geographical and spiritual imagination. Distant, mysterious islands emerged into an expanding mental world, shaped by Plato's Atlantis (in *Timaeus* and *Critias*), More's *Utopia* and Bacon's *New Atlantis*. These texts shaped the expectations of voyagers, and audiences at home. If the Dutch failed to exploit their hard-won insight their raids demonstrated Juan Fernández had become a serious problem for the Viceroyalty of Peru. The islands offered an excellent offshore base for hostile shipping, but the Viceroy lacked the manpower or money to sustain a permanent occupation against such a hazy, intermittent menace. As long as the silver kept flowing north to Panama the royal authorities in Spain were prepared to risk an occasional attack, relying on intelligence from Europe to send advance warning to Lima before hostile ships could round Cape Horn. Between 1662 and 1665 the Jesuits occupied the island for a second time, but even they lacked the dedication needed for island life. After that the Viceroy of Peru attempted to destroy the island as a food depot, landing packs of savage dogs to annihilate the goat population in 1675. Although the measure would be repeated many times the goats proved elusive and adaptable, outlasting canine and human predators, and evolving into a distinct genus.

In England a new, more sober literature emerged in the last decades of the seventeenth century. After the fashion of Elizabethan voyage collector Richard Hakluyt and his Stuart successor Samuel Purchas these voyage narratives were used to encourage the expansion of English trade.[21] Such voyages resumed under the Commonwealth, a dynamic expansive maritime state that served trade and faith by making war on Catholic Spain. Cromwell showed particular interest in the closed markets of South America, considering a project to attack Chile and Peru. The Lord Protector had studied Hakluyt and Raleigh. Such thoughts proved abortive but the idea, once raised, remained at the heart of English ambition.

After the Restoration of 1660, maritime monarch Charles II understood 'the great and principal interest of this nation' to be overseas trade.[22] This insight prompted Charles and his brother James, Duke of York to send an expedition to the Straits of Magellan in 1669. Captain John Narborough, HMS *Sweepstakes* had orders to chart the entrance to the Pacific, and 'if possible lay the foundations of a Trade there', by finding an unoccupied region to colonise, to avoid war with Spain. Narborough got no further than the port of Valdivia in southern Chile, although he produced an excellent chart of the Straits. He turned back without stretching into the open ocean, let alone reaching Juan Fernández. Even so the islands appeared on John Seller's 1675 'Chart of the South-Sea'.[23] Seller a London instrument maker, teacher of navigation and publisher of charts and pilots, had been appointed hydrographer to the King in 1671, backed by a monopoly and an import ban designed to break Dutch domination of charts and navigational texts. Seller's *Atlas Maritimus* of 1675, the first English sea atlas, featured the royal warrant, and the two English circumnavigators, Drake and Cavendish. His South Sea chart included the Juan Fernández Islands and the San Félix–San Ambrosio group to the north, all 'borrowed' from Dutch charts. The meaning of the latter was as yet little known in England: while Juan Fernández had a history in English, the distant Desventuradas would not trouble the English for another century. Seller's work may have been imperfect, even by contemporary standards, but his appointment and his publications created an English hydrography, aimed at merchants and mariners travelling to the far flung corners of the globe.[24] The English had yet to visit Juan Fernández, but it could be found on an English chart, one that carried the Royal Warrant.

3

Pirates and Freebooters

—◦◦◦—

While the King opened the door to the South Seas the initiative to exploit the opportunity came from an altogether less dignified quarter. Behind the carefully chosen language of Stuart expansionism lay the age-old lure of gold and silver. Plunder and trade along the rim of the Spanish empire was the object, rather than the vast, unknown ocean that lay beyond. The offshore islands would be the service stations that refreshed incoming expeditions before they struck the coast, not the launch pad for new and distant enterprises. At the heart of the English Pacific lay the silver mines of Peru,[1] the contemporary standard for fabulous wealth. Drake and Cavendish had demonstrated that the ships carrying the precious metal north to Panama were effectively unguarded. By the end of the sixteenth century the Spanish convoyed bullion across the Atlantic, but not between Callao to Panama, or the annual Acapulco to Manila voyage that funded Spanish trade with China. This combination of wealth and weakness proved irresistible to financially compromised Stuart Kings and wild, piratical men from the lawless margins of empire.

The 'South Sea' exerted a powerful pull on men already beyond the bounds of lawful business, their appetites whetted by Henry Morgan's 1670 sack of Panama, and a growing familiarity with the Pacific voyages that terminated at the great isthmian depot. While buccaneers introduced their contemporaries to the exotic unknown their deeds became a significant literary genre, introducing Juan Fernández to a wider English audience. In 1678 French chronicler Alexandre Exquemelin published a record of Caribbean piracy, *De Americaensche Zee-Roovers*, in

Amsterdam. Exquemelin went to the French West Indies in the mid-1660s and spent almost a decade with Henry Morgan, the prince of buccaneers. Returning to Holland in 1674 he qualified as a surgeon, and compiled an account of his experiences. His tales of lawless men on the wild Caribbean frontier became an instant best seller, quickly translated into German, creating an enduring fascination for golden, exotic and violent stories at the heart of central Europe. A Spanish edition followed, for an audience more concerned to exterminate than emulate. This version added new material and occasionally garbled the original text. The first English edition of 1684 seems to have followed the Spanish text. A French edition of 1686 was effectively a new work, and this may have led to the second English edition, which contained an account of the Pacific voyages of English mariner Basil Ringrose, who touched on Juan Fernández.[2] By this time Exquemelin's book had become a franchise operation, each country effectively creating a distinctive version. One thing is clear: the myriad forms of this text became a key resource for early eighteenth century South Sea pioneers and projectors.

Exquemelin reported that Englishmen first reached Más a Tierra on Christmas Day 1680. Their route to the island had been unusual. A loose confederation of Caribbean buccaneers had crossed the isthmus and captured three large ships off Panama, together with local pilots. Suitably equipped they set off to raid the Pacific coast. Over the next two years the buccaneers would seize 25 ships, kill at least two hundred Spaniards, and cause damage estimated at four million pesos. Such success was all the more remarkable for a small group of ill-disciplined, violent men prone to mutiny and frequent changes of leadership.[3] The island witnessed a recurring pattern of disasters, as the raiders brought mutiny, disaffection, shipwreck and death in their wake.

Relying on a captured Spanish pilot Captain Bartholomew Sharp initially anchored on the south side of the island, close to the southern end of the modern airstrip, a desolate spot bereft of wood and water, before rough weather forced them to shift into what became Sharp's Bay and later Puerto Inglese.

This was a poor anchorage; ships were frequently driven out to sea by fierce offshore winds. These events were recorded in five journals, for among the crew were navigator author William Dampier, cartographer author Basil Ringrose and surgeon author Lionel Wafer. Dampier, the most engaging of them, was an inveterate recorder of data, be it hydrographic, cartographic, animal, vegetable or mineral. Born in Somerset, he had taken the chance of a seafaring career, wandered into the Caribbean, and fallen in with the buccaneers. Navigational skill and endless curiosity ensured he would be employed long after his less attractive character traits – drunkenness, cowardice and double-dealing – had been exposed. Samuel Taylor Coleridge pillaged Dampier's work in the 'Rime of the Ancient Mariner' (much as the old buccaneer had pillaged Spanish ships), but acknowledged him as 'a man of exquisite refinement of mind', although the compliment may require revision.

Dampier's works were brought to print with considerable editorial support, improving a pedestrian, unpunctuated prose that was just one thing after another. Having dismissed Más Afuera as 'a mere rock', Basil Ringrose landed on Juan Fernández to shoot goats and obtain fresh water, 'a very refreshing Place to us'. He recorded several gales of wind, shooting at least six goats, and fish 'so plentiful that in less than one hour's time two men caught enough for our whole company'. Once refreshed, discipline collapsed; the buccaneers deposed Sharp from command, 'the company being not satisfied either with his courage or behaviour'.[4]

On 12 January 1681, eighteen days after their arrival, the buccaneers sighted three Spanish ships; one of many squadrons organised by the Viceroy of Peru to protect vital silver shipments to Panama. In their haste to get away the buccaneers, now led by Captain John Watling, left behind a 'Miskito' Indian named Will. Men from the Mosquito Coast of Central America were often recruited for buccaneering voyages, being expert fishermen.[5] Out hunting goats when the alarm was raised, Will could not get back to the beach in time.

After their hasty departure the buccaneers took more than twenty ships, considerable treasure and a priceless haul of cartographic knowledge. On 29 July 1681 Sharp captured the ship *El Santa Rosario*, and 'secured a Spanish Manuscript of prodigious value', a 'great Book full of Sea-Charts and Maps':

It describes all the ports roads, harbours, bayes, sands, rocks & riseing of the land & instructions how to work a ship into any port or harbour between the Latt. of 17° 15 N and 57°S Latt. ... The Spaniards cried when I gott the book (farewell South Sea now) ... They were going to throw it overboard but by good luck I saved it.[6]

The Spanish charts and sailing directions included maps and coastal perspectives of Juan Fernández. It was no accident that the chart of the island was the last in the manuscript, Juan Fernández was the key to an entire ocean. Ringrose and Dampier found the charts reliable. Soon after Dampier and Wafer took their leave and recrossed the Isthmus of Darien.

The Spanish manuscript saved Sharp's neck. Hauled before the Admiralty Court on a well-merited charge of piracy his judges included several senior officers, including Narborough. With the charts in hand Sharp was acquitted on 10 June 1682, to the disgust of the Spanish Ambassador. They were translated into English, and Thameside chart-maker William Hack produced several manuscript copies, 'including handsome presentation copies given to Charles II, ministers and courtiers'. The work was not published, to keep the intelligence from yet other hands. Charles rewarded Sharp with a Captain's commission in the Royal Navy. Hack noted Juan Fernández was:

not inhabited, but if it were it would prove the sharpest thorn that ever touched the Spaniards; for it is naturally fortified: & with a £100 charge & good management 100 men may keep it from 1000 if it should be invaded; it lyes 120 leagues (330 nautical miles) west from Valparaiso. In a word if this isle was inhabited it would be very profitable in matter of trade in time of peace with the Spaniards; & if a war very useful to the English.[7]

While the island is actually a little further out to sea the basic argument remained sound until the end of Spanish America.

On 22 March 1684 two buccaneer ships met off Juan Fernández: John Cook's *Batchelor's Delight* (a captured Danish slaver, complete with a cargo of female slaves) and John Eaton's vessel. When they landed the next day Will had prepared a fine stew of goat meat and tree cabbage for his scorbutic guests. The fresh victuals came too late for John Cook, who took sick at the island, and did not recover. Dampier records that his funeral on the coast of Costa Rica involved rather more ceremony than was usually accorded his kind. The *Batchelor's Delight* had another strikingly literate pirate crew, Dampier, Wafer and Ambrose Cowley keeping journals. The two ships remained at the island for 16 days, exploiting the food and water to recover from the inevitable scorbutic epidemic. They also recovered Will, who had survived for three years, using his skills to find food and evade capture. While such resourcefulness made him a model for Robinson Crusoe, Will became Man Friday. Friday was described as tall and olive-skinned, with long straight black hair, a typical Miskito. Will had been met on the beach by fellow Miskito Robin, their striking greeting ceremony transferred into Defoe's book from Dampier's account. In 1687 four men from the homebound *Batchelor's Delight* were marooned on the island at their own request, having gambled away all their prize money. In 1689 they drove off a Spanish landing party.[8]

Whatever the financial rewards were, the buccaneers had a striking impact on Spain. By 1686 they had seized 72 coastal traders, close on two-thirds of all local shipping. The Spanish fortified the coastal ports, and often mobilised armed ships, but the era of cheap security based on distance and ignorance was over. Trade disruption crippled customs revenue, a key income stream, making any local action even more difficult. The Peruvian squadron, a miserable under-funded half-measure, was left to rot when the threat abated. Imperial Spain simply would not fund effective seapower in the Pacific. Short term measures, landing dogs on Juan Fernández in 1675 and searching the Straits of

Magellan for English settlements were the best the Spanish could manage. Finally they resorted to private enterprise; a local company provided ships, armed with royal cannon, to cruise against the buccaneers. Having cleared the coastal zone by the late 1680s the company wound up. The respite would only be temporary. An empire of isolated ports, dominated by the extraction of bullion, and connected by unarmed coastal shipping was little more than an open invitation to enterprising raiders. That it existed without naval protection, preferring the local comfort provided by a handful of forts reflected Spain's continental mindset, and the chilling economics of seapower.

Between 1686 and 1690 Peru spent 6.5 million pesos on local defence, remitting only 750,000 to Spain.[9] This was not the purpose of empire. Moving silver from Callao via Panama to Madrid mattered; sea control and insular possessions did not. Silver sustained the Habsburg Imperial system; Juan Fernández did not. In an extractive empire of exploitation the cost of defending silver shipments had to be balanced against the value of the metal being moved. Three times in the seventeenth century the cost of defending Peru rose to unusual, unsustainable levels: in 1624, in response to an advanced warning of l'Hermite's fleet; in 1658, to rebuild the South Seas Armada; and in 1679–80, in response to the buccaneer incursion. In all three cases security costs threatened to outstrip the value of the silver being moved along the coast, and led to the suspension of all other seaborne commerce.

In the next major war, which began in 1688, England and Spain were allied against France, so the next English privateer to head into the South Pacific, Captain John Strong's *Welfare*, carried trade goods and a commission to take French ships. Even so, the investors considered occupying Juan Fernández. 'If these two islands with Mocha were fortified by the English they would be capable, in cases of a Breach with Spain, of doing them a great deal of mischief.' In 1690 the *Welfare* stopped at Más Afuera, and picked up the four buccaneers left on Más a Tierra three years before. The men had undergone a religious experience while marooned; they proved awkward shipmates, not least when they reverted to their piratical opinions despite the voyage being intended to trade peacefully. Near Concepción a boat party was lured ashore by the Spaniards and captured. Among the prisoners two Juan Fernández maroons were executed, to prevent them spreading their knowledge. The rest were imprisoned. While the *Welfare* voyage had been a financial disaster, it completed a remarkable decade that put Juan Fernández on the English world map. Soon it would occupy a central place in the national imagination. Even though the next expedition to call at the islands was French it had an English pilot. Captain Franco's ship not only remained at Juan Fernández for five months in 1691, but it returned in December 1692. The privateers had little to fear. Spanish Peru lacked the resources to control the sea, falling back on old methods, occasional patrols, removing the sheep and horses and attacking the goat population with savage dogs.[10]

When Dampier's description of the *Batchelor's Delight* voyage appeared in the 1697 as *A New Voyage Round the World*, it created a market for buccaneer tales. Although largely descriptive, written to serve practical seamen, Dampier's broad curiosity secured him a far wider audience. If Dampier's description of the meeting between Will and Robin was the literary highlight of the island visit, it segued neatly into a discussion of survival for maroons, one which would have served a later inhabitant well. Only then did Dampier locate and describe the island. 'It is about 12 leagues round, full of high hills and small, pleasant valleys; which if manured, would probably produce anything proper for the Climate. The sides of the Mountains are part Savannahs, part Wood-lands.' Among the trees some could be used for building but, he lamented, 'none fit for masts'. The cabbage trees were small, 'but produce a good head, and the Cabbage very sweet.' He contrasted the goats on the east and west ends of the island, unable to explain why those in the arid west were fatter. Equally mysterious was the fact that while the island could feed 4 or 500 families, it remained uninhabited. The fish were 'in great Companies …, so plentiful, that two men in an hours time will take with Hook and Line, as many as will serve 100 men'. This cornucopic line, originally Schouten's, would be repeated endlessly, along with Dampier's description of seals and elephant seals by each new visitor to the island. Elephant seal oil was 'very sweet and wholesome to fry meat', but the flesh was 'indifferent'. Finally he came to the essentials: anchorages and water.

There are only two bays in the whole Island where Ships may anchor, these are both at the East end, and on both of them is a Rivulet of good fresh water. Either of these Bays may be fortified with little charge, to that degree that 50 men in each may be able to keep off 1000.[11]

Finally he noted that for 16 days the doctors from Captain Eaton's ship fed the scorbutic men on goat meat and herbs, with good results. Dampier's report located the island and its anchorages, catalogued the edible resources, and provided a survival guide for future maroons. Yet the island itself had yet to enter the wider popular consciousness. To rouse interest in the book Dampier named many of his more exotic landfalls, from Tierra del Fuego to Formosa in the extended title, but not Juan Fernández. Wafer produced a 'Secret Report' for the Earl of Halifax in 1698, and advised occupation:

This I look upon as a Place fit for a settlement to make it a Store House of all Provisions. Here may be Black Cattle, Sheep and Goats Easely breed, and it is a good place for a Look Out or to Set Wounded or Sick men on Shore, In order for their recovery.[12]

The buccaneers did not fade away; a new cycle of wars turned them into legitimate instruments of state power with privateer commissions. Their exploits, as pirate and privateer left an enduring legacy in English literature. The best-selling texts of Exquemelin and Dampier revived the market for seafaring narratives, little troubled by novelty or profit since the days of Hakluyt and Purchas. They met an audience primed by increased domestic interest. Charles II made voyaging central to purposes of his new Royal Society, founded in 1662, reflecting the interconnected, expanding commercial and intellectual horizons of

Restoration England. Royal Society secretary Robert Boyle soon published a guide for seamen reporting distant voyages in the society's journal *Philosophical Transactions*. Royal patronage of voyages and trading ventures focused the commercial and landed elite on useful knowledge. It was no accident that Dampier dedicated his 1697 *A New Voyage Round the World* to the Earl of Halifax, President of the Royal Society, or that Society Secretary Sir Hans Sloane became the leading collector of voyage texts.[13] While most educated Englishmen were content with published accounts of the South Pacific Sloane, a wealthy doctor, assiduously acquired the primary documentation of buccaneer voyages. His purchases reflected personal interest and scientific curiosity, and ensured their survival in the British Museum collection.

Dampier set the fashion for oceanic travel books, including the first English glimpses of Australia. Piling up details, sketches and reports entranced his land-bound audience. Plunder, weirdness and bizarre food made it clear the Southern Ocean was another world. Dampier described the relish with which he consumed flamingo tongues alongside an intelligent, if graphic discussion of scurvy, along with the refitting, watering and other facilities of the coasts he visited. He hoped to make his fortune, and achieve gentlemanly status on the back of his book, but such dreams proved elusive. *New Voyage* sold five editions in six years, making publisher James Knapton a genre specialist, while rapid translation into Dutch, French and German spread Dampier's name across Europe. He was, briefly, a man of significance. In 1698 he addressed the Royal Society, dined with Samuel Pepys and John Evelyn, learned men who appreciated a good sea story, and took command of HMS *Roebuck* for a Pacific voyage that proved beyond doubt that whatever else he could boast Dampier was no leader of men.[14]

After the failure of his brief naval career Dampier's book became a promotional tool for further buccaneering. Dampier's writings and local knowledge lured unsuspecting or plain gullible investors into a new privateer voyage that set off for the South

Seas in 1703. England was now at war with France over the succession to the Spanish throne, so the government was deeply involved. The Treasury provided for Dampier's family in his absence. He also got to kiss Queen Anne's hand, when he took his leave of her husband, Prince George of Denmark, the Lord High Admiral. Dampier commanded the 200 ton *St George*, previously a merchant vessel named *Nazareth*, along with the *Cinque Ports Galley* and a coterie of old cronies. His name was well-known to the Spanish, who feared his cartographic insight and first-hand experience. The old buccaneer knew that pilot books and other navigational information was a key resource, seizing texts from prize vessels, the better to understand the Great South Sea: 'these we found by experience to be very good guides.'[15]

The privateers set the usual rendezvous at Juan Fernández. Stopping at Madeira and the Cape Verde islands, they committed the usual buccaneer outrages, getting drunk, plundering the locals and enslaving a few unwary Africans. Then Dampier put his first lieutenant ashore at St Jago (modern São Tiago), where he died. Such riotous antics destroyed discipline, and Dampier lacked the skill or the will-power to command. Men deserted. Then Captain Pickering of the *Cinque Ports* died. When the ship reached Juan Fernández on Christmas Eve 1703 most of the crew, disgusted with replacement Captain Thomas Stradling deserted and ran ashore. Dampier sailed past the island, apparently unable to identify a place he had visited three times before. When he finally cast anchor he persuaded Stradling's crew to re-embark by promising to consult them, and honour the distribution of prize money under the articles of association. Meanwhile almost all the scorbutic men recovered on a diet of fresh food and clean water. The ships were careened, water casks refilled and barrels of seal oil stowed for cooking and lighting. The last involved frightful animal cruelty: the men enjoyed tormenting the elephant seals for sport, jabbing them with boarding pikes, much as bulls and bears were baited back home in England.

Having put his ships and men into some sort of order, Dampier bungled an attack on the French ship *St Joseph*, spotted off the island. He also left some of the crew, with the ship's boats and other stores ashore. When the English ships returned they found two larger French ships had arrived – the *St Esprit* and *Baron de Breueuil* – so they headed off for the mainland. The French ships had come to trade, in violation of Spanish law, generating 357 per cent profits. A second French squadron that operated between 1707 and 1709 did equally well. With Spain a battle ground between rival Habsburg and Bourbon kings little trade reached South America, leaving a market only too willing to evade the law. French trade officially ended with the Treaty of Utrecht, closing a brief golden age of interloping in the South Seas.[16]

When the English ships began raiding Spanish shipping, their crews quickly realised Dampier was incompetent, cowardly and usually drunk. Worse still, he took bribes from captured ships, to prevent his men from plundering their cargo: hiding the cash from the investors. On his return to England Dampier was assailed in print, his chosen medium, and on his chosen ground of navigation. William Funnell, second mate of the *St George*, had deserted in the Pacific and returned home embittered. His references to magnetic variation and pointed criticism of Dampier's inability to navigate Cape Horn stressed technical expertise, while a dedication to Admiralty Secretary Josiah Burchett implied career ambitions.[17] By questioning Dampier's status as the lone literate navigator, Funnell seriously damaged the old buccaneer's reputation.

4

'The Absolute Monarch of the Island'

~~~

The *Cinque Ports Galley* returned to Juan Fernández in May 1704 hoping to refit, but the French had taken the men and stores abandoned the year before. Morale was so low that Scottish sailing master Alexander Selkirk decided to maroon himself on the island. He despised Stradling, and reckoned the worm-eaten ship was about to sink. Although he regretted the decision as the boat rowed back to the ship, giving Stradling the satisfaction of refusing to let him rejoin, it proved to be wise. Returning to the Chilean coast, the *Cinque Ports* sank; half the crew drowned, the rest ended up in a Spanish prison.

For Selkirk, abandoning the ship meant the loss of his home, his 'family', his purpose in life and the relaxation of the mess-deck. For some months he lived a dark, introverted life, slowly coming to terms with his situation, and his environment. Eventually he adjusted to the realities of a solitary existence on a small island, finding food and a sexual outlet among the goats. Diana Souhami suggested his habit of marking the ears of goats recorded these bestial interludes. There was no need to 'own' the livestock in any other way on an island that was his and his alone.[1]

While Selkirk lived his curious life, surrounded by goats and cats, waiting for rescue, petrified that the Spanish would catch him and send him to the silver mines, the expedition collapsed in mutual recrimination, deceit, and despair. Dampier botched his attack on the Manilla galleon and finally reached England without the ship, in circumstances that left the investors penniless, but some of the officers in funds. The old buccaneering ways were based on mutual support, democratic decision-making and complete contempt for lawful authority. It was hardly surprising that the concerns of far-distant investors, men of money with little understanding of the oceans, were ignored. The buccaneers were men seeking pleasure and reward, they had no reason to adhere to the law codes of a polite society that held them in contempt, and was not above hanging them when expediency required.[2]

Dampier's expedition may have been a disaster, but hope springs eternal. In 1708 Bristolian merchant ship captain Woodes Rogers raised funds for a two ship South Seas expedition, inspired by the successful French voyages. Rogers had suffered significant losses at the hands of French privateers, while a recent Act of Parliament removed the Crown's right to share in privateer profits, specifically to promote privateering enterprise. This expedition proved far more successful than its precursors, and it established Juan Fernández on the English world map. If the voyage of the *Duke* and *Duchess* relied on William Dampier's navigational skill, he did not receive a command. Rogers proved a far better expedition leader.[3] On 31 January 1709 the expedition reached Juan Fernández, for the essential stop-over to recover from scurvy and refresh the water supply. This was no easy matter, for, as Rogers noted:

We are very uncertain of the latitude and longitude of Juan Fernandez, the Books laying 'em down so differently, that not one chart agrees with another, and being but a small island, we are in some doubts of striking it.[4]

The importance of fetching the island was the main reason why Dampier had been taken on as the pilot, but the old pirate had forgotten the latitude!

That night the privateers could see a fire burning ashore in Windy Bay, and suspected they would find a French ship nearby. The following morning *Duke* and *Duchess* crept into the Bay, despite frequent offshore squalls. When the first boat reached the shore it encountered a strange figure: 'our Pinnace returned from the shore and brought an abundance of Craw-fish, with a Man cloath'd in Goat Skins, who looked wilder than the first Owners of them'. This was the first sight most members of the expedition had of Alexander Selkirk. Not that the taciturn Scot was the best of story-tellers: 'at his first coming on board us, he had so much forgot his Language for want of Use, that we could scarce understand him, for he seemed to speak his words by halves'.[5]

Strange, stuttering Selkirk proved a very useful acquaintance, making goat and vegetable soup for the sick, and helping harvest the fish, flesh and vegetation of the island for scorbutic sailors. Selkirk claimed the turnips had been sown by Dampier's crew; he also enjoyed the leaves of the indigenous cabbage tree, sandalwood seeds and a form of pepper. Selkirk understood the seasonal weather, flora and fauna, reporting the island 'capable of maintaining a good number of people, and being made so strong that they would not be easily dislodged'.[6] The synergy with Dampier's sentiments a decade earlier suggests textual borrowing by Rogers or his editor.

Rogers observed 'the greens and the goodness of the air' ensured the sick 'recovered very fast of the scurvy'.[7] A diet of turnip tops, tree cabbage, watercress and parsley limited mortality to two of the twenty-one scurvy patients. Meanwhile the ships were prepared for action, undergoing a full refit: stripped down, their masts lowered and the hulls careened. A forge was set up ashore, along with a tented encampment for men deprived of their wooden home. Rigging was mended, ironwork repaired, and the cooperage shaken down, cleaned and remade. Meanwhile the seal population paid a heavy price; many were butchered and rendered down, providing eighty gallons of oil for lamps and cooking. On 14 February the two ships set sail for the mainland.

The magical island of Juan Fernández had cured the sick, replenished the ships and saved a solitary sinner from damnation. Voyage narratives by Rogers and Edward Cooke, the latter including a rough map of the island, linked the remarkable story of Selkirk with a unique place, and helped to make it British. Cooke's map renamed Windy Bay 'Duke and Duchess Bay', pointed out the best fishing grounds, and stressed that the south-east end of the island had few trees, but many goats. A profile emphasised the mountainous nature of the place, and a singular large tree on the ridge, in all probability the same one that George Anson's men lamented they could not reach in 1741. The presence of a single tent where Anson later pitched camp suggests his bower was rather less 'natural' than he had suspected.[8]

Selkirk had lived on goat, crayfish, cabbage trees (*Juania australis*) and turnips sown by Spanish settlers. The latter now covered several acres. He had given up fish, Rogers noted, because without salt it upset his stomach. Rogers also observed the effect of isolation on Selkirk's spiritual life, and the value of plain, temperate living for bodily health and mental vigour. The quasi-religious nature of Selkirk's existence during a residence of four years and four months provided an important element for Defoe's reworking. The slow adjustment to solitary life and endless search for sails make it clear that Selkirk had not intended to wait for years: he expected to be picked up by another English ship within a few weeks. Instead he saw only a few passing Spanish ships, and a single Spanish landing. Well aware that if captured he would be enslaved and sent to the silver mines of Potosi, Selkirk scuttled up a tree for safety. Despite stopping to piss on the very tree where he was hiding, the Spaniards were unable to spot the terrified Scotsman amid the branches. They shot some goats, wrecked his camp and left.

Almost as soon as he rejoined the world of men Selkirk became encrusted with myths. His legendary physical agility and prowess as a goat hunter is easily explained. According to modern islanders, for whom goat hunting is the national sport, the goats use the same well-worn paths and when moving in flocks are easily caught by hand from ambush.[9] Similar confusion attends his many alleged island residences. Recent excavations at Aguas Buenas accepted the old story that Selkirk lived in a hut halfway up the mountain, on the track to the famous look-out. This makes little sense. The site is more than an hour's climb from the beach, and the food supply. It is dominated by the remains of a Spanish gunpowder magazine, littered with the shards of a large water pot made in southern Chile. It did not exist in Selkirk's day.

Selkirk never left Windy Bay and he had no reason to climb the mountain. He was expecting to be rescued by a ship, and needed to light a signal fire on the beach. The discovery of the broken tip of a pair of eighteenth century dividers in the powder magazine adds very little. While contemporary English and Scottish dividers were made of brass, the find is bronze. While Selkirk had his navigational equipment on the island, he brought it on board when he joined the Rogers expedition; he had no reason to use it, let alone break or discard it while stuck on Juan Fernández. The excavation report ignores Anson's occupation, and in an effort to sustain the building's link with Selkirk indulges in a line of argument that starts from a flawed premise, and proceeds through strikingly flimsy data 'clearly not amounting to much as evidence', linked by all too many 'speculative' and 'probable' connections to reach a dubious conclusion. The only 'meagre' rationale for the claim 'We believe that the remains left at Aguas Buenas were left by Selkirk' seems to be that 'our work has provided some justification for renaming the island Robinson Crusoe'.[10] Such 'evidence' would not get very far in a court of law.

The location of Selkirk's camp was described by Dr Thomas Dover. Hobbling ashore, weakened by scurvy and months at sea, Dover recorded the camp lay within half an hour of the beach, hidden from the sea, close to a stream, in an area where a distinctive white grass grew. Selkirk used the grass to stuff his mattress. The 2010 Caligari film expedition discovered a location that satisfied all of these requirements, just outside San Juan Bautista, and easily reached by following a stream. Intervening high ground offers a fine view of the bay, while hiding the camp from passing ships. The soil appears to have been under grass for many centuries, being too wet to sustain trees. This would be the ideal hideout for a nervous beachcomber, anxious to see but not be seen. It would allow him to find food without undue effort, and made a fine goat pen.

As the two ships sailed away Juan Fernández was once again unoccupied and silent. In December, Rogers's ships took a

Manila galleon, worth around £200,000, and brought it home in triumph to the Thames in October 1711. Sorting out the money proved as problematic as ever, but the treasure helped sell a financial scam to a credulous nation. Set up in the same year the South Sea Company promised to buy up the floating national debt, about £10 million, and pay it off in return for 6 per cent interest and a monopoly on British trade with Spanish South America. While the scheme had far more to do with domestic politics and speculative finance than the South Pacific it fed off the growing sense that this was the ocean of opportunity, one that had an obvious if minute epicentre at Juan Fernández. Critically, the Company acquired a copy of Hack's edition of Sharp's *Waggoner*, and hired Herman Moll to produce a large map. The Tory ministry supported the Company because it was anxious to exchange the bloody battlefields of Flanders for the profitable pursuit of trade war against Spain. This strategic shift was popular and largely correct once the key issues of the Spanish Succession had been resolved. The projectors, profoundly ignorant of the South Seas, relied on Rogers and his men for South Pacific voyaging. Juan Fernández, the obvious base for any new venture, was high on their list of priorities. Cartographer Herman Moll produced a chart to represent the limits of the new Company's remit, placing Juan Fernández at the centre of the sheet. While the island's location remained imprecise, it was loaded with meaning. Moll, like fellow navigator of buccaneer voyages Daniel Defoe, understood the limits of the buccaneers as accurate reporters of fact, lamenting their irritating habit of renaming features already named. Moll's chart sold well; it seems Defoe owned a copy.[11]

Once the market had been aroused by a spate of South Sea yarns, spurious and then fictional versions quickly followed. Defoe was the best-known creator of South Pacific fiction, but there were others. William Chetwood's 1726 tale *Voyages and Adventures of Captain Robert Boyle* provided a connection with the theatre. Chetwood, the prompter of Drury Lane, added a degree of veracity by introducing William Dampier as a historical character and landed his hero on Juan Fernández, before taking the Manila galleon. Jonathan Swift brilliantly subverted the fantastical quality of the genre with *Gulliver's Travels* of 1726, another South Sea story to name Dampier, in the very first sentence, along with cartographer Herman Moll.[12] This was a sea of wonder, and the lands it contained, little known but much imagined, contributed a disproportionate element to the evolving imaginative concept of Britishness just as an Act of Union linked two ancient polities with very different traditions of empire.

Defoe's expertise on the region may explain why his erstwhile paymaster Chief Minister Robert Harley chose not to consult him about the South Sea project. While Defoe favoured extending colonial settlement and avoiding open conflict with Spain, he was among the most prominent critics of the South Sea speculation. Inspired by the success of French traders on the Chilean and Peruvian coasts in the previous decade, Defoe pushed for a sustainable colonial trading policy, not occasional raids seeking plunder. Harley's plan to acquire a base in Spanish America under the Treaty of Utrecht faltered, and he accepted the lesser prize of the *Asiento*, a contract to supply slaves to Spanish American Colonies, and tariff concessions. By the time the South Sea Company went public any hope of a trading profit had evaporated. The fortuitous arrival of Rogers with the Manila galleon helped distract attention from this unpleasant reality. Amid a frenzy of publishing new information appeared, derived from pilot books taken from the Manila galleon, information quickly accessed by the Company, through Rogers and Edward Cooke, second Captain of the *Duchess*.[13]

While Woodes Rogers waged a fraught, prolonged legal battle over the prize money, Cooke rushed into print with *A Voyage to the South Sea, and Round the World* in March 1712, barely five months after his return to London. Such haste meant Cooke devoted less than half the 640-page text to the voyage, packing the remainder with a curious combination of borrowed history, Spanish coastal pilots and commercial intelligence. It was 'both propaganda and an intelligencers hand book for commercial aggression'. The fold-out map and coastal profiles were the very things a mariner would require, while woodcuts of animals, birds and fish reflected the influence of Dampier's *New Voyage*. However, Cooke lacked the intellectual curiosity and expository power of the older text. His object was to curry favour with a powerful patron, dedicate Robert Harley, the dominant figure in British politics. Cooke dismissed the Selkirk story, 'the most barren Subject that Nature can afford', revealing a monumental failure by author, editor and publisher to understand the book market. When the audience demanded to know more about the wild man dressed in goat skins Cooke complied, with striking ill-grace. While Cooke interviewed Selkirk to gather more material, he refused to introduce romantic fables, or turn the Scot and his survival instinct into a philosophical enquiry.[14] In his defence Cooke reflected the views of most contemporary seafarers; rocks and solitude were just plain dull.

Although Cooke beat his captain into print by three months, Rogers's text became the standard account. Rogers's compelling descriptions, notably his extended treatment of Selkirk, caught the attention of the reading public. Rogers's introduction revealed much of the logic of the South Sea Company, emphasising the wealth of Spain in the Pacific, and the prospects for trade demonstrated by French merchants. A British base on Juan Fernández 'might be of great use to those who would carry on any Trade in the South Sea'.[15] It has been suggested that Daniel Defoe helped compile Rogers's introduction, stressing the wider strategic and commercial imperatives that might have escaped the attention of a hard-bitten privateer. Defoe had debated the merits of the South Seas in the pages of the *Review* between June and August 1711, but fellow journalist/author Sir Richard Steele provided editorial support for Rogers. Dampier did not add a book to the list, distracted by litigious investors and crewmen from the *St George* fiasco. Some demanded pay and prize money; others, like John Welbe and William Funnel, attacked his conduct. Selkirk testified against Dampier, on behalf of the *St George* investors. His savage indictment of incompetence, cowardice, greed and knavery was confirmed by other witnesses. Dampier's day in the spotlight was done; no one wanted to go voyaging with the sick old man, on board ship, or across pages of text. He had made the market for travel books, and visited Juan Fernández more often than any other Englishman, but Rogers's voyage threw his tales into the shade. Dampier died in debt in 1715.

Steele's editorial interventions turned Rogers's simple narrative of Selkirk and his rescue into a Christian morality tale: necessarily stripped of goat abuse, the Scot became a Christian gentleman, British patriot and imperial governor.[16] This public version of the story endured for three centuries largely unchallenged. It was charming, effective, and quite untrue. Even if the philosophy and reflection of Selkirk's island years had been genuine, they proved strikingly ephemeral. Returning to the flesh-pots of London, he reverted to his old boozing and brawling habits, signing on for a final voyage to escape a complex marital situation.

By 1712 Selkirk's experience had been recorded, and placed in the wider context of English voyaging, alongside the stories of Sharp, Ringrose, Dampier and Will the Miskito Indian. In December 1713 Steele returned to the subject, in all probability to fill out the pages of his new journal *The Englishman*. Recalling conversations with Selkirk soon after his return to England, he reported the Scot, who had done very well from prize money, observing, 'I am now worth eight hundred pounds, but shall never be so happy as when I was not worth a farthing.' Although struck by his faith, Steele realised the sailor was slowly slipping back into another life, that of a common seafarer ashore. In truth Steele had completely forgotten the man behind the story, failing to recognise Selkirk when they met in the street. Steele's article revealed how far the Act of Union of 1707 had changed English attitudes. Selkirk may have left England a foreigner, but he returned a British mariner, and his deeds were suitably recorded. Selling the Act of Union with Scotland had been a major project for the author who turned Selkirk and his island into a literary masterpiece.

Selkirk's was one of many buccaneer tales that created a market for voyages, a national thirst for knowledge about the rest of the world, one that would be serviced by a rapidly expanding, newly uncensored book trade. These island-hopping texts fuelled a new round of travel collections, fictional writing and geographical speculation, turning the South Seas into an obsession that lured otherwise sane men to risk their money on visionary voyages and speculative investments.[17] Rogers, Cooke and Selkirk replaced Dampier as regional experts; soon all three would be embroiled in the scandal of the South Sea Company. When Rogers met key players at South Sea House in late 1711 it seemed that Juan Fernández would soon become a British colony.

In January 1712 the South Sea Company projected a massive combined operation by the Navy and the Company to smash down the gates of the South Pacific. The directors planned a settlement on 'the Gibraltar of the Pacific', but Ministerial support for such plans reflected the need to leverage peace with Madrid. Once a general European peace had been signed at Utrecht the expedition vanished, leaving the South Seas Company with a Treaty concession to supply slaves and an annual trading ship to Spanish America. The expedition had been little more than diplomatic posturing. A year later bankrupt South Sea veteran John Welbe circulated a project to control the South Seas by occupying and fortifying Juan Fernández, as a springboard to new lands to the west, which he conveniently assumed were rich in gold. By 1715 Welbe had cut his scheme to suit the straightened times, merely sending a ship via 'Juan de fardinandos ... to get wood and water'.[18]

In 1720 the madness of the 'South Sea Bubble' saw shares sold at thirty-two times face value. It could not last. In the wake of the 2008 banking disaster, the stunning, shocking collapse of the Company became a morality tale for contemporary audiences. While 'Bubble' entered the lexicon to describe hyper-inflated markets, the original 'Bubble', which combined the key elements of greed, ignorance, misleading promotion and political interference, remains the ultimate case study. Harley adopted the scheme to pay off the National Debt, as part of a complex political programme. Long after he left office the government had to cover-up embarrassing links to the new Hanoverian monarchy.[19]

Meanwhile, the island was briefly turned to account. A French/Chilean fishery of 1712 collapsed when the solitary ship was wrecked. The War of the Spanish Succession had weakened Spain, and emphasised the shipment of Peruvian bullion. The restoration of peace changed little; Philip V, the new Bourbon King of Spain, wanted to recover his lands in Italy, with American cash. Nothing was done about the offshore privateer haven. It remained the secret haunt of interlopers, illegal traders and pirates from Britain, France and Holland, only to be catapulted into international celebrity by a work of imaginative fiction.

By the close of the Spanish War, British buccaneers had rendered the seas of Peru familiar. Dampier's texts, complete with maps, by leading cartographer Herman Moll, created a Pacific voyage genre, mixing navigation, strategic analysis, science and wonder, shaping the national debate. Woodes Rogers added the exoticism of Selkirk's story and the lure of treasure galleons, transforming the South Seas into the field of dreams, a place to find fortune and found an empire.[20] After the collapse of the South Sea Bubble Sir Robert Walpole's government ignored the subject for twenty years, reflecting an alliance with France, the primacy of the European Balance of Power, and less risky economic opportunities in the Atlantic region. The South Sea projectors fell silent, they would resurface when relations with Spain began to spiral down to war.

The emergence of England as a global player prompted the publication of two major travel anthologies in 1704 and 1705, books that kept the South Seas at the forefront of an emerging world view. Not only was travel literature essential to any gentleman's library, it also quickly became a mainstay of the book trade. Booksellers Awnsham and John Churchill consulted the voyage collector Sir Hans Sloane and the philosopher John Locke for their four-volume *A Collection of Voyages and Travels*.

The preface, which may have been compiled by astronomer and magnetic voyager Edmund Halley, included a ringing endorsement of the economic value of oceanic exploration, backed by 1,600 folio pages of travel narratives, mostly unknown in England. To help clear unsold copies, two more volumes were added in 1730 and 1732. The description of Juan Fernández echoed Schouten's journal:

They say besides, that coming to this, which they call the *Fine Island*, they found a port very safe for their ships, having twenty or thirty fathoms depth, the shore al sandy and even, with a delicate valley full of trees of all sorts, and wild boars, and other animals feeding in it; but they could not distinguish them, by reason of the distance they were at. They extol particularly a most beautiful fountain, which coming down from high rocks, rowls into the sea by different canals, which form a pleasant prospect, and its water is very sweet and agreeable.[21]

They saw also great store of seals, and other fish, which they caught in great plenty. In short, they were so in love with this island, for the good qualities they discovered even at its entrance, that they were very unwilling to leave it, though pressed in point of time: 'I do not doubt, but that this is a very pleasant situation ... And without doubt these islands will be peopled in time, when the continent grows populous.'[22]

This brief account would influence the scorbutic ramblings of later British visitors, building a chorus of rapture that turned a useful watering place island into a magical island. John Harris produced a smaller and less original text, while Dampier received the accolade of a collected edition in 1729. Interest in the South Seas revived when Britain went to war with Spain in 1739, prompting fresh works and new editions. Prolific author John Campbell produced an enlarged edition of Harris in 1744–8. These were costly productions, often funded by advance subscription, reflecting both public taste and economic interest. 'The literature of travel now found a public, not only among dilettanti who read for amusement, but also among merchants and brokers who had invested money in commercial ventures to

Africa, Asia and the Pacific.'[23] Cheaper books, and the growing market for monthly and quarterly reviews, spread this knowledge across polite society. The profusion of voyage literature, historical and contemporary, designed to push the pace of exploration and economic exploitation, profoundly altered the British world view.

5

The Magical Island of Daniel Defoe

In 1719 the forty-year engagement between English mariners and Juan Fernández was finally consummated by journalist, author, spy and economic propagandist Daniel Defoe. *The Strange Surprising Adventures of Robinson Crusoe, Mariner* reflected the hopes and fears of a dynamic, prosperous nation in the grip of the South Sea Bubble, facing the threat of Jacobite insurrection. For Defoe the solution was obvious. Increased overseas trade would calm the masses at home, and repay the astronomic debts piled up by two major wars. Everyone assumed the long-closed markets of Spanish America were the best place to find extra trade; indeed the mere suggestion had deluded an entire nation into believing the South Sea Company could pay off the National Debt.

Books by Rogers and Cooke put the Selkirk story into wide circulation, and found their way into Defoe's extensive library, joining Dampier and other buccaneer/survivor tales. Voyage narratives had become very popular in the previous thirty years, while the fact that both Rogers and Cooke named Selkirk on their title pages demonstrated the allure of the island for potential buyers.[1] The return of peace after almost twenty years of war prompted discussions of the new, inclusive Britishness. While Selkirk's story put a Scotsman into the mainstream of oceanic voyaging just after the Act of Union, Defoe wrapped the new monarchy into his novel. Crusoe was half German – his real name was actually Kreutzenaer, 'my father being a foreigner of Bremen'. That this Anglo-German hybrid became, like King George I, an exemplary Englishman, was testament to changed times and the imaginative power of islands, great and small.

George was Crusoe's German father, mentioned on the first page of the book, and Crusoe was an example of Britishness set before the new monarch.

For all his mastery of invention Daniel Defoe was strikingly well read. In an age without public libraries he owned more than 2,000 books, far more than other contemporary authors, including Swift, Locke, Addison and Johnson. Furthermore, this was a carefully developed working collection, focused on history, travel and geography, enabling him to make striking, rich and curious journeys without leaving his house in Stoke Newington. Literary men of later generations had little difficulty spotting his sources, although Defoe only named those he used for direct quotations in non-fiction works. A commercially successful author, he despised pedantic displays of bookish learning. Voyage narratives included maps and drawings, descriptions and detailed observations that informed his imagination. Along-side key collections, including both editions of Hakluyt and Purchas, were more specific items needed by anyone thinking about Juan Fernández, identity and trade, including Bacon's *Essays*, Raleigh's *History of the World*, William Camden's *Elizabeth*, Grotius, Bynkershoek and Selden on maritime law, Flamsteed and Kepler on astronomy, Pepys's *Memoirs of the Navy*, Thucydides, and Hobbes's *Leviathan*. South Seas expertise came from Lionel Wafer, Betagh, Cooke, and the second edition of Exquemelin, which included Basil Ringrose's Juan Fernández narrative. These books and pamphlets provided the raw material for invention, making 'the tour of world in books', travelling 'by land with the historian, by sea with the navigators'.[2] Defoe collected navigational, cartographic and legal texts, along with those addressing the diseases of the sea.

Crusoe, a complex, multilayered text, reflected a deep engage-ment with various literary genres. While a significant literary industry has grown up over the past two centuries, attempting to attribute the basic story to other sources, or to 'prove' Defoe met Selkirk and stole his journal, Defoe was far too skilled an author to pirate a single buccaneer tale for a storyline. The idea that Defoe took Selkirk's non-existent journal was created (or at least retailed) by John Entick in 1757. Entick offered no evidence to back his assertion.[3] Selkirk's story was 'the most obvious source', but the wealth and variety of conscious and unconscious borrowing by a veteran author and exponent of maritime exploration meant it was only one element in his creative process.

The presence of Sir Walter Raleigh, colonialist, promoter of an Orinoco Empire and national hero in Crusoe's DNA is impossible to ignore. That the spellbinding literary creator of the Jacobean age should attract the admiration and emulation of his literary successor a century later should come as no surprise, but no one seems to have noticed. Defoe drew a great deal of material from Raleigh's *History of the World* for his imperial and geographical writings.[4] Raleigh sought gold on the Orinoco, and Defoe deliberately located Crusoe's island off the mouth of the river, exploiting the fact that Dampier had visited and described the island of Aves off the Orinoco, the river that, according to Columbus, flowed into Paradise.[5] Building on Steele's interpretation of Selkirk's island sojourn as a moral tale of British redemption, colonial domination and success Defoe reimagined Juan Fernández, using maps and eye-witness accounts. Then he added new features, notably the cave that has haunted romantic imaginings of Juan Fernández ever since.[6] There is no cave in any Selkirk narrative; he lived in a hut made of sticks and grass. Crusoe lived in a fortified cave, a residence suitable for a colonial overlord in savage lands, not an unarmed maroon expecting to be rescued by English sailors. Indeed the whole island has been reimagined by later visitors to satisfy Robinsonian dreams, without taking the trouble to separate fact and fiction. Armchair travellers who commingle Selkirk and Crusoe, Juan Fernández and an imaginary island off the Orinoco make a serious error. Defoe did not stoop to plagiarise; he created the narrative and employed telling details borrowed from his rich library to make it 'real'. If he wanted to be taken seriously, he needed to be believable.

Defoe's hero was a curious compound of Anglo-German attitudes, a hybrid who could be held up as the exemplary Englishman. He met triumph and disaster with equanimity and worked hard to improve his lot, to develop his 'empire', rescue benighted savages from the darkness of cannibalism, and reconcile Europeans of different faiths. He was building a better world, a modern world, if only in microcosm. Crusoe may have been the first truly middle-class hero. There was nothing of Selkirk in this. Crusoe's stoicism, self-control and determination in the face of adversity became quintessential 'British' virtues. By the nineteenth century his cool courage under fire and under pressure had come to define the British, a convergence that kept him at the top of any literary list. *Crusoe* survived the shifting patterns of culture and taste across three centuries, endlessly read, reimagined in new locations, and subjected to a staggering industry of academic enquiry, a curious fate for a piece of hastily executed polemical ephemera littered with glaring continuity errors.

Defoe had far more important things on his mind than a simple tale of a marooned sailor. His audience were the movers and shakers of early eighteenth-century London, and his targets were contemporary. He had never believed South Sea Company hype, doubting the Spanish would allow the company to profit from an *Asiento* wrung out of them by force. For him the Company was a front for a Jacobite Tory revival, something that alarmed a man of progressive democratic views. After publishing *Crusoe* he produced a savage indictment of the Company. He preferred an English colony in South America, suggesting various locations including the mouth of the Orinoco River, site of Raleigh's misadventures, and those of Crusoe, or further south in what is now Argentina.

In February 1719, while drafting *Crusoe*, Defoe advocated the Orinoco scheme in the *Weekly Journal*. These links explain the timing of the book, the strongly colonial theme and the precise location of Crusoe's island. He expanded on the colonial theme in the second, largely forgotten, Crusoe story. Defoe did not connect Crusoe to Juan Fernández because it was too far away to be a practical option for colonial projects, but the island was never far from his mind. His next novel – *The King of Pirates* of 1720, a fictionalised life of pirate John Avery – had Avery crossing the Isthmus of Panama and returning to England with Bartholomew Sharp, a voyage that visited Juan Fernández.[7]

Alongside the three Crusoe stories and pirate novels, Defoe also wrote extensively on the South Sea Bubble scandal, commerce and economics, in fact and fiction. The fictional travelogue *A New Voyage Round the World* of 1724 reshaped and refreshed the seemingly inexhaustible reservoir of knowledge he had accumulated across a long and busy career. Defoe used this 'voyage' to stress the distinction between travellers who merely record what they found, and when they found it, and those who analysed the meaning of what has been discovered. In this way he empowered imaginative, reflective armchair travellers over mariners and buccaneers who brought home confused tales of seas and islands, ports and storms. The obvious inspirations for the book were two familiar texts, Dampier's book of the same title, the author being conveniently dead, and Woodes Rogers's *A Cruising Voyage Round the World* printed in 1712 and 1719. He may also have had access to the latest Juan Fernández narrative, George Shelvocke's voyage, in manuscript. Defoe reckoned these voyagers 'illiterate sailors' who had learned a thousand times more than they recorded. He included an extensive description of Juan Fernández. Once again his object was to prompt exploration and colonisation for commercial purposes, not celebrate piracy. Defoe created a synergistic vision of the world ocean as a fit space for British enterprise and exploitation. His analytical turn of mind included imaginative writing, some of the best centred on Chile, in which he returned to the theme of British colonies in South America. The old idea of colonising Valdivia survived and prospered in an imagined land, uninhabited and yet heaped with gold.

In 1727 the prospect of war with Spain gave Defoe another opportunity to expound his commercial, colonial maritime vision.

Dismissing Spanish sabre-rattling as 'Quixotisme', he coined the maxim 'England may Gain by a War with France, but never Loses by a War with Spain.' The old glory of Drake and Raleigh was once again to the fore, Defoe revelling in the heroic deeds of the greatest pirate, and the elegant prose of an admired imperial projector.[8] In 1728 Defoe published two major works on trade: *A Plan of the English Commerce* and a 300-page contribution to 'an extensive survey of the commerce of the whole world'. The ambitions of this 862-page text were revealed by the full title: *Atlas Maritimus and Commercialis: Or, a General View of the World, so far as Relates to Trade and Navigation: With a Large Account of the Commerce carried on by Sea to Which Are added Sailing Directions for Coasts and Islands on the Globe.* In other words, a guidebook to the commercial opportunities of global trade, aimed squarely at the mercantile men of London and, like *Crusoe*, published by William Taylor with a syndicate of London printers and cartographers.

Taken in the round, Defoe's writings form a manifesto for an ever-expanding global economy, centred on London, linked by sea. This would create more employment, leading to a happier working population, and ultimately 'An Encrease of Colonies encreases People, People encrease the Consumption of Manufactures, Manufactures Trade, Trade Navigation, Navigation Seamen, and altogether encrease the Wealth, Strength, and Prosperity of *England*.'[9] In this he recognised the deeper meaning of the British experience. Britain would be a maritime trading empire, like the Carthaginian state he discovered in Raleigh's *History of World*. He lamented the downfall of Carthage at the hands of the Romans, those 'Destroyers of Industry and Trade'.

The lesson was clear: first Spain and now France were new Roman Empires, Continental Universal Monarchies that opposed the liberties and the commerce of Britain, the new Carthage. The message would be repeated down to his death in 1731. A self-made man of the Augustan age Defoe believed history and geography had replaced ancient languages and ancient knowledge as the key to progress. His argument was exemplified by the Americas, lands beyond the classical world. This was just one more way in which his unique mind grasped a distant future. That Montesquieu reached a very similar conclusion at the same time, based on severely classical models, provides a striking endorsement for the Englishman's insight.[10]

The advocacy of colonisation in the Americas, North and South, addressed an ongoing debate. While many saw the colonies as profiting at the expense of the mother country, Defoe disagreed: 'The Wealth and Strength of our Colonies is our own Wealth and Strength ... we are great in their Greatness'.[11] He preferred trade and agriculture to the Spanish model of asset-stripping mineral wealth while leaving the land to subsistence cultivation and blocking foreign trade. British Colonies, he argued, generated more real wealth than those of Spain. As the Empire became global, the options for colonisation spread. Crusoe the castaway quickly becomes an idealised colonial and commercial pioneer, a diminutive King George, and Juan Fernández, like More's Utopia, a diminutive Britain. Juan Fernández was never far from his thoughts.

Defoe established the central place of this tiny island in eighteenth-century English culture, melding rough tales of buccaneering men and the economic ambitions of a dynamic maritime state into an original text for mass consumption. *Crusoe*'s enduring success reflected Defoe's understanding of his audience and the timeless quality of his vision. Within a year the book had been translated into French; Dutch, German and Russian versions followed over the next forty years. Cut-down editions, as badly printed as edited, became staple fare for eighteenth-century chapbook peddlers, the cheapest and most accessible English texts. While *Crusoe* provided the English with a world view at once moral and commercial, Defoe continued to push the idea of a global empire of trade on his fellow countrymen in fiction, geography, history and journalism for another decade, a decade in which Juan Fernández would witness a striking example of Karl Marx's jest that history always repeats itself, first as tragedy and then as farce. As Diana Souhami observed, 'Selkirk transmuted into Crusoe's mythical world. His own reality blurred. His time on The Island claimed first by journalists, was reinvented in the bright world of fiction. What had really happened and who he was were incidental.'[12] The Crusoe version avoided subjects that worried British audiences, sex, death, religious doubt and above all boredom. The real Selkirk died at sea, off the coast of West Africa, on 13 December 1721. As if to mark the meaning of his passing, Selkirk's ship, HMS *Weymouth*, captured a pirate vessel a few days later, and hanged the crew. The age of the buccaneer was over.

6

Shelvocke's Sojourn

———◦◦◦◦———

While Defoe built an imaginary empire from the island narratives of marooned mariners, others tried to exploit that hard-won knowledge in pursuit of treasure. Woodes Rogers's voyage revived the English dream that Juan Fernández 'might be at first of great use to those who would carry on any Trade to the South Sea'. With Rogers's text in hand another English privateer voyage headed for the South Pacific. John Clipperton and George Shelvocke set Juan Fernández as the squadron rendezvous and refreshment stop. The British investors secured an Austrian privateer commission to get round the problem that Britain and Spain were in perfect amity. Fortunately a brief Anglo-Spanish war relieved them of the need to get a flimsy cover story from Habsburg Ostend.[1]

Any voyage to the little-known, lightly charted South Seas put a premium on local knowledge. Senior Captain John Clipperton had been Dampier's chief mate on the *St George*, although he hardly endeared himself to the old buccaneer, deserting and stealing the legal commission or letter of marque. Predictably, the new voyage did not begin well; the two captains were at daggers drawn from the outset. Former naval officer Shelvocke was drinking heavily, while Clipperton refused to share the charts. From the outset it was obvious that Shelvocke wanted to operate alone, and he made sure the ships separated. Clipperton's *Success* made a fast passage, arriving at Juan Fernández on 7 September 1719. After waiting a month for his companion, using the time to refit, revictual and refresh Clipperton set off on a successful raiding campaign. He left a message in a bottle for Shelvocke, while two of his men deliberately marooned themselves. They were captured by a Spanish landing party two months later, their presence betrayed by prisoners taken from one of Clipperton's prizes. The Spanish also removed the bottle.

Shelvocke paid a high price for his laggardly voyage; the *Speedwell*'s passage round Cape Horn proved long and terrible. As hope faded, Simon Hatley, the gloomy, superstitious mate, shot an albatross, providing Samuel Taylor Coleridge with the plot for his verse epic 'The Rime of the Ancient Mariner'.[2] While Shelvocke was understandably anxious to make Juan Fernández, a near mutinous crew, seduced by French misinformation, insisted on a diversion to Concepción, which Shelvocke used to justify abandoning his instructions.[3]

Speedwell finally arrived off Juan Fernández on 11 January 1720. Despite the sickly state of his crew Shelvocke displayed little interest in the 'magical' island, belatedly sending a boat ashore on 15 January. He found no sign of Clipperton, and after waiting four days for the *Success* cruised over to the mainland, where he picked up some small prizes. With the crew in better spirits, although rather scorbutic, the *Speedwell* returned to the islands in May, initially fetching up near Más Afuera on the 6th, and at Juan Fernández on the 11th. Even so Shelvocke was unwilling to anchor in Windy Bay; he preferred to stand on and off while a boat went ashore for water. Later he claimed that they were unable to get enough water to replenish the casks and reluctantly decided to anchor, to raft the large water butts ashore. The butts were filled in a single day, but then the weather turned and the *Speedwell* was trapped in the Bay for four days. On 25 May the anchor cable failed during heavy gales from the seaward, which Shelvocke noted was 'a thing very uncommon' and the ship was wrecked. From Shelvocke's description 'if we had struck but a cable's length further to the eastward, or westward of the place where we did, we must inevitably have perished' it appears *Speedwell* had been anchored off Bahía Pangal, the usual watering place, which lies between two sheer rocky cliffs, while the rest of the bay has a relatively gentle beach gradient. *Speedwell*'s hull was stove, and all three masts went over the side, the crew used them to build a raft and reach the shore. Only one man was lost. Shocked and stunned, the castaway captain forgot the well-known fecundity of the island, recalling 'the dread we had upon us of starving on the uninhabited isle we were thrown upon', 'the remotest part of the earth'. At least he managed to save his privateer commission, some bags of bread and most of the gunpowder. That night a huddle of wet, frightened men were:

saluted by the melancholy howlings of innumerable seals on the beach, who lay so thick that we were obliged to clear our way of them as we went along, and nothing presented itself to our sight but rocky precipices, inhospitable woods, dropping with rain, lofty mountains, whose tops were hid by thick clouds, and a tempestuous sea, which had reduced us to the low state we were now in.[4]

Misery and despair transformed the expedition into a tale of shipwreck, chaos and recrimination. Marine Captain William Betagh claimed Shelvocke deliberately wrecked the ship, to defraud the investors. Although Betagh had reason to hate Shelvocke, and was nowhere near the island at the time, his claim demands closer attention. The rarity of onshore winds in this area, and Shelvocke's troubling character make the accusation plausible – but the case remains unproven.[5]

With the ship in pieces the social structure of the new islanders changed. Shelvocke's commission, the basis of his authority over the crew, concerned an irretrievably wrecked ship. Released from legal obligation, the men proved reluctant to work, or even acknowledge his leadership. Among his few methods of exerting control the erstwhile Captain found 1100 silver dollars the most effective. The rest of the plundered cash, securely stowed below the bread room was hopelessly lost. By playing on the men's fears of falling into the hands of Spanish, and being sent to the mines of Potosi Shelvocke managed to pull them together, up to a point. The camp was set up half a mile from the sea, with a good water supply and plenty of wood to build huts and make fires. This may have been the site of the original Spanish settlement at Bahía Pangal, and even if it was not, five months occupation, tree felling and burning by seventy men quickly cleared a space to be grazed by the ubiquitous goats. Soon the officers were comfortably situated, dining on roast crayfish.

Getting off the island would prove more difficult. Salvaging timber and equipment from the wreck helped, while charcoal for forges was created by burning local timber. Soon after laying the keel, made from the *Speedwell*'s bowsprit, the carpenter refused to work. Shelvocke had to bribe him to carry on. Cutting timber proved tedious, 'we were obliged sometimes to go a great way from the water-side, and after having cut it down, it must be dragged up steep hills and other fatigues which tired the people to a great degree. But in two months we made a tolerable show.'[6] With the men working day on and day off, bolstered by a good diet all promised well for an early departure.

Then the men refused duty, the officers backed them, and Shelvocke lost control of the weapons and the island. After two months Juan Fernández was weaving another kind of magic, the magic of mutiny. Just like the better-known *Bounty* mutiny sixty years later, the crew began to identify with their island home, disputing authority figures from their previous existence. They seemed indifferent to their fate, unconcerned at the prospect of a long stay. In the absence of a ship the men assembled at a large tree, standing in for the mainmast, and adopted the old Jamaica buccaneer rules of prize distribution, in defiance of their erstwhile captain and the investors at home. *Speedwell*'s voyage was over; the men would strike out on a new basis, led by erstwhile cobbler Morphew. Morphew complained Shelvocke was too much the man of war officer, 'too lofty and arbitrary for a private ship'.

If Morphew played the part of John Adams, Lieutenant Brooks was happy to be Fletcher Christian, lending a fig leaf of gentlemanly character to proceedings. This 'gang of Levellers' made Shelvocke sign their articles. Despite later claims that he tried to defend the interests of the investors, Shelvocke's words were a smokescreen for deeper schemes. Work on the new vessel slowed to a crawl, while only a single black man, a descendant of Will, was left to fish and forage for the captain's table. This mattered because without food Shelvocke's 'family' of supporters shrank as quickly as his pot. His repeated warnings of Spanish cruelty finally took effect on 15 August, when a large ship came in sight. In an instant Shelvocke recovered his authority, directing the sailors to remove the black and Indian men from the beach, to prevent them betraying the castaways. In the event the vessel did not come close enough to spot the remains of the *Speedwell*, the new ship, or the crew. With the men answering his command Shelvocke reminded them that a life of slavery at Potosi was the only reward the Spaniards would offer them. Eventually the older sailors, those with most to lose at home accepted his authority, and work on the ship was pushed to completion. Even so eleven of the more advanced 'levellers' decided to stay on the island, abandoning the camp for the interior.

One small cannon had been salvaged from the *Speedwell*'s quarter deck to arm the suitably recondite *Recovery*, along with a pump, essential to keep the leaky, ill-caulked ship afloat. On 5 October the ship was launched with her casks already in place, and most of the rigging up. Wasting little time, she sailed on 6 October, every spare inch of the hull of the ramshackle barque crammed with smoked conger eel, the only fish or meat they had been able to preserve. They also carried four pigs, fed on putrid seal meat. The eels were fried in seal oil and eaten with the last of the cassava flour salvaged from the wreck.[7]

When the ship crept out of Windy Bay twenty four men were left behind, the 'levellers' and the black and Indian men recruited after the ship left England, who had no choice in the matter. This colony of maroons was removed as soon as the Spanish learned of their presence. William Betagh named eleven 'levellers'. The ultimate fates of John Wisdom, Joseph Manero, William Blew, John Biddleclaus, Edmund Hyves, Daniel Harvey, William Giddy, John Robjohn, Thomas Hawkes, John Row and Jacob Bowden are unknown.[8]

Four days after departing Juan Fernández the *Recovery*, on course for the Bay of Concepción spotted a Spanish ship. Desperate to escape their overcrowded, evil-smelling, un-seaworthy craft they made short work of the capture.[9] After that the expedition resumed privateering, preying on local shipping and returned home with a solid, rather than fabulous prize fund. Arriving in England in 1722 officers and disappointed investors began quarrelling over money, authority and power. Several resorted to print. While Shelvocke had the best of the literary and financial exchange doubts about his integrity persist. He cleared £8,000 as his personal share of the prize fund of £137,000. Despite a successful voyage, ruinously expensive litigation ensured the investors did not share in the proceeds. This would be the last Pacific privateer voyage.

This was not what Shelvocke had expected; he framed his book, once he had explained the loss of his ship and the failure to reward the investors, as a guide for future expeditions. Amid the self-justification and rancorous abuse of his officers were competent passages on navigation, complete with a global track chart of the world re-encompassed, including a suitably spacious 'Great South Sea' and navigational fixes. He also discussed the resources of Juan Fernández, the key to any British Pacific venture. Shelvocke's description of Juan Fernández as a fruitful, wholesome healthy location, one where dying men recovered, and 'levellers' returned to their proper station, helped cement its place in the mental world of subsequent Pacific voyagers. Shelvocke knew his place in the literary imagining of the island; he followed Defoe, Dampier, Rodgers and Selkirk, works that ensured the island was sufficiently well known to feature in the long title of his book. Clearly Juan Fernández fascinated his audience.

After excusing his failure to provide 'an exact description' of the entire island, six months had not been enough time, given the need to build a barque and deal with a mutinous crew, Shelvocke's fifteen-page survivor guide stressed the island was rocky, and vertical, 'insomuchas that there is no walking a quarter of a mile without going up or down a steep declivity'. He advised future navigators to avoid getting close to the shore, and warned that previous accounts, which minimised the risk of northerly winds, were unreliable:

In going in, beware of the flaws which come down the narrow valleys so violent as to be often times dangerous; these too in the night, are surprising as you lie at anchor ... it is my opinion, that the anchorage is far from being safe.[10]

After the wreck the weather had been so bad that they could not fish, nor could they abide the taste of seal meat, so they lived on seal offal. The sheer scale of destruction necessary to feed seventy men in such an inefficient way quickly drove the seals away, forcing the castaways to eat seal meat; they avoided the fishy taste by stripping away the fat and roasting the steaks 'till they were as dry as a chip'. Like any Briton abroad, Shelvocke lamented the absence of alcoholic beverages to help digest these ill-conditioned husks. The men found better eating among the descendants of Selkirk's cats, easily caught by the ship's dog. Only the Captain balked at such feline fancies. With little powder or shot, or shoes to clamber about in the rocky heights where they lived, goat meat was hard to come by. There were plenty of goats, despite the packs of wild dogs. The dogs, no better equipped to catch mountain goats than the newly arrived British sailors, also dined on seal flesh. After losing the only boat crude fishing coracles were constructed from sea lion hides. Crayfish were caught with seal guts, simply attaching the offal to a line brought in any number of hungry crustaceans. The fish was fried in seal oil, and eaten with a little wild sorrel. Among the other vegetables only the cabbage palm was worthy of note, each tree providing no more than two pounds of edible material. The sailor's dwellings were of the Selkirk type, branches, grass, scraps of sail and animal skins, easily blown away by storms.

When he came to describe the island, Shelvocke repeated much that was already known, but neatly reinforced with telling personal detail. Seventy men lived there for five months without a day's illness, while stout and gouty Shelvocke, deprived of alcohol and salt, recovered his health and vigour. He added an updated list of flora and fauna, crediting previous buccaneers with sowing turnips, pumpkins, sorrel, watercress and other crops. Fresh water dominated every account of South Pacific navigation down to the end of Spanish rule, and Shelvokce was no exception. 'Water was plentiful at the western end of the bay, and kept as well as any in the world.' Having set out the qualities of the place, and the value it possessed as a healthy and fruitful strategic base for operations against Spanish trade and settlements Shelvocke was moved to lyrical heights by the scenery:

down the Western peak, contiguous to the Table Mountain [El Yunque], descend two cascades at least 300 foot perpendicular, close by one another, about 12 foot in breadth, (which probably supply most of the other runs of water). What with the rapid descent of these waters, and the palm-trees which grow quite up close by the edges of them, adorned with vast bunches of red berries, it yields as agreeable a prospect as can be seen.[11]

The soil was loose, making the burrows of flightless birds, pardelas, dangerous to the unwary. When it came to natural wonders, Shelvocke gave pride of place to seals and elephant seals. Bull elephant seals would provide a butt of oil each:

if this island lay nearer to England, 2 or 3 large ships out of the River Thames, or elsewhere, might find a lading [cargo] of train oil, since, in the winter months, there is an infallible certainty of finding them there.

In short, every thing that one sees or hears in this place is perfectly romantick,– the very structure of the island, in all its parts, has a certain savage irregular beauty, which is not to be expressed; the many prospects of lofty inaccessible hills, and the solitariness of the gloomy narrow valleys, which a great part of the day enjoy little benefit from the sun, and the fall of waters, which one hears all around, would be agreeable to none but those who would indulge themselves, for a time, in a pensive melancholy. To conclude, nothing can be conceived more dismally solemn, than to hear the silence of the still night destroyed by the surf of the sea beating on the shore, together with the violent roaring of the sea-lions repeated all around by the echoes of deep vallies, the incessant howling of the seals, (who according to their age, make a hoarser or a shriller noise) so that in this confused medley, a man might imagine that he heard the different tones of all the species of animals upon earth mixed together. Add to these the sudden precipitate tumbling of trees down steep descents; for there is hardly a gust of wind stirring that does not tear up a great many trees by the roots, which have but a slight hold in the earth, especially near the brinks of precipices. All these, or any one of these frightful noises would be sufficient to prevent the repose of any who had not been for some time inured to it. Thus have I given an account of such parts of this Island as I have had a sight of, and of every thing worthy observation on it, which occurred to me; but this only relates to the *Northern* half, the mountains being impassable to go to the *Southern* parts of it, therefore I can say nothing of them.[12]

While the wild, natural and romantic aspects of the island were more likely to alarm his readers than enchant them – the taste for such sublime experience was as yet limited – Shelvocke's text became a resource for later voyagers.

The distinctly unimpressive economic returns of voyages to the South Seas meant Shelvocke would be the last British privateer to cruise the South Seas. While Rogers brought home prize goods worth £148,000, and healthy profits for investors, the Dampier and Shelvocke expeditions were commercial disasters. A decade later John Campbell lamented that the painful combination of avarice, buccaneering and chaos 'gave the public a bad idea of all Expeditions to the South Sea, and induced many to suppose, that ... they were calculated purely for the private Advantage', while taking tales of mutinies and disasters too seriously was keeping the nation asleep, unaware of the riches to be had by men of enterprise and energy. Despite these problems the cultural impact of buccaneer and privateer voyages would be out of all proportion to their number, or their financial success. *Robinson Crusoe*, *Gulliver's Travels*, *The* 'Rime of the Ancient Mariner' and other voyage narratives transformed the intellectual landscape of eighteenth-century Britain. However, the licensed predator had run his course; no more would put in at Juan Fernández to refit and refresh, recover goatskin clad castaways and feast on crayfish. Henceforth British power would be projected into the Pacific by the Royal Navy.[13]

Before the next British voyagers arrived they had an opportunity to reflect on the last Dutch attempt to contest the future of the South Pacific. Hoping to cut into the Dutch East India Company's Asian monopoly the West India Company sent an expedition under Jacob Roggeveen in 1721. Following the Schouten/Le Maire voyage, the three-ship squadron set Juan Fernández as their rendezvous, and the flagship arrived on 24 February 1722. All three vessels remained for several weeks. Suitably refreshed, the expedition sailed off into the unknown, finding and naming Easter Island. In British accounts Roggeveen claimed Juan Fernández 'would afford subsistence for 600 families at least'. John Campbell added emphasis:

Whatever nation shall revive and prosecute Mr Roggewein's plan, will become, in a few years, master of as rich and profitable a commerce, as the Spaniards have from their own country to Mexico and Peru, or the Portuguese to Brazil.[14]

This foreign endorsement was doubly convenient, investing long held British views with a degree of impartiality, and a hint of urgency. In fact the Dutch studiously ignored Roggeveen, he was arrested at Batavia (modern Jakarta) by the Dutch East India Company and arrived home a prisoner. The Dutch never came back to Juan Fernández, and later it became clear that contemporary accounts of the Roggeveen voyage were garbled, misleading and in some cases invented. Roggeveen's journal noted the island had 'extremely good water and firewood, and fish', which were 'in such great abundance that four men with the hook are able to catch in two hours for a hundred men so many than they have enough for a midday and evening meal'. The fish were fried in fresh seal oil. He dismissed the buccaneer narratives of abundant greenery as romances and above all said nothing about settlement, or the strategic value of the islands.[15] That Campbell happily bolstered his own argument with some very doubtful Dutch courage should not mislead. The Dutch showed no interest in Juan Fernández, and Roggeveen was the last Dutchman to enter the Pacific via Cape Horn.

After Shelvocke and Roggeveen, the islands slumbered for almost twenty years, visited by a few discrete smuggling voyages while the occasional Spanish expedition landed dogs to destroy the goat population, long the staple diet of freebooters and interlopers. In truth, the silence of those years was only the lull before the storm. The British had been planning and projecting their way into the South Pacific ever since the high drama of Drake and Cavendish, fuelled by the lure of silver and the promotion of vital export trades. Britain produced a surplus of woollen goods and manufactures, which were hard to place on the global market. The prospect of new American markets encouraged merchants and manufacturers to engage with the wider world, embark their money in new voyages, or push the ministers for another Spanish War.[16]

George Anson's Voyage

———⟨∂∕∂⟩———

In 1738 the invariably strained Anglo-Spanish relationship plumbed new depths. Long-standing quarrels over the terms of the *Asiento*, South Seas Company political influence and British arrogance spiralled into war. Company complaints about unfair restraints on market access met a growing desire among the wider commercial community to resume the old habit of plundering Spanish America, overriding the wisdom and caution of Prime Minister Sir Robert Walpole. His deluded opponents supposed the possession of a vast costly Navy meant a war with Spain would be short and successful. Plans were legion, including South Seas projects pivoted on Juan Fernández. The strategy could not be faulted for modesty. Valdivia in Southern Chile would be an ideal settlement, while Juan Fernández might be occupied and fortified as 'a settlement, retreat, or as a place of rendezvous'. South Seas 'experts' Hubert Tassell and Henry Hutchinson, men connected to the Company, recommended occupying Juan Fernández, building a small fort and houses and cultivating the land as a settlement, retreat or rendezvous. Such designs had more than hint of the massive, overblown 1712 scheme, combining an impressive fleet with a landing force of 1,500 troops. Both men sailed with Anson's expedition, linking naval force with commercial ambition.[1]

Eventually a force of six warships and two transports was placed under the command of Captain George Anson, an officer with considerable American experience, albeit North American, and an expertise in celestial navigation. His flagship was HMS *Centurion*, a sixty-gun battleship. Resources were so tight that Anson's tiny landing force consisted of Chelsea Pensioners and raw, untrained Marines. Although his troops were distinctly unimpressive Anson embarked a formidable library of South Pacific books, using the most recent, Shelvocke's text, to encode signals. British information security was shocking. By January 1740 the French knew of plans to attack Spanish America, perhaps at Buenos Aires, which had been an early objective, or establishing a colony in Patagonia. Intelligence from Paris finally roused the Spanish to recognise the danger, and by the middle of the year warnings had been sent from Madrid to the governors of Manila, Mexico and Peru. Spying became circular when the British captured a Spanish dispatch, advising the Viceroy of Mexico 'that the King of Spain had heard of our fitting out six ships, with 700 land forces on board, for to go round Cape Horn to the South Sea'. The Viceroys should be on guard, using the annual royal revenue to enhance local defences. Long before he sailed from Spithead Anson knew the element of surprise had been lost.[2] To make matters worse the Spanish sent a powerful squadron to destroy his force before it could reach the Pacific.

A delayed departure meant Anson's squadron rounded Cape Horn in winter storms. Only four ships made the rendezvous at Juan Fernández, their crews decimated by hypothermia, typhus, dysentery and, above all, scurvy. Eighteenth-century mariners knew how scurvy affected the human body, but they had no idea what caused it, other than long sea voyages. The symptoms were terrifying. Teeth became loose in the gums, old wounds reopened and began to bleed, men lost their strength, limbs became swollen, joints tightened, and sections of skin blackened. Sixteenth-century Spanish mariners had appreciated the preservative quality of lemons, and some English seamen learned the lesson, notably those sailing to India. Yet no one made a systematic attempt to analyse the disease until after it had decimated Anson's expedition.

While eighteenth-century men sought divine intervention and looked for land, modern medical knowledge has expanded our understanding of what went wrong. The expedition spent months anchored at Spithead before sailing, a period when the men had little access to fresh food. The long voyage south did little to improve the situation, living on salt meat, hard biscuit and other preserved rations. By contrast Anson and his officers had eaten fresh provisions at Spithead, arriving at Juan Fernández in better condition.

Scurvy is a wasting disease brought on by a critical deficiency of vitamin C. The human body can store enough vitamin C to last a few weeks, but this must be replaced by regular supplies obtained from fresh vegetables, citrus fruits, milk, raw fish or seal meat. Older men have a smaller reserve of vitamin C than boys and younger men, explaining the earlier onset and disproportionate losses among the old soldiers. Even so it would be six months after sailing that the first scorbutic outbreaks occurred, longer than modern science would suggest. HMS *Gloucester* recorded the first cases on 11 March 1741.

However, the problem was more complex; the men were also suffering from deficiencies of niacin and other vitamins, leading to idiotism, lunacy and convulsions, while the lack of thiamin and vitamin A caused night blindness. Rough weather rounding the Cape Horn left the men exhausted, filthy, frozen, bruised and short of hot food, all of which reduced their resistance to scurvy, and other shipboard diseases.

Having rounded Cape Horn and narrowly avoided disaster due to navigational errors, Anson waited for some days at the first rendezvous, Socorro on the Chilean coast. It proved to be a desperate disappointment. Where Narborough's journal recorded landing on a fine sandy beach Anson saw only a rocky shore and crashing waves. There was no food or succour to be had, and after a few hair-raising days trying to hold station in storm conditions he headed north for Juan Fernández, 'the only road in that part of the world where there was any probability of our recovering our sick, or refitting our vessel, and consequently our getting thither was the only chance we had left to avoid perishing at sea'.[3]

Unfortunately Anson had an inaccurate location for the island, a common feature of existing accounts, including Shelvocke's.

The position given was too close to the mainland and one degree of latitude too far north. To make matters worse Anson lost faith in the navigational abilities of the ship's master after the close brush with disaster rounding Cape Horn. A fine observational astronomer and experienced navigator Anson made a cautious approach, missing Juan Fernández and sailing right up the Chilean coast before admitting his error. In the nine days that were wasted close on one hundred men died, a tragedy that inspired some powerful lines in the official voyage narrative, lines that established the island at the heart of the story: 'Under these disheartening circumstances, we stood to the westward; and, on the 9th of June [1741], at daybreak, we at last discovered the long-wished for island of Juan Fernandez.'4

Although their books (notably Shelvocke's) told them the island would be their salvation, first indications suggested it was a tough, rugged and mountainous place. The following day HMS *Centurion* coasted along the northern shore, with a northerly wind, looking for the main anchorage, Windy Bay. The sight of this verdant island with waterfalls cascading into the ocean was enough to revive some invalids, they struggled onto the deck simply to see and smell salvation. The officers, more concerned to find the anchorage, quickly realised there was no one on the island, either Spaniard or Englishman. Four more men died that day. With a desperately weak crew, one that depended on the officers, boys and even a cleric to carry out the simplest manoeuvres and a current carrying them close to the shore Anson wisely anchored at sunset. Early the following morning the cutter was sent to locate Windy Bay, while Anson waited for a fresh easterly gale and high seas to abate. The crew set about fishing, quickly hauling in a prodigious quantity. The boat returned seven hours later with grass and fresh seal meat, having located the anchorage to the west, and the following morning (12 June), the anchor half-raised, the crew were too weak to haul it up to the cathead, the ship drifted into Windy Bay, luffing up towards the watering place at Bahía Pangal. During the day three more men died. The 'dreadful and fatal' voyage of 148 days from Brazil had finally ended.[5] The disaster was a direct result of poor diet before the ships left England, and the length of passage from the last landfall.

Shortly after the *Centurion* anchored, the sloop *Tryal* appeared. Anson hoped she could help to shift the *Centurion*'s anchors further inshore, but the tiny warship was in no condition to oblige. Anson sent Lieutenant Philip Saumarez and a boat crew to carry the hawsers on board and help work the ship, they found that only Captain Charles Saunders, a lieutenant and three men were able to work the sails. The sloop had lost 34 men from a crew of only 100. Most of those still living were close to death; they lay on the deck, literally awash in their own excrement, amid the wreckage of the rigging, alongside the unburied dead. Saumarez's men helped *Tryal* moor inshore of the *Centurion*. By the next morning the two ships were anchored. Saumarez recorded both ships 'sending materials ashore to raise tents for the sick, who now died apace. It being impossible to conceive the stench and filthiness which men lay in or the condition that the ship was in between decks.'[6] With so few men fit for duty, Anson and his officers had to work the ship, and carry the scorbutic invalids ashore. As the first boats headed for the island the officers were enraptured by 'this enchanting landskip, which still improved upon us the further we advanced.' However such delights would have to wait: the first priority was the health of the remaining men, then refitting shattered, filthy ships. Anson's mission depended on the mythic restorative qualities of Juan Fernández.

On 15 June the *Tryal* was blown out of the bay by 'the violent flaws of the wind', and had to be helped back by *Centurion*'s pinnace. She returned on the 17th, to find that a tented camp had been established at Bahía Pangal, close to the original Spanish settlement and Shelvocke's camp. The landing was not easy, 'by reason of pretty much surf, and great stones like rocks, instead of sand or gravel on the shore'. To improve access Anson had the men build a wharf.[7]

By the 18th all 135 invalids had been brought ashore, a monumental task for the handful still strong enough to carry them in their hammocks across a rough, stony beach, and up a steep hill. A dozen men had died as they were being brought ashore. After three weeks the daily death toll ebbed. Once ashore, the sick recovered quickly, a century and half before anyone understood the causation this apparently miraculous transformation only reinforced the notion of a magical island.

Once the invalids had been housed, tents were set up for the cooper and sailmakers, while two copper ovens were brought ashore to bake bread. Not only was fresh bread good for morale, but it reduced the strain on scorbutic teeth and gums. As the men recovered they were put to work catching fish, goats and seals. The main task was feeding the fires that baked their bread, and made charcoal to work the blacksmith's forges. Those remaining on board faced a major task. Badly damaged rounding the tempestuous Cape Horn, the ships had been left in a state of almost indescribable filth by the combination of a large number of sick and dead men and the destruction of the seamen's heads (the flimsy 'seats of ease' that projected out over the bowsprit). The crew were unable to clear either the effluent or the dead. Few British warships ever sank to the state and condition of Anson's squadron, floating charnel houses with raw sewage slopping across the lower decks, infecting the ballast and stores. *Centurion*'s 'Teacher of the Mathematicks' Pascoe Thomas reported the ship to be in 'a very nasty condition'. He was not exaggerating. Anson was equally blunt; the ship was 'intolerably loathsome'.[8]

Once the ships had been cleaned, the casks taken ashore, shaken down, refreshed and rebuilt by the coopers, a full store of water was quickly placed on board. Anson's men had discovered broken pottery, a fire and food scraps; evidence of a recent Spanish landing. They had reason to expect the Spanish would return, and were in no position to fight. With so many men at work or recuperating ashore the *Centurion* was desperately short handed. On 30 June a violent offshore gust parted the cable on the small bower anchor, with only a dozen men on board Anson watched in some trepidation, until it became clear that the best bower would hold. The smaller cable had been cut by the rocky holding ground; it was quickly bent onto the spare anchor. The ship was warped closer inshore on 1 July, secured for the rest of the stay. In July two forges were set up ashore to repair the chain plates and other ironwork. Major repairs to the rigging would depend on the *Gloucester*, which carried spare stores.[9] In a stark reminder of just how savage the passage round the Horn had been the flagship's sails and running rigging were so far gone that an anchor cable had to be unrove to make ropes, and despite using every scrap of worn canvas there was barely enough to make a single suit of sails.

On 21 June midshipmen on the lookout hill reported a large ship attempting to beat up into the wind and enter the bay. Before she could be identified a thick haze descended and the ship was not seen again for almost a week. Finally, on the 27th, HMS *Gloucester* limped into view, attempting to sail into the bay from another direction. Something was desperately wrong. The ship, her masts and yards damaged and deranged, was being handled by a tiny crew of sick men. Once she was within reach of the shore, about three miles out, Anson dispatched a boat with fresh food and water. Climbing onto the deck Philip Saumarez 'found her in a most deplorable condition, nearly two-thirds of her men being dead but very few of the rest able to perform their duty'. One-third of Captain Mitchell's skeletal crew were small boys, best able to resist scurvy. Rats scampered over the inert carcasses of the dead and dying, lying on the decks amid their own filth, in search of an easy meal. Many of the sick, too far gone to defend themselves, lost fingers and toes to the ultimate survivors.[10] The voyage from Brazil had cost the lives of 254 men, only 92 remained to crew a floating morgue, once the most beautiful ship in His Majesty's Navy.

Even with Saumarez's boat towing, the *Gloucester* could not fetch the bay, the exhausted boat crew had to let go and watch the ship drift away with the offshore breeze. On 3 July she came within two miles, and fired two guns, a signal of distress. Another boat load of food was sent out, but the ship could not be brought in. This time she was swept off to the west, fetching up close to the island of Más Afuera, where rich fishing grounds provided vital nourishment. Only on the 25th did the horrific voyage of HMS *Gloucester* come to end when the anchor went down in Windy Bay. By this stage the crew had been reduced to a mere 80 men, few of whom were able to work. A working party of newly recovered men went on board with fresh food, and brought the ship to the anchorage, which Anson patriotically renamed Cumberland Bay, in honour of the King George's II's favourite second son. Much to Anson's surprise the survivors of this horrific voyage recovered far quicker than those of the *Centurion*.[11] The fish of Más Afuera had been their salvation.

Once the men regained their strength Anson allowed many of them to live ashore. Two heavy guns were laboriously landed, placed in a battery close to the forge and bakery at Bahía Pangal to fire signals. The first test for this precaution came on 16 August when a ship was spotted. On entering Cumberland Bay she proved to be the storeship *Anna*, the fourth and last member of the squadron to reach the island. *Anna*'s crew were in far better health than their naval colleagues, restored by a two month refreshment stop at Socorro. They had found Narborough's beach by accident, communicated with local Indians and acquired a good stock of fresh food and water. Their voyage demonstrated that with a less crowded ship, better quality seamen and a long refreshment stop it was perfectly possible to round the Horn and make Juan Fernández. Although only a hired transport and not under naval discipline the ship's master had not considered turning back, unlike the warships *Severn* and *Pearl*, which had abandoned the voyage, rather than face Cape Horn. *Anna*'s arrival enabled Anson to put the men back on a full measure of preserved rations, and bake more bread.[12]

While the expedition slowly returned to health the Spanish response collapsed. Forewarned by French intelligence the Viceroy of Peru armed four ships to locate the English intruders.

Three headed south along the Chilean coast, the fourth cruised off Juan Fernández for several weeks departing only three days before the *Centurion* staggered in. By that calculation Anson's last navigational problem had avoided a battle he was in no condition to fight. Reckoning Anson could not have remained at sea for so long without a landfall the Spanish concluded he must have been wrecked rounding Cape Horn. Heading back to base at Callao they were caught in a severe storm and put out of action for several months.[13] The evidence they left on the beach ensured Anson kept *Centurion* ready to sail at short notice.

8

The Magical Island

The British set a course for Juan Fernández because it was unoccupied, and it had food, water and, above all, a suitable anchorage. They knew Selkirk and Will had lived on the island for years on end; they had the texts of Dampier, Rodgers, Shelvocke and others on board. Absorbed in an English history of the island, they blithely assumed that they had found some of Selkirk's goats, animals whose ears he had marked thirty-odd years before! The more likely occasion for goats with torn ears was the frequent arrival of Spanish dogs, trying to clear the livestock.

Saumarez reckoned the food supply 'providentially calculated for the relief of distressed adventurers who find such vegetables as are particularly adapted for curing the distempers contracted on long sea voyages and bad diets, especially those of the scorbutick kind'.[1] Pascoe Thomas agreed:

here are Greens and Salads of several sorts, and very wholesome, by the assistance of which our sick men began to recover apace, and those greens and fish were our principal food while here, tho' we often for the sake of variety, killed and eat the young seals and Sea Lions, and found them very good.[2]

The seeds and leaves of the pepper trees helped to season such fishy steaks. Fruit trees, perhaps descended from early Spanish plantings provided enough berries for Anson to order a pie. Thomas credited the Spaniards with sowing turnips and radishes, which had spread across Cumberland Bay in great profusion, with dock leaves, sow thistles, mallows, clover, wood and watercress, chicken sorrel, dandelion and several other edible herbs. He also found a species of wild oats, which could easily be cultivated. The rich soil was 'the best and fattest I ever saw, and I doubt not would produce, in the greatest abundance, all sorts of European fruits, grains, herbs, or flowers, either for profit or delight'.[3] Having no role in the refitting process, Hubert Tassell began reducing the island to a very English kind of order, laying out gardens. The link between husbandry, possession and title was clear, making gardens constituted ownership. Not only was this an earthly paradise, but it was an entirely practical one, holding out the promise of excellent crops, grown and harvested by any sensible Englishman.

Everyone agreed the key foodstuffs on Juan Fernández were watercress and wild turnips, goats, seals and sea lions, and especially bacalao, a large, white-fleshed cod-like fish. With so many dogs on the island, goats were hard to find, mostly in the higher reaches of the mountains; Anson had 'many' of the dogs shot. At a loss to explain how so many dogs could survive when the goats were so wary, Thomas concluded they must live on cats, rats and marine mammals. Saumarez reported they had entirely wiped out the goats on the level, barren western end of the island, disappointing hopes raised by the buccaneer narratives.[4] Some of the lazy brutes were eaten by Anson's men. Reports that they had a fishy taste confirmed Saumarez's hypothesis that they were living on young seals. He reckoned there were no more than 150 or 160 goats on the island, but they tasted like venison. Saumarez also noted the island was overrun with rabbits.

With 'turnips and Sicilian radishes' ready to crop, Anson 'sowed both lettuces, carrots and other garden plants, and sett in the woods a great variety of plum, apricot, and peach stones' which, according to Spanish visitors to London in 1748, 'have since thriven to a very remarkable degree' (i.e. the peach and apricot trees were in fruit).[5] There could be no more English method of asserting ownership than laying out gardens and deliberately planting fruit trees that would take years to grow into productive maturity. In word and deed Anson turned a fleeting residence into an enduring demonstration of a new reality, maps and charts, coastal views and gardens reinventing the island as an English landscaped park.

With few goats being caught (around one a day, Walter reported), the crew, growing 'tired' of fish, were persuaded to eat seal meat. To aid digestion, or perhaps mask revulsion, they referred to seal meat as 'mutton', while the flesh of the majestic sea lion became 'beef'. Such meals were not without risk: one sailor had his skull crushed in the jaws of an enraged female sea lion as he was skinning her pup. The 'extraordinary' elephant seals were a major resource, resting on the beach in vast herds they could be killed with ease; a single pistol shot through the mouth was usually enough. The blubber was rendered down for lamp oil, and the highly nutritious flesh served up as steaks. Thomas suggested that the seal furs 'might be of good value in England'.[6]

The massive elephant seal prompted more reflection, and a picture in the official account. For all their bellowing and posturing, Thomas reported they were easy to drive off. Young elephant seals were harvested for food; the large males provided some rough sport once the seamen had recovered their sprits they began baiting the beasts into a rage before worrying them to death with boarding pikes. Such random cruelty was a commonplace for eighteenth century Englishmen, with bear and bull baiting among the more popular entertainments. The bulldog was bred for such 'sport'. The more reflective gentlemen took the trouble to record the habits and anatomy of their prey. Purser Lawrence Millechamp was particularly struck by the fact that the male had a bone in his penis.

When it came to the insular food supply Millechamp noted the shallow waters of the bay were home to vast shoals of a cod-like fish, 'the most delicious repasts at this island', which was easily hooked and often salted down for future consumption; indeed 'two or three people could never fail to take as much as in about two hours as all the ship's company could use'. Occasionally large sharks came into the bay to interrupt fishing. Thomas distinguished 'several species of cod, rock-cod, cavallos, bremes, snapper, cray-fish, black-fish, several sorts of flat fish and abundance of others, some of a hundred weight and above, all taken with the hook' because the bays were too rocky for a seine. Fish, he explained 'were not only the chief refreshment we met with, but the principal branch of our food during our stay in this place'. The mighty salt water crayfish, so numerous that Selkirk had become sick of them, provided an alternative, a 'delicacy in greater perfection, both as to size, flavour and quantity, than is perhaps to be met with in any other part of the world ... of a most excellent taste.' They were easily picked up from the shallows with boat hooks.[7] The only seabirds he bothered to name were the spectacular albatross, observed by Edward Cooke thirty years before, and pintados. The rest were 'not worth mentioning'.[8] Thomas's offhand observation suggests that with so much else on the plate oily seabirds were not eaten.

While the ships were overhauled the officers inspected 'the only commodious place in those seas where British cruisers can refresh and recover their men after their passage round Cape Horn, and where they may remain for some time without alarming the Spanish coast':

Indeed Mr Anson was particularly industrious in directing the roads [harbours] and coasts to be surveyed, and other observations to be made, knowing from his own experience of how great consequence these materials might prove to be to any British vessels hereafter employed in those seas.[9]

He began with a more accurate record of the location; most of the astronomical and hydrographic work fell to Philip Saumarez. Having settled the latitude of the island, and provided a brief description Saumarez focused on Cumberland Bay, including a coastal view and chart to improve recognition. The other bays were dismissed as 'scarcely more than good landing places' for watering. Ships were advised to anchor at the western end of Cumberland Bay in about 40 fathoms, only two cables from the beach, sheltered from the 'large heavy sea' that rolled in whenever east or west winds blew. As the holding ground was rough it was advisable to armour the last six fathoms of cables, to prevent them being rubbed through. The Bay was open to northerly winds, like the one that wrecked Shelvocke's ship, when these blew, waves broke over *Centurion*'s forecastle, fortunately they were infrequent. Sharp southerly gusts could blow ships out of the anchorage.

On shore, the mountainous terrain around Cumberland Bay was largely covered in thick woods. On the upper slopes the soil was thin, and the trees rarely grew to any size, as their scant roots often gave way. A sailor fell to his death over a cliff after two trees failed to hold; Lieutenant Piercy Brett was luckier, escaping without serious injury. Of the indigenous trees only the myrtle was large enough to work for timber, with pieces up to forty feet long being shaped. This tree also hosted a moss that tasted and smelled like garlic, which was soon employed in cooking. Saumarez confessed he was no botanist, but his journal formed the basis of the official narrative, rendering his singular ineptitude into a plural.[10]

9

Making Juan Fernández English

———◦◦◦———

'This Island was a happy haven to us'[1]

With a veritable garden of delight unfolding beneath his feet, Anson had the luxury of occupying and enjoying the landscape, a pleasure he shared with some of his more observant companions. They were 'captivated by the numerous beauties', wooded hills, free from thick or spiny underbrush, waterfalls and rivulets descending through 'romantic vallies', rendered fragrant by aromatic trees possessing 'such elegance and dignity as would with difficulty be rivalled by any other part of the globe'. Here nature elegantly triumphed over artifice. The squadron remained at Juan Fernández until September, slowly recruiting their health and refitting their shattered ships. Local foodstuffs lived up to the praises bestowed by previous English voyagers, while the striking mountainous landscape excited Anson's artistic sensibilities. Indeed he chose to place his tent away from the workaday camp of the crew, in a beautiful valley that might have been created by Lancelot 'Capability' Brown, who would sculpt the grounds of the family seat at Shugborough. Distance and separation recreated the social space between classes that shaped eighteenth-century British society. The lawn lay at the end of a broad avenue cut through the trees, providing a gently sloping view down to the ships in the bay, some half a mile distant. Anson combined elegance with efficacy. Yet nothing was quite what it seemed. The 'natural' clearings and ideal lawns reflected earlier human invasions, tree-felling and camp-building, any clearing sustained by ever-hungry goats. The 'lawns' of Juan Fernández were no more 'virgin' than the Official Narrative's striking vision of Tinian.

From his cabin on the *Centurion*, schoolmaster Pascoe Thomas enviously detailed Anson's 'small square environ'd by a Grove of Myrtle trees, the passage to which was mostly natural, and something like to a labyrinth. Near it ran a fine large rivulet of water, to which a passage was cut thought the woods; the whole together forming a pretty romantic scene.' All told, about a hundred men lived ashore. The official narrative echoed Thomas's lyricism, and offered an engraving that Walter, or perhaps Anson himself, observed only gave 'some faint conception of the elegance of this situation'.[2] To enhance his enjoyment of the garden Anson had his men build useful features, including small bridges across ravines and rivulets.

After the terrors of the voyage and the hard work of refitting, Pascoe Thomas devoted ten pages to a lyrical excursus on the island paradise. He began with the distant view of the northeast end, 'a huge heap of irregular and craggy rocks and mountains, one of which known by the name of the Table Land [El Yunque], lying behind and above any of the rest'. This mountain opened out as ships entered the bay, revealing 'a fair valley and gently ascending hills'. Thomas doubted anyone would ever climb to the top, and few enough have. The mountain tops were often shrouded in mist and cloud, while the hills were covered 'with beautiful groves of trees, interspersed with many openings and ever-green valleys, which form a very agreeable prospect'. Small rivulets ran down the hills, often from 'fine natural cascades; and the channels through which they afterwards run being generally pretty rugged, and sometimes much upon the descent, causes the murmuring of those rivulets to be very agreeable to a rural scene'. Once ashore, the savannahs and shady groves, mostly of aromatic myrtle trees, were in squares, circles and triangles, 'far outdoing such as are made by art'. Suitably inspired, Thomas was moved to quote *Paradise Lost*, to convey his sense of the island as an English heaven:

If we add to those beauties before us, the gentle murmuring of the neighbouring brooks, which are often near those bowers, and the musick of the Birds among the branches, I think there can scarce anywhere be found a more happy Seat for the Muses, and the Flights of Fancy, or Pleasures of the Imagination.[3]

The combination of an ordered English world with a seemingly magical recovery from disease, a striking landscape, the euphoria of survivors and a well-stocked library provided Thomas with a sense of wonder, and the language with which to convey it.

Smitten with his new abode the schoolmaster lambasted his predecessors for lacklustre ornithological research, they had missed most of the bird species, the buccaneers noted the easily caught, ground-dwelling pardelas, but ignored hummingbirds, hawks, blackbirds, thrushes and owls, as well as 'a beautiful little red bird' slightly smaller than a goldfinch. He also described another small bird, with a green back spotted with gold and a white belly, although he had not seen it himself. Well aware of the tastes of his audience, Thomas did not linger on the other half of the island, the barren 'Goat Place' of Sharp's *Waggoner*. It was, he reported, 'much more flat and level than this, and the goats more numerous, but wood scarcer; but not having been there, I can say nothing of it to the purpose'. Saumarez, who had been round the island, added that this area was 'dry, stony, and destitute of trees'. Having little or no water and no anchorage, it was of no use to ships.[4]

Voyage drawings, engraved for publication, captured this sense of wonder. Although he reckoned no description necessary, in view of the extensive literature, Saumarez was deeply moved by 'the most romantic and pleasant place imaginable, abounding with myrtle tress, and covered with turnips and sorrel, its bays abounding with variety of fish, and seems calculated for the reception of distressed seamen'. Writing home from Macao, Lieutenant Peter Denis attributed their safe arrival at 'the hospitable island' of Juan Fernández to God, while the plentiful supply of food ensured the people recovered their health. Lawrence Millechamp of the *Tryal* was another moved to write despite the island having been 'so well described by privateers and others

who have resorted there'. Allowances must be made for the fact
that the expedition carried most of the books that mentioned
the island; Thomas, Saumarez, Walter and Millechamp may have
had little else to read for two years.[5] Little wonder texts about
Anson's time on Juan Fernández display a degree of similarity in
subject matter, tone and judgement. While this may reflect the
limited horizons that the island offered, the texts also suggest
discussion among authors and copying.

Thomas, entrusted with teaching the young gentleman their
navigation, provided a detailed location, 87° 37' west from
London, along with the magnetic variation in July. He also
printed a captured Spanish manuscript list of all the ports and
cities of the Pacific Coast, complete with magnetic variations.
Saumarez claimed to have reached the same figures by 'repeated
observations'. Thomas reported the location was 105 leagues
from the mainland, about 12 leagues around.[6] It was also a
very safe rendezvous. The weather was mild, with a few sharp
offshore gusts dropping down off the mountains, twice parting
cables, it seldom blew onshore, reducing the risk of wrecking,
but it occasionally gusted along the shore for a day or two,
when a heavy swell set into the bay, making it impossible to land
from boats. Saumarez had the advantage of compiling the chart,
circumnavigating the island and voyaging to Más Afuera.

Anson followed up *Gloucester*'s involuntary visit to Más
Afuera by sending Charles Saunders and Philip Saumarez in the
Tryal to look for the rest of the squadron, and record the island
in more detail. The British were aware of other island, if only
from Spanish and Dutch accounts.[7] Returning in late August,
Saumarez reported that Más Afuera, some 22 leagues distant,
west by south, was not the small, barren rock hitherto reported,
but a substantial, well-wooded and watered mountainous island
rather larger than Más a Tierra. The main drawback was the
inability to moor; the only anchorage, on the north side, was
small, close to the shore and exposed to most winds. Once
ashore the island had much to offer, including 'a peculiar sort
of red earth whose brightness equal vermillion and with the

proper management might furnish the composition for the potters of an extraordinary kind'. In contrast to its neighbour, the island 'abounds with goats', who were easy to catch, being unaccustomed to humans. There were no dogs, or European vegetables. Although far from ideal, Anson recognised Más Afuera could be a life-saving resource, 'especially for a single ship, who might apprehend meeting with a superior force at Fernandez'. The island having been 'more particularly examined than I dare say it had ever been before, or perhaps ever will be again', Anson published the information for future voyagers, with coastal perspectives of the northeastern and western sides of the island, ensuring it would be recognised.[8]

By August the human toll had slowed to a trickle; there were only eight deaths that month, mostly from the *Gloucester*. Soon there would be ships to take and towns to raid, if they had the strength. After purchasing and stripping the leaky, worm-eaten *Anna*, it was found that broken deck beams rendered her unsafe for further navigation, providing additional resources to refit the warships. Shifting spars and setting up a temporary rope works ashore brought the three warships back to a serviceable condition, and the extra men were a god-send for the *Gloucester*, now reduced to a crew of 82. By early September the scorbutic invalids had either died or recovered, the ships were clean and seaworthy, the store rooms filled and the season for navigating on the Chilean and Peruvian coasts about to open. Saumarez believed Spanish ships scarcely looked out of port until late September, those heading south from Callao to Valparaiso generally passed within sight of the island.[9]

Any hopes Anson had entertained of executing his orders evaporated on the 148-day voyage from Spithead. His three remaining warships had sailed with 961 men; they left Juan Fernández with only 335. Death struck the veteran soldiers and raw marines hardest, annihilating his tiny army, while his siege artillery had disappeared, along with HMS *Wager*. There were not enough men in the squadron to fight the guns of his flagship. However impressive his force may have seemed at a distance, the slow and stately manner in which the sails were handled would have revealed his weakness to experienced eyes. While the squadron remained desperately weak, the 100-day occupation of Juan Fernández had given Anson a chance.

Anson considered heading north to link up with Admiral Sir Edward Vernon's fleet in the Caribbean via the Isthmus of Panama, reversing the old buccaneer strategy of Sharp, Dampier and Ringrose. The British were surprised to see a sail away to the northeast late on the morning of 8 September. Assuming the ship, which came close enough to be identified as Spanish, must have spotted the squadron, Anson took *Centurion* in pursuit. Light winds left her becalmed until the following day, when the Spanish ship was long gone. Continuing on course for Valparaiso Anson spotted a ship on the 12th: the unarmed *Monte Carmelo* was easily taken. The ship spotted on the 8th had been sailing in company from Callao to Valparaiso, both carried passengers and valuable cargo. Of far greater worth was the intelligence that Pizarro had failed to round the Horn, and the Viceroy of Peru, following the advice of his officers, had concluded Anson had been lost in the same location. The weak British squadron was now the most powerful naval force in the Pacific, and coastal shipping would be unprotected. Anson switched his plan, copying the old-time buccaneer campaigns, raiding a largely defenceless coast, and sweeping up unarmed merchant shipping. He could keep ahead of any Spanish response, coasting north with the current.

Returning to Juan Fernández on 14 September, Anson gave the other crews their first sight of a prize, re-energising the squadron before he sent *Tryal* and *Gloucester* to cruise off Paita and Valparaiso, leaving *Centurion*'s crew to refit the prize with guns from the *Anna*, and attempt to clean the flagship's weed-infested hull.[10] Anson sailed from Juan Fernández on 19 September, losing sight of the island on the 22nd.

In July 1741 the *London Magazine* reported that as Anson had rounded Cape Horn, and Pizarro had been driven back to the River Plate, Vernon should attack Porto Bello and cross the

Isthmus. Vernon had forwarded Spanish reports of the Pacific squadron's proceedings, which he hoped would cheer the government. In early 1743 Lewis Lidger, hitherto Anson's cook, arrived in London via Lisbon, having been captured ashore in Peru, providing slightly garbled corroboration of the facts. These brief reports only whetted the appetite for more.[11]

Anson sacked Paita and captured many ships, and after a horrific voyage across the Pacific took the Manila galleon. He returned home in 1744 without hair, teeth, or much of his original crew, but rich beyond the dreams of avarice. His world-shattering circumnavigation was seized upon by a nation desperate for glory, and a world fascinated by human suffering, heroic feats of endurance, triumph and treasure. At the epicentre of the story lay the magical island of Juan Fernández, an earthly paradise where the sick suddenly became well, where nature surpassed art in the creation of romantic vistas, the waters were sweet and the sea teemed with life.

Making Books

This extraordinary expedition generated many books, crafted to suit all tastes, and all pockets. They referenced buccaneer literature, and Defoe's insular hero: both had informed the planning and shaped the attitudes of the voyagers. In the years since Rogers and Dampier new tastes had rendered the uninhabited wilderness a more idyllic space than it may have appeared to previous generations. The books of the 1740s made Juan Fernández romantic, the better to imagine heroic Robinsonian narratives. Anson's expedition cemented the identification of this island with Defoe's hero, a process far from complete before the voyage sailed.

Anson's occupation of Juan Fernández was the culmination of an English project dating back to the 1660s, to an island first mentioned in an English book a generation earlier, some 120 years before the *Centurion* dragged her anchor into Windy Bay. The British had managed to locate the island, if not with any great precision, occupy it for discrete periods of time, and describe the food supply. By 1750 the ocean beyond Cape Horn and the Straits of Magellan had been opened, and Juan Fernández lay at the centre of a developing British world view, the ideal base from which to exploit the weak, moribund Spanish Empire.

Voyage narratives began to appear soon after *Centurion* returned to Britain. The anonymous *An Authentic and Genuine Journal of Commodore Anson's Expedition* of 1744 had enough internal evidence, not least a striking illustration of the camp above Bahía Pangal, to indicate the author had at least discussed the voyage with a survivor.[1] This first rough sketch emphasised the importance of the voyage to leading professional author John

Campbell, who followed his best-selling *Lives of the Admirals* with a multi-volume 'complete collection of voyages' based on Harris's forty-year-old *Navigantium atque Itinerantium Bibliotheca*. He dedicated the book to 'The Merchants of Great Britain', a critical section of his intended audience, using the introduction to urge his countrymen to find new markets and develop new trade through discovery and industry. As English minds found examples more effective aids to understanding than theory he rehearsed the rise and fall of Genoa as a model of how to lose a sea empire. Luxury and idleness were bad enough, but 'endless negotiations and fruitless alliances' were worse, topped off by a shift to business and security models dominated by banking and allies, rather than manufacturing and national naval power, concluding: 'may her fall prove a warning, not a precedent'. This was no mere impulse to trade; this was a national policy based on seapower, commerce and insular detachment from the travails of European politics.[2]

Campbell spoke to a very specific British identity, a distinct culture wrapped up in the ocean. He pointed to a tiny, far-distant island, another Gibraltar that would open the Pacific to British enterprise. Defoe's *An Inquiry into the Pretensions of Spain to Gibraltar* of 1729 demonstrated just how quickly newly-won possessions could be taken into British hearts. Conquered in 1704, the 'Rock' replaced Dover Castle as the icon of British security, power and aggressive commercial diplomacy, a British bastion controlling access to distant seas.[3] The shift of focus from the Mediterranean to the Pacific reflected an expanding concept of British seapower, on which all such overseas possessions ultimately depended, and appealed to the commercial classes whose taxes sustained the fleet, and the global network of island bases that gave it strategic reach.

To satisfy demand for Anson material, Campbell pasted a hastily compiled section into the *Voyages*, largely based on the *Authentic Journal*. Writing in the middle of a war that was hardly glorious, a year before the last Jacobite uprising, he followed Defoe's argument that increased overseas trade would improve internal cohesion and political stability. To catch his public he placed the South Pacific, the current theatre of dreams, in the first volume. Spanish weakness and lethargy could no longer be obscured by disinformation. He advised the South Sea Company to occupy Juan Fernández as the base for trade and further exploration. 'History', he asserted, 'affords us no example of a maritime power that remained long at a stay. If we do not go forward, we must necessarily go back.' England must replace Spain as master of the Pacific.[4]

If Campbell provided context and meaning for the epic voyage, readers demanded more detail. Pascoe Thomas's *True and Impartial Journal* of 1745 duly obliged, but Anson's quasi-miraculous return, laden with Spanish booty, Chinese silks and a narrative of disaster and redemption, the greatest event of the age, demanded an official explanation. Well aware that he faced competition, Thomas wryly noted that a 'Certain Honourable Gentleman' had stolen his notes, and returned home early from Canton, seeking 'to discourage others.' The 'Gentleman' was the Reverend Richard Walter, Anson's chaplain.

Walter's book turned this British story into a universal possession. On the surface the authorised account could be read as a travel narrative, a modern version of the buccaneer texts that had been read so closely when the squadron arrived at Juan Fernández, as guides to local navigation and natural resources. Consciously or otherwise they shaped the organisation and language of their successors. Yet the new version was subtly different. Anson, the central figure, as leader, decision-maker and hero, always appeared in the third person as 'Mr Anson', enlightened despot of the island, detached, serene, judicious and wise. Although this was a deliberate literary construction, other accounts confirm Anson wore the 'mask of command', a potent blend of authority and detachment, with the same pride and purpose as his rank. Anson had no need to be the hero of his own tale; he had acquired wealth, power and status beyond ambition. After his return he had married the Lord Chancellor's daughter and defeated a French fleet off Cape Finisterre, becoming Lord

Anson. He would revitalise the Royal Navy and direct British strategy until his death in 1762.[5] Famously taciturn, he avoided the public gaze, taking solace in his garden. Rather than blowing his own trumpet Anson put a great deal of his own time and money into the *Voyage* because it had been a major learning experience for the British state, and above all for the Royal Navy that he led. Consequently the book addressed a far wider range of issues than older voyage texts.

Fuelled by a universal hunger for information, the official account attracted over 1,800 advance subscriptions among the social, political, naval and commercial elite, several from the middling sort, and a few subscription libraries. Curiously, while most Cambridge colleges subscribed, none of those at Oxford bothered. Among the dukes, earls and archbishops, admirals John Byng and Edward Hawke stand out, along with Swynfen Jervis, father of another naval hero, joining Lord Hardwicke (Anson's father-in-law), Admiralty Secretary Thomas Corbett, former Jacobite apologist and historian Viscount St John, patriotic engraver/publisher John Pine and the Book Society of Stowmarket. By contrast, Pascoe Thomas recruited seafarers, including voyage veterans and the middling sort in southern towns, including many from Gosport, not least peruke makers Daniel Dickens and John Miller – men who may have profited from the ravages of scurvy.

With strong advance sales, the *Voyage* easily carried the cost of well-drawn charts and pictures. Where other texts used illustrations for dramatic effect the official illustrations, many based on Lieutenant Piercy's Brett's drawings, were integral to the process of annexing and anglicising the island, giving it a place on the global chart, an existence in the contemporary visual imagination and a strong visual identity.[6] In the same way that the woodcut frontispiece of *Robinson Crusoe* fixed the castaway in British culture, Anson's illustrations defined his island. Despite the high price the book went through four editions in a year, remaining in print ever since, a distinction it shares with *Robinson Crusoe*. By 1776 Anson's book had reached a fifteenth

English edition, making it the most successful travel book of the century. As Glyn Williams observed, it was a work in the mould of Richard Hakluyt's Elizabethan narratives, a striking adventure story that carried a strong message about the need for exploration, trade and colonies. That this message was shared with a massive 2,000-page compendium suggests these texts were the alpha and omega of contemporary imperial thought, one a vast canvas of time and space, the other a record of singular achievement. Neither should be confused with works of history: they were entirely forward looking, urging the ambitious to act, not rest on past glories.

While he did not have the time to compile the book, he was running a world war against France between 1745 and 1748, and never displayed any great enthusiasm for putting pen to paper, Anson micro-managed the project. Acutely aware of the strategic and political significance of the expedition and anxious to exploit his hard won knowledge Anson produced a guide for future voyagers. Although Richard Walter compiled the text it soon became clear the parson, an author so clumsy that he managed to leave God out of his book, lacked the insight, judgement and literary skill to impose Anson's agenda on the material, let alone produce a technically competent guide for future British expeditions. The draft had to be reworked by larger minds. Anson handed it to mathematician, artillerist and engineer Benjamin Robins FRS. Not that his Lordship allowed either author a free hand. Robins waited on Anson every morning, to read aloud the latest passages, so his Lordship could check the facts and shape the message. Robins's scientific skill and ability to see the big picture is especially clear in chapters X and XIV, which abandon the narrative to analyse Spanish trade flows and the strategic opportunities open to a squadron rounding Cape Horn in better condition. These chapters digested the experience of the voyage, earlier narratives and captured Spanish material. When Robins left London, to take up a high profile post in India, Walter was left to take the manuscript through the press. Ultimately Anson was responsible for the book; it reflected his aims, his experience and above all his objectives – and he checked every page.[7] Anson and Robins gave the text its purpose, inner logic and precision. As Robins boasted:

no voyage I have yet seen, furnished such a number of views of land, soundings, draughts of roads and ports, charts and other materials, for the improvement of geography and navigation, as were contained in the ensuing volume; which are of the more importance too, as the greatest part of them relate to such islands or coasts, as have been hitherto not at all or erroneously described, and where the want of sufficient and authentic information might occasion future enterprises to prove abortive, perhaps with the destruction of the men and vessels employed therein.[8]

The drawings were all based on accurate records, and approved by Anson, unlike the 'bold conjectures and fictitious descriptions' of other authors. Captured Spanish charts and pilots, critical to Anson's success, had proved very accurate. The value of this handbook for invading the South Pacific was evident ninety years later, when hydrographer Captain Philip Parker King checked Anson's charts. He found them 'old-fashioned' but serviceable.

Anson's official history informed and instructed future commanders on every aspect of their work, from navigation and operations, to cruising formations and boat patrols, advice that remained relevant a century later.[9] For his personal delectation Anson commissioned marine artist Samuel Scott to capture key events of his voyage in oils, but there would be no picture of Juan Fernández. With Brett's sketches and Anson's input Scott would have had no difficulty presenting the magical island in suitably verdant form, but Anson made a different choice. He focused on the taking of the Manila galleon, the burning of Paita, and his later triumph off Cape Finisterre. He chose to memorialise glory, not providential recovery. The assessment of Juan Fernández in his book was at once more fulsome and more practical. He had no need of a pictorial reminder.

Published accounts agreed that Juan Fernández was an island paradise, a romantic vision of loveliness amid a vast, desolate ocean, a vital source of life and health amid the horrors and death of a scorbutic catastrophe. Printed text, manuscripts and images concurred in blessing the island as an ideal British location – part country estate, part health spa, and packed with the finest foods. The expedition locked the island into an English world view, one of three idealised locations, along with Tinian and Cape Town, where a fleet could refresh should another such venture be attempted. Anson's handbook for future British circumnavigators put a premium on accurate navigational information, including a major contribution to contemporary understanding of magnetic variation. If anyone was in doubt as to the strategic purpose, the list of refreshment stops was repeated on the very last page, pointedly returning the reader to the 'vallies of Juan Fernández' before they closed the book.[10] These 'English' refreshment stops for scorbutic circumnavigators opened the age of British global power.

Anson used his prize money to buy Moor Park at Rickmansworth. The magnificent house had recently been rebuilt in the Palladian style, and decorated by Sir James Thornhill, creator of the ceiling in the Painted Hall at Greenwich Hospital, by Benjamin Heskin Styles. Styles a South Sea speculator and insider dealer, had sold up before the Bubble burst. Anson's expedition could be seen as a heroic vindication of the original project, rebuilding commercial confidence in the South Pacific, bolstering the link between seapower and the City. The delusions and designs of 1711 had come full circle. With an eye to the future Anson also invested heavily in the family seat at Shugborough, home of his elder brother Thomas, where Lancelot 'Capability' Brown landscaped the grounds to create an idyllic 'rolling' topography. Anson added an Ionic temple, in the Greek revival style, moving local author Samuel Johnson (no admirer of Anson) to write:

> A grateful mind! praise! All to the winds he owed,
> And so upon the winds a temple he bestowed.[11]

If the Shugborough temple recalled his voyage the extensive gardens at Moor Park recalled the island that saved his men from disaster. They would be his only solace after the death of his wife.

The voyage became a universal possession. In 1748 Anson's friend Henry Legge, British minister in Berlin, was moved to write: 'it is a work which, as an Englishman, I am proud of, and, as a mariner, I think will be of perpetual use to the faculty'. The Prussian king, Frederick the Great, expressed 'a strong curiosity to see you'. John Hawkesworth, editor of the first of Captain Cook's journals, promised to 'do my best to make it another *Anson's Voyage*'.[12] The book created a new literary genre, prompted an enlightenment fascination with the Pacific that lead to the voyages of Cook, Bougainville and others, and reshaped the European garden. When Jean-Jacques Rousseau picked up the French 'translation' it provided a plot device, while the illustrations opened up a new insight into the relationship between man and nature. St Preux, the hero of *la Nouvelle Héloïse*, a thinly disguised autobiography, joined Anson's voyage. Where Anson carefully set out the strategic value of Juan Fernández, Tinian and the Cape of Good Hope as refitting stations for British warships, Rousseau, often following the French text very closely, used the first two as metaphors conveying virtue and purity. Finding an artificial *Elysée* at the home of his erstwhile lover the hero, both Rousseau and St Preux, lost interest in formal gardening. The wild garden forms 'a sentimental and moral turning point for St. Preux, reshaping his state of mind, as the islands are physical turning points and supply the physical needs of Anson's sailors'. Anson, who had seen these places, preferred classical idylls, combining artificially informal landscaping, ancient buildings and trophies, a three-dimensional version of a canvas by Claude Lorraine.[13]

The official narrative did not include a portrait, allowing 'Mr Anson' to keep his distance, but his pan-European celebrity created a market for a picture. Amsterdam, centre of the European print trade, duly obliged. Among the many variations on the theme of naval heroics, geographical achievement and plunder, two prints offered the newly made peer alternative heraldic

supporters to the rather predictable lion and seahorse assigned
to Baron Anson of Soberton in Hampshire. Artists developed an
image from the official narrative to identify the insipid gentleman
in the portrait, replacing the medieval sea monsters that littered
the open spaces of old charts, with a truly monstrous creature
– a male elephant seal. The image in Shelvocke's book, revised
for the *Voyage*, caught the eye of the artist. Not only had Anson
taken a fabulous treasure, survived a perilous voyage and
browbeaten the Chinese, but he had captured the likeness of an
awe-inspiring beast. Jan Wandelaar gave the beast a degree of
animation and expression worthy of a professional artist. The
sea monster is tamed by Neptune, trident in hand, with Anson's
portrait held aloft by Britannia, her crown adorned with the
sterns of warships with a mountainous background suggestive
of the seal girt island. Another elephantine image merely copied
Brett's beast, while Neptune, Amphitrite and a triton do homage
to the hero, his voyage represented on a globe, complete with the
stop-over at Juan Fernández, illuminated by the sun of undying
fame, bursting through the metaphorical clouds which had
hung over the expedition.[14] In both images Anson maintains the
same curiously reserved expression, unwilling to smile lest the
viewer note that the expedition had cost him his teeth! As Carl
Skottsberg noted a century ago there are no more elephant seals
on Juan Fernández.[15]

Closing the Stable Door

However reluctantly Anson appeared on the international stage, his voyage and the international success of his book made him famous across the literate world. It also exposed Spanish weakness, pointing out Juan Fernández as 'the only commodious place in those seas, where British cruisers can refresh and recover their men after the passage round Cape Horn'. Possession of the Falkland Islands and Juan Fernández would 'make us masters of those seas'.[1] Those words forced the Spanish government to occupy and fortify Juan Fernández, in case the British returned in strength. If they did the silver fleet would cease sailing.

In 1748 Anson, as First Sea Lord, planned a follow-up project to survey the Falkland Islands, Tierra del Fuego and Patagonia, thereby ensuring a swift passage to Juan Fernández, the inevitable destination of all those who entered the Pacific from the south. Chapter XIV, examining what might have been done had the squadron arrived in the Pacific without a scorbutic catastrophe, reflected his thinking. By January 1749 Anson planned to send two sloops, calling at Juan Fernández to water and refresh before crossing the Pacific, seeking new lands to the west. Juan Fernández would also support a leap across the Southern Ocean towards New Holland (modern Australia). In Anson's strategic vision new charts would link a chain of British insular bases stretching from the Falkland Islands by way of Juan Fernández to a new Pacific destination, replacing those other idyllic stopovers Tinian and the Cape of Good Hope.[2]

The Spanish were under no illusions. Anson's raid had done far more damage than the value of the bullion he brought back to

Britain – an estimated eight to ten million dollars had been taken or destroyed, and a similar amount in lost trade, delays and the deterioration of cargoes. Above all Anson had crippled the flow of specie from Peru to Spain. Juan Fernández had become a serious strategic problem, and they had already examined the options. In September 1740 advanced warning of Anson's expedition reached the Viceroyalty of Peru. The Viceroy, the Marquis de Villagarcia was fortunate that two brilliant young naval officers, Jorge Juan and Antonio de Ulloa happened to be in the country, working with a French scientific mission. They advised him how to improve coastal defences at Callao, built two galleys and helped equip a four-ship squadron to cruise off the coast. When the squadron returned without sighting the British the young officers concluded that Anson had failed to round Cape Horn, and were released to resume their scientific mission in the Andes, only days before Anson broke cover. They returned to Lima on 26 February, and took command of two ships the Viceroy had fitted out as cruisers 'for the security of the coast of Chile and the island of Juan Fernández against any reinforcement coming to the enemy'. While Anson told his prisoners he was heading north the Spaniards knew other British ships had failed to round the Horn in 1741, and might try again. Their first object was to inspect Juan Fernández, the key to Anson's success, and recommend a suitable response.[3]

The two ships finally left Callao on 4 December 1742, running past Más Afuera to anchor at Más a Tierra on 9 January. They found ample evidence of English 'occupation', but no Englishmen. A merchant ship sent three months earlier from Chile had recovered two cyphered messages in bottles from Anson's campsite. Without Shelvocke's book the papers were impenetrable, although their purpose must have been obvious – Anson advising any laggard ships to follow him up the coast. Examining the campsite in minute detail Jorge Juan and Antonio de Ulloa found only 'the picquets and poles of the tents, with their small wooden bridges for crossing the branches [of rivers], and other things of that kind'. Such marks in the landscape may have been little more than garden furniture, but they represented a significant act of occupation.

The Spanish officers spent the next fortnight conducting the most accurate scientific survey of the islands to date, departing on 22 January. They observed that the dogs on Más a Tierra, which had driven the goats up onto the mountainous heights, no longer barked. They recovered their voices when placed with other dogs, with the same hesitation and uncertainty as Selkirk had spoken on first meeting his fellow countrymen. The culinary highlights of the expedition were crayfish weighing up to nine pounds. After joining the unfortunate Commodore Pizarro at Valparaiso the two ships continued cruising along the Chilean coast between Valdivia, Valparaiso and Juan Fernández until the middle of the year, calling frequently at Juan Fernández, just in case more British ships arrived. Ulloa paid another visit while sailing home round Cape Horn. Ulloa and Jorge Juan's reports, public and confidential, demonstrated the moribund state and defensive weaknesses of Peru. Their *Relación Histórica del Viage a la América Meridional* of 1748, an Ansonesque travelogue, would be available in English before the next Anglo-Spanish War.[4] Their private report for the King, the *Noticias Secretas de América* of 1749 (only published in English in 1826, after the fall of Spanish America), highlighted the incompetence and injustice of the regime. Their strategic analysis was clear. Spain needed a fleet and arsenal at Guayaquil to control the silver route. They also provided detailed instructions for navigating into Cumberland Bay, and the best location for fortifications. Although the anchorage was not ideal, exposed to strong northerly winds, with poor holding ground, occasional violent southerly wind sweeping down from the mountains and a difficult landing, they recommended that the island be occupied and fortified.[5]

Whatever the Viceroy of Peru thought of these reports he had little incentive to act, and even less ability to do so after a catastrophic tidal wave swept over Callao in October 1746, killing thousands. The Spanish Court proved more receptive.

Early in 1749 King Ferdinand VI ordered the new Viceroy of Peru, the Count of Superunda, to fortify Juan Fernández, 'at all costs against the hated and covetous English'. Rumours abounded that the British were planning to settle the Falklands and Juan Fernández. These rumours became concrete in April 1749 when Jorge Juan, in London at the time, uncovered plans for HMS *Porcupine* and another sloop to enter the South Pacific. He collected a formidable library of texts that addressed the English view of the island, one that he continued to update after returning to Spain.[6] His timely warning gave Madrid the opportunity for a diplomatic protest.[7] At this point Lord Sandwich, First Lord of the Admiralty, communicated the scheme to his political mentor the Duke of Bedford, Secretary of the State for the Southern Department (the Foreign Secretary for Southern Europe). Bedford wrote to the British Minister in Madrid, arguing the report may be open 'to many misrepresentations', creating 'uneasiness and suspicion' between the two courts as major commercial negotiations were in progress. The Admiralty planned to chart the Falkland Islands, and the mythic Pepys Islands, before retiring to Portuguese Brazil to refit. The second stage involved entering the South Seas, 'in order to make further discoveries there. As this latter part of the scheme cannot be carried into execution without wooding and watering at the Island of Juan Fernández, and possibly coming sometimes within sight of the Spanish Coasts of Chile and Peru' it should be abandoned, lest Madrid thought the British were 'preparing to be ready to attack them upon a future rupture, in a part where they were undoubtedly weak, and of which they must consequently be more than ordinarily jealous. The reduced scheme, Bedford concluded, could not 'give any umbrage at Madrid'.

Such hopes were quickly dashed. Spanish Chief Minister Carvarjal recognised any such endeavour would bring British and Spanish possessions and trade into close proximity, leading to collisions more serious than those that had led to the outbreak of war in 1739. Furthermore, 'neither he nor anyone else could be a stranger to the rise and intent of such an expedition, since it is so fully explained in the printed relation of Lord Anson's voyage'. He dismissed claims that the voyage was purely exploratory, and would benefit Spain more than any nation.

Carvajal also claimed Spain had already charted and settled the Falklands, and the non-existent Pepys Islands. The object of the British plan was obvious and hostile, to create a refitting station at the mouth of the Straits of Magellan, to avoid the problems experienced by Anson in his Pacific adventure. Carjaval launched a furious verbal assault on the British minister. Spain had no desire to increase the oceanic and navigational knowledge in the Pacific, or any other sea over which it claimed control. When Carvarjal was called away by King Ferdinand the Navy Minister, the Marques de Ensenada took up the subject, and the attitude. In his report the British Minister stressed the Spanish had not offered any legal reason why the British should not sail in the Pacific, condemning their 'whimsical notions of exclusive rights in those seas', to 'keep those possessions as mysterious as they can, and the utility and preservation of them depend upon their not being known, nor having any other possession or competition in their neighbourhood'. The British decided to lay aside the scheme 'for the present', to safeguard larger political and economic agendas in Europe, while reserving the right to enter the Pacific at a later date. The British project depended on occupying Juan Fernández, which Anson knew would 'make us masters of those seas.'[8] Although sacrificing the 1749 expedition to wider considerations was reasonable, given the marginal commercial value of the Pacific, Anson regretted the lost opportunity to the end of his days.

The British were not alone in dreaming of a Pacific future. A French translation of Anson's *Voyage* inspired savant Charles des Brosses's 1756 *Histoire des Navigations aux Terres Australes*, which recommended his countrymen settle Juan Fernández, citing Roggeveen's text, and a boyhood engagement with *Robinson Crusoe*. Entirely unaware that the source was flawed, des Brosses developed Roggeveen's argument to stress that France should pre-empt Britain. A decade later the British could read his text in translation. Des Brosses had analysed 65 narratives of Pacific voyaging in search of a great Southern Continent, creating 'the most weighty combination of history and propaganda as yet devoted to the enterprise of the South Sea', a more sophisticated argument than that advanced by Campbell.[9] The distinction reflected both the intellectual merits of the authors, and those of their intended audiences. While des Brosses targeted savants and scientists, Campbell addressed the great commercial companies of London, the East India, South Sea and Royal African. Where Campbell spoke of commercial opportunity, des Brosses affected to see only national glory. That the Frenchman profited from the industry of Campbell and his British precursors is impossible to deny, not least in his focus on Juan Fernández. Des Brosses's writings prompted a series of French voyages into the Southern Ocean seeking *Terre Australis*, but none would anchor at Juan Fernández.[10] That did not stop the British assuming that they would.

Late in 1749 King Ferdinand's orders to occupy Más a Tierra reached Lima, where an engineer was directed to fortify Cumberland Bay, Bahía Pangal, Puerto Inglese, and any other sites associated with English raiders. The occupation was necessarily substantial, and therefore costly. As the island had no economic prospects these were sunk costs, so much money poured into the sea in gilded tribute, a vain attempt to compensate for the absence of effective naval defence. The initial settlement comprised 62 soldiers, 175 colonists, 22 convict labourers and 18 cannon, with ample supplies of food and military stores. Once ashore Lieutenant Colonel Juan Navarro Santaella laid out the town of San Juan Bautista around the Church of San Antonio and Fort Santa Barbara. While this was standard Spanish colonial practice, it was far cry from Anson's tented camp, let alone the transient occupations or earlier Dutch, English and French mariners. The new governor began charting his territory with Anson in hand, noting where he improved on the English record. Maps have always been tools of power and control and his purpose was to establish the Spanish Crown's superior title to this long abandoned outpost, backing a claim based on prior discovery with superior cartography.

A second wave of soldiers, settlers and convicts arrived from Concepción, the main base for the island throughout the remaining years of the Spanish empire. On 25 May 1751, before the infant colony had time to settle, a massive earthquake struck the Chilean coast, devastating Concepción, Valparaiso and San Juan Bautista, where the effect was doubled by the subsequent tsunami. Around forty people drowned, including the governor, and most of the new buildings were ruined. With help from the mainland the settlement recovered and a new fort was begun on higher ground. This nine-gun work stood ready for service by December 1751. Although the engineer, now safely back on the mainland, claimed his works were adequate to keep the entire British Navy out of Bahía Cumberland, such bombast was only meant for Imperial consumption. The defences were adequate to mark Spanish ownership, and keep out private vessels: had Anson returned they would have been overwhelmed. Proving that even a natural catastrophe could not destroy the island's reputation the engineer declared it so healthy that 'only the old could die'.[11] That may have been true, but the colony itself was entirely dependent on the mainland for supplies and manpower, and the Spanish Empire was already chronically over-stretched financially. Simply rebuilding the fort cost $12,000, and the island had no economic value to justify either the capital outlay or the continuing costs of garrisoning and feeding a substantial village with little agricultural activity and no trade whatsoever, some three days sail from Valparaiso. Every six years governor and garrison were replaced from the Concepción regiment. In 1762 the governor of Chile proposed ending the colony, on the reasonable grounds that an island unseen by a foreign vessel for seventeen years needed no defences. He was overruled by the Viceroy. With the English agitating new ventures in the Falklands and openly discussing the Pacific Spain was unable to cut its losses and withdraw. In the long term the cost of the settlement had to be carried because the tiny Spanish Armada of the South Seas, dedicated to the safe transport of silver, had no pretension to command the ocean. Spain faced an obvious conundrum, a costly naval force could secure the seas, but forts were cheaper, in the short term. Ultimately the decision to favour land defences reflected deep-rooted cultural assumptions. Not that the fortifications were deterring anyone; Spain, as was customary, kept their existence a profound secret.

Having frightened the Spanish into occupying the island, Anson also generated a 'treasure' story. Cornelius Webb claimed Anson had buried gold on Juan Fernández before setting off for Acapulco, and after returning to England sent him to recover it. As Anson had acquired no treasure before leaving Juan Fernández, the story made little sense: the only things he buried there were dead sailors. The denouement, in which Webb deliberately burnt his own ship while on passage to get a new mast at Valparaiso, was simply laughable.[12] Treasure hunters, preferring myth to reality, would arrive in the twentieth century.

Mastering the Pacific

—ᘒᕉᕉᙢ—

After the disastrous losses of 1739–48, Spain wisely stood aside when the Seven Years' War erupted in 1756. However, a change of monarch and French blandishments brought Madrid into the war early in 1762, when France was defeated. Britain already had plans for the South Pacific, and they did not envisage sneaking to Juan Fernández like fugitives on a Spanish Lake. They would seize the Falkland Islands and then Valdivia, the best harbour in southern Chile.[1] Anson's last great project, a two pronged assault on the Spanish Empire reflected the startling increase in British knowledge, power and ambition. He revived the Manila mission originally conceived in 1739, adding a devastating strike at Havana, the beating heart of Spanish power in the Americas. In the intervening two decades the strategic balance had swung decisively in Britain's favour; in place of straggling raids across vast ocean spaces they would strike high value targets. Rather than loiter at Juan Fernández the British would pick up silver from Peru and Mexico at Havana. The little island in the Pacific was no longer adequate to sustain British ambition. Although Anson died before the operations began the British captured Havana and Manila, shattering Spain's global empire.

When the war ended in 1763, Imperial Spain had been reduced to the second rank. The British returned the captured cities, because they could come back at any time, and launched new missions seeking bases in the South Atlantic and the Pacific. British interest had been piqued by the 1764 translation of des Brosses's *Histoire des Navigations aux Terres Australes*, and Louis de Bougainville's attempt to pre-empt them at the Falkland Islands – gateway to the South Pacific. The response from London was swift.[2] While the British saw no need to challenge Spain for Juan Fernández, they responded to French interest in the South Atlantic archipelago by dispatching John Byron, a survivor of the wreck of the *Wager*, with HMS *Dolphin* and HMS *Tamar* around the world on the expedition Anson had planned in 1749.

After Anson's death in 1762 his circumnavigators continued the Pacific agenda of expanding trade and tapping the riches of Spanish America, in peace or war. Byron's mission was planned in profound secrecy; it seems that only the Admiralty and the King were in the know, and further disguised by giving Byron command of the East Indies squadron with orders to sail via Brazil and the Cape of Good Hope. This was a strategic voyage, using the Falklands and Juan Fernández as way stations to a Pacific empire of trade. After annexing the Falkland Islands in January 1765, Byron passed the Straits of Magellan and returned to the South Pacific in 1765, seeking new lands and trade opportunities that would 'redound to the honor of this Nation as a Maritime Power, to the dignity of the Crown of Great Britain and to the advancement of the Trade and Navigation thereof'.[3]

Byron approached the Juan Fernández Islands from the south in late April. With Más a Tierra shrouded in a sea haze he sighted Más Afuera, Anson's carefully delineated fallback position for an isolated cruiser in those seas and hove to (i.e. furled sails to loiter) on 27 April. After inspecting the northern end of the island from the deck of his ship the following day, producing three excellent coastal perspectives, Byron looked for Saumarez's anchorage: 'This island is very high & mostly cover'd with wood, the only clear spots I saw upon it were towards the N[orth] end. They appeared very green & pleasant & there were hundreds of goats feeding there.' The boat failed to find the anchorage, or a secure landing, but returned full of fish. Desperate for wood, water and goat meat, Byron sent another boat, equipping the crew with cork lifejackets to help them swim, and protect them from the rocks. His boats secured useful quantities of wood and water, despite the heavy surf and large sharks 'that come into the very Surf when they see a Man in the water'.[4]

They also shot some goats that tasted 'as good as any venison', including one with the obligatory Selkirkian slit ear. Because Juan Fernández had achieved mythic status, all the best stories could be retold without question. In reality Selkirk had never been on Más Afuera. On the 30th the surf was so heavy that a sailor who could not swim preferred to take his chances ashore. He was forcibly rescued from his Selkirkian ambition by a junior officer. Byron weighed anchor and headed off into the Pacific, his water butts replenished, and plenty of firewood in the hold. The 'other' island had provided useful refreshment, compromised by heavy seas, poor landing sites and aggressive sharks. Little wonder the Spanish had made no effort to colonise the outer island. Byron had missed Más a Tierra, and the fortifications in Cumberland Bay.[5]

Byron's oversight ensured the next expedition, led by Samuel Wallis and Philip Carteret in the *Dolphin* and the *Swallow*, left England with plans to stop at Más a Tierra. Having lost contact with Wallis during a tough passage through the Straits of Magellan, Carteret, a lieutenant on the *Dolphin* under Byron, realised his crew needed fresh food and water. On 10 May 1767, HMS *Swallow*, profiting from a strong southeasterly wind, fetched the eastern end of Juan Fernández, and opened into Cumberland Bay, fully expecting it would be as empty as it had been on the day Anson departed.

But I was not a little surprised to observe a great number of men all about the beach, with a house and four pieces of Cannon over the waterside with two large Boats lying off of it, a Fort about two or three hundred yards up on the rising of the hill and on which they hoisted Spanish Colours, it was faced with stones and masonry has 18 or twenty embrasures with a longhouse inside of it, which I took for Barracks for the garrison, it did not seem to be fortified on the back or land side next the hill, all these works are on the westernmost side of the land of the Bay; there are round about the fort of different kinds about 25 or 30 houses, much Cattle feeding on the brow of the hills which seemed to be cultivated, many spots being parked and enclosed.[6]

There was another block house at Puerto Inglese. While English strategists and French savants speculated Spain had finally acted. The secret had been well kept, even the Spanish Ambassador in London knew nothing, warning Madrid that the Wallis/Carteret expedition might attempt to colonise the Falkland Islands, Juan Fernández and the Galápagos.

Finding the Spanish in control of Cumberland Bay Carteret quickly bore away (changed course) without showing any colours. He did not have a Spanish flag, while hoisting an English ensign would have caused problems. Instead he made for Más Afuera, although 'not the most eligible place for a ship to refresh (as Anson described it)', it had been vacant when he last saw it. Arriving on 16 May, the *Swallow* remained standing off and on for several days, unable to anchor in the rough weather, sending the cutter inshore whenever the weather abated to fill the casks with much needed water. Having landed on the island two years earlier Lieutenant Erasmus Gower reported the water supply much reduced. It had been a very dry summer that year, then one night a furious storm filled the gullies and washed away some of *Swallow*'s casks. Watering was difficult, dangerous work, leaving the men bruised and battered, soaked and chilled. One night Carteret was lucky to get the cutter on board and stowed before 'a terrible hard squall broke on us, & laid down the ship in a surprising manner, had we been but half a minute later in getting the boat in, we unavoidably must have lost her'. Several of the crew were fine swimmers, including three men who had to coast round the treacherous island, risking shark attack, after heavy surf prevented the boat reaching them. Whenever the weather allowed, Carteret sent the cutter inshore for water, fish and seals, but only managed to get his anchors down on 21 May, and on the 23rd the *Swallow* was once again driven out to sea. Carteret feared he had lost two boats and 28 men; their recovery was fortunate, ample proof that Más Afuera was no substitute for the salubrious bay at Más a Tierra.

From the 16th of May to ye first time we was drove off from the anchoring ground, we had scarce anything else but a series of dangers, troubles fatigue and misfortune ... it was a kind of miracle we had not lost the boats several times by the constant hard gales and violent sudden squalls and gusts of wind; which would at times be attended with Lightening & dreadful Claps of Thunder and hard rain, ... A thing I could never have credited if I had not been witness to it, as it was so very different from what we had two years before with Commodore Byron, and the Constant NW, NNW & WSW winds we met here & in out Passage did surprise me much, for former Authors have mentioned and it has been generally thought that the winds are constantly from ye S to ye SW on this Coast.[7]

He also took the care to correct the navigational details of Anson's narrative, which he attributed to the Reverend Walter rather than the Commodore. Carteret reckoned the island was surrounded by anchorages, but poor holding ground meant none were safe in a storm, an account confirmed by modern visitors. At least the fishing was excellent:

All the time we were about this island, we lived upon the fish we caught, in order to lengthen our stock of provisions; and not a piece of meat, was made use all this time, either by me or any other person.[8]

For once Byron's nickname 'Foul Weather Jack' proved misplaced; the hard weather fell to Carteret.

Carteret departed on 25 May, with most water casks filled, but abandoned a lot of cut firewood on the island. His men scarcely ate a pound of goat meat apiece. His chart, considered exemplary by Spanish navigator Alejandro Malaspina, had been obtained 'at the cost of innumerable hardships and perils'. Returning to Britain in 1769, Carteret's report of a Spanish garrison on Más a Tierra warned off other navigators. Even the Spanish were energised: Manuel de Amat, Viceroy of Peru from 1761 to 1776, sent expeditions from South America to Easter Island and Tahiti, reinforcing the Juan Fernández labour force with common criminals and soldiers from the mainland to support these voyages. Convicts and guards alike found the isolation depressing. Spaniards, Creoles and Indians saw nothing romantic in a sea-girt rock at the end of the known world. They were not, one imagines, avid readers of Defoe. It required an English sensibility to reach such eccentric conclusions.

By the late eighteenth century Crusoe, Anson and Rousseau had transformed Juan Fernández, or at least the verdant and accessible parts, into a 'happy' island.[9] Rousseau deliberately shifted the location from Defoe's mythic compound to Walter's quasi-realistic medicinal romance. He hoped men of greater education and insight would join Pacific voyages, to replace seaman's tales of wonder and the unimaginative ramblings of half-educated prelates, with precise information, fit for the elevated minds of Enlightenment Europe. In the late 1760s the first such voyager set sail: Joseph Banks joined Captain James Cook's Pacific voyage, itself a curious compound of navigational concerns, to observe the transit of Venus, and strategic geography. Profiting from Samuel Wallis's discovery of Tahiti the expedition entered the Pacific without stretching north along the Chilean coast. With Más a Tierra occupied it made sense to head directly to friendly Tahiti, or enter the region via the Indian Ocean.

Cook's voyages transformed the map of the Pacific, filling in most of the unknown area, creating new cultural connections, while Banks and his artists opened European eyes to new wonders. Exploration vessels carried experts to hitherto unknown lands, their scientific and artistic endeavour on the European mind shifted attention away from the Juan Fernández group. Bernard Smith's pivotal study slips past Selkirk's island without a word.[10] His Pacific, Cook's Pacific, is entered by way of Patagonia, stopping briefly to savour the curiosities of Easter Island before reaching the Polynesian paradise of Tahiti, and the more challenging lands of New Zealand, Australia and Melanesia. On the Cook voyages navigators, scientists and artists, shared a workbench in the great cabin and read each other's journals, breaking down disciplinary boundaries. The new Pacific studies of Joseph Banks did not address Juan Fernández, leaving island imagery necessarily impoverished. The new ways of seeing that came to the Pacific with Cook simply by-passed the old way point, leaving Juan Fernández without modern images, or taxonomic categorisation. There would be no struggles between classicism and realism in images of Juan Fernández. Only seafarers and navigators addressed the scene, their distant perspectives of El Yunque emphasising pedestrian concerns.

The French expedition of Jean François de Galaup, comte de La Pérouse, set a rendezvous for Juan Fernández, should the two ships become separated rounding Cape Horn. La Pérouse cancelled the plan after his ships made a quick, easy passage, disposing of the 'old prejudice' based on Anson's horrific account. Instead he headed for the cheap provisions of Concepción.[11] The Franco-Spanish 'Family Compact' ensured a friendly welcome.

13

Scurvy Resolved

La Pérouse's decision reflected his anxiety to avoid the ravages of scurvy, a central concern for all eighteenth century Pacific voyages. While the Spanish authorities in Madrid and Lima took practical steps to close the stable door to their Pacific sea lanes, the British began to address the primary cause of Juan Fernández's enduring attraction. Anson's voyage had been a truly hellish experience, the triumph of death left only a shattered fragment of the original force to complete a mission set for three times their number. These deaths had been accompanied by madness and disaster.

The salutary tale of the store-ship *Wager* might have been created especially for the purpose. Wrecked on an inhospitable coast discipline collapsed, Captain David Cheap lost his mind and at least one of his young officers went over to the enemy, entering the Spanish Navy and the Roman Church. This was hardly surprising, the wrecked mariners saw Cheap shoot one of his own midshipmen, for no obvious reason.[1] *Wager*'s people never made it to Juan Fernández, dribbling home in sorry groups. Once they had recovered their health the officers were more concerned to apportion blame than account for their conduct: and the petty officers made useful culprits. Walter, or more likely Robins, used the *Wager* disaster to create an alternative expedition, to highlight Anson's exceptional, heroic leadership. Having served this exemplary role, the unfortunate Cheap was not subject to further punishment.

To leave the story there would disguise other differences. Anson's ships only survived because they sought salvation on a well-known uninhabited island. Unlike Cheap Anson had several experienced officers under his command and his ships, however distressed, arrived in one piece. Without their ship *Wager*'s men, like Shelvocke's, had no legal or structural basis for discipline. Finally, and perhaps critically, Anson arrived at a near perfect refuge, packed with fresh food, good water and decent weather. Cheap and his crew did not. Once his men began to recover from scurvy Anson was able to clean the ships, ending the ravages of typhus and dysentery. Cleanliness was the key to oceanic voyaging, defeating most transmissible human epidemics. Landing on an uninhabited island, the crews escaped exterminating horrors like dysentery, typhus, malaria, yellow fever and local violence that awaited sickly, emaciated scorbutic men in pestilential port cities and tropical islands.

While ocean-going merchant seafarers had known about the danger of scurvy on long voyages for two centuries, frequently citing the useful properties of citrus fruits, the Royal Navy of 1740 had little experience of global navigation. Most naval operations involved relatively short cruises in Home Waters or the Mediterranean, punctuated by frequent returns to port to clean the hull, restock the water butts and obtain fresh food. Furthermore big manpower-intensive ships did not put to sea in winter, while those in the Mediterranean had access to a year round supply of fresh food. In the Caribbean, where fruits were easily obtained, men died of yellow fever long before they could become scorbutic.

The Royal Navy belatedly created a permanent Sick and Hurt Board in the early 1740s. Hitherto medical care had only been organised in wartime. This development coincided with the scurvy epidemic on Anson's ships. The link between a newly global navy, the greater focus on disease and the arrival of Anson at the Admiralty saw the Sick and Hurt Board tasked to find a solution. In 1747 Physician James Lind examined the disease, recording that it led to lassitude, immobility, depression, irritability and anger. Painful joints were a common early symptom. Scorbutic men bruised easily, their hair and teeth fell out, old wounds reopened and the skin discoloured. In the same year, elixir of vitriol, a mild sulphuric acid, had been identified as a cure. While an oral dose of vitriol might clear up the mouth ulcers that commonly afflicted scorbutic men it had no other benefits. During the Seven Years' War (1756–63), a truly global conflict, the Board reviewed many more remedies. The basic rule for selection was full disclosure of contents, cheap ingredients and ease of storage on long voyages. While the first and last stipulations were obvious the central question of cost reflected the unprecedented scale of British naval operations. Even the Royal Navy could not afford gold plated solutions.

New naval hospitals built at Haslar and Stonehouse in the early 1760s provided naval doctors with ideal opportunities to try new remedies. These hospitals had bars on the windows, to stop the men deserting. Trials on board cruising ships after the return of peace in 1763 pointed to the importance of fresh vegetables and fruit, but storage remained the key problem, especially on overcrowded battleships. The American War of Independence (1776–82) transformed naval understanding of scurvy. Gilbert Blane, Physician to the Fleet in the West Indies provided fruit and fruit juice to improve health, while Captain Roger Curtis commanding the gunboat flotilla at Gibraltar used Moroccan lemons to cure scorbutic men.

The first post-1763 British expeditions to the South Pacific, those of Byron and Wallis, used far smaller vessels than Anson, allowing the officers to devote more attention to crew comfort, cleanliness and health. Both expeditions had outbreaks of scurvy, but they did not prove fatal. This was hardly surprising, expedition vessels provided a very different environment from the crowded warships of 1741, and they had the option of stopping or changing course to find fresh food. After his untimely death much credit was accorded to the beatified Cook for defeating scurvy, but his approach, and his understanding, differed little from that of Byron and Wallis. None knew how to prevent or cure scurvy, so they did everything they could to avoid the problem. Of the numerous remedies embarked, most possessed only prophylactic value. Anxious to keep his men healthy Cook forced them to consume sauerkraut, malt wort and spruce beer, dosing himself with the same delights. By contrast Joseph Banks, having consulted widely, brought carefully bottled lemon juice. As *Endeavour* crossed the Arafura Sea Banks noticed the physical symptoms of the disease, he drank the juice, and was cured. He recorded that Cook and fellow scientist Daniel Solander, who were obviously scorbutic, became very 'nostalgic' or homesick.[2]

Twenty years later Captain Arthur Philip, an officer with considerable experience in Portuguese colonial service, deliberately reduced the voyages of the first convict fleet to Botany Bay to no more than nine weeks duration. He understood that scurvy normally appeared after twelve weeks at sea. At Rio de Janeiro he purchased large quantities of oranges, issuing several a day to his crews and the convicts they were transporting. Oranges are excellent sources of vitamin C. Philip lost only forty-eight from a complement of over a thousand, many of whom, like Anson's men, had been in poor health before they left Britain. In the 1790s Spanish hydrographer Alejandro Malaspina voyaged and charted the Pacific coast of the Empire, avoiding lethal outbreaks of scurvy with frequent stops. Instead he lost twenty men to land-based diseases. By contrast, Bruny d'Entrecasteaux's chaotic French Pacific expedition lost over 40 per cent of the crew to scurvy and dysentery after political divisions destroyed the discipline needed for effective man management.

Despite the citrus successes of the American War the Royal Navy hesitated until a scurvy epidemic in the Channel Fleet in 1795 threatened national security. Finally the Navy standardised Cook's paternalistic man-management system. It was no coincidence that Admiral Sir Roger Curtiss was the Captain of the Fleet, or that Fleet Surgeon Thomas Trotter recommended fresh meat and vegetables as the ideal preventive, keeping lemon juice to cure those already affected. The Sick and Hurt Board agreed. In 1795 Admiral Peter Rainier's sixteen-week voyage to the East Indies demonstrated beyond doubt the value of lemon juice, his men had been issued three-quarters of an ounce of juice per day. They were beginning to show scorbutic symptoms at the end of the voyage. Rainier stopped the rot by increasing the dose to one ounce. His report led other admirals to demand lemon juice. That year physician Sir Gilbert Blane joined the Sick and Hurt Board, and within months the Board recommended a regular issue of juice. This posed serious problems of supply, and cost. Finally in 1800 Anson's nephew John Jervis, Admiral the Earl St Vincent insisted on a regular issue for all ships on home stations. Preventing scurvy was vital to maintaining a close blockade of the main French naval base at Brest.

Much of the delay in addressing scurvy was occasioned by eighteenth-century notions that the sea was an unhealthy place; that sea air was bad, and land air good. At sea men expected to get sick, and duly did. Only in the early twentieth century did scientists finally understand the cause of scurvy was vitamin deficiency, which enabled them to provide both preventives and cures little different from those suggested by empirical tests a century before. It was in 1934 that the cause was finally isolated, along with the impact of thiamine deficiency on mental health. Finally the insanity, nostalgia and overwrought sensory inputs of scorbutic mariners, the very strangeness of seafaring, made sense.

Nor was scurvy the only vitamin deficiency disorder to afflict seafarers. Across the ages mariners had been affected by a strange phenomenon, seemingly healthy men suddenly became convinced that the ocean was a green field. Under this delusion, calenture, afflicted men left the ship, often with fatal results. While Erasmus Darwin linked their sensibility to nostalgia, naval physician Thomas Trotter blamed the reading of novels and romances. Yet Trotter recognised the link between scurvy and homesickness, which he categorised as 'scorbutic nostalgia'. Afflicted men suddenly felt a profound yearning for home and food, green fields and fresh water. Several visitors to Juan Fernández displayed these symptoms. Men were overwhelmed by the sight and smell of land, tiny fresh water run offs were magnified into mighty waterfalls, some insisted on being buried, or placed face down in freshly dug earth. On Anson's voyage it was claimed that men recovered after such earthy inhalations. That these two maritime diseases entered the English cultural mainstream reveals just how deep the sea had penetrated into the life of the nation, and how seriously scurvy had confined the development of British commerce, strategy and self-image.

Richard Walter's account of the approach to Juan Fernández is critical to any study of calenture and scurvy. He found it hard to convey the emotional state of the crew as they caught sight of land, lacking the literary power to describe feelings which he must have shared. Sights, sounds and smells made men feel better. Walter opened the enclosed mental world of the scorbutic. Sufferers have no space for the sensibilities of others, entirely wrapped up in their own feelings and visions. Endlessly rehearsing trifling grievances they become obsessive, as mad as David Cheap. They imagine things, and find it impossible to escape the descending spiral of their own delusions. A lethal disease that leaves the mind unfettered, scurvy turned the commonplace into wondrous visions.

While commonly associated with seafarers, scurvy was not restricted to the sea. It was common enough among the rural poor in eighteenth-century Britain, where seasonal food supplies and grinding poverty reduced winter vitamin intake. At sea the disease was more dangerous because remedies were harder to find, and seafarers inured to hardship, danger and risk, were reluctant to acknowledge their suffering. Sailor culture placed a premium on manly resolve, standing up to adversity and trivialising death as the only defence against despair and collapse. The madness of seamen was notorious; they provided a disproportionate number of inmates for mental asylums in eighteenth-century London. It did not help that sailors, as a group, were heavy drinkers, and more likely than landlubbers to have contracted tropical and venereal diseases.

The body needs a daily intake of ten milligrams of vitamin C to avoid scurvy, and sixty milligrams to remain healthy. While eighteenth-century men saw listlessness as a cause of scurvy, we know that the opposite is true. The mental symptoms are easily explained; scorbutics have almost no vitamin C in their brains, once the brain has scavenged any remaining vitamin C from the rest of the body vitamin deficiency causes oxidisation tissue damage in the brain, disrupting neuro-transmitters. This causes depression, reduces spontaneous activity, and heightens interest in taste, flavour and smell. Vitamin deficiency means brain function is both changing and deteriorating, including the loss of fine motor skills and strength. On 23 March 1741 the *Centurion* lost 'one of our ablest seamen', who fell overboard from the rigging.[3] This tragedy, commemorated in William Cowper's poem 'The Cast-away', was undoubtedly scorbutic.

Anson's voyage turned scurvy, the iconic disease of the British Empire, into an adjective used to describe other unpleasant manifestations. It became a commonplace of expeditions to the Frozen North, the dusty Australian outback, and the wild Patagonian shore Anson had coasted. Everywhere the British pushed at the limits of knowledge they found scurvy, it stopped explorers in their tracks, set a span on human endurance and played a dark role in many more disasters, from John Franklin in the Arctic to Robert Falcon Scott at the other end of the earth. Occupying an equally significant place in the imaginary world of the explorer it made an Edenic paradise of green islands, transfixing the imagination of countries and continents with a blizzard of adjectives.

Spanish voyagers, fresh from the ports of Peru and Chile, found little to spur the imagination on Juan Fernández. It was a useful navigational marker, and a strategic problem. They were mystified by English descriptions, and curiously flawed English navigation. Even when they recognised the words they did not see how they applied to this island. Lost in wonder, scorbutic British mariners mistook their location, and misplaced their paradise.

Modern science has an explanation: the loss of vital amino acids allows the nervous system to suffer sensory overload, for good or ill. In this state men can as easily die of despair as recover their health from the smell of freshly dug earth. Half a century after Anson, scientist Humphrey Davy experienced many of the same effects when breathing nitrous oxide (laughing gas). Suddenly he became the centre of the universe, with profoundly heightened sensitivity, by turns irritable, blinded by dazzling visions, startled by enhanced hearing, and isolated from reality in a parallel world of his own imagination. Gas, like scurvy, LSD and other hallucinogenic drugs, reduces the natural restraining mechanisms that modulate human sensory perception.

The heightened imaginative capacity of scorbutic men created the fabulous island of Juan Fernández, the one that greeted weary mariners after many months battling mountainous seas and epidemic disease. These were expeditions into the darker recesses of the human psyche, to places that could only be accessed by novel stimulants, or potentially lethal deficiencies. Here, in the self-absorbed mental world of sick men, emerged fictive seas, magical islands and redemption, investing Crusoe's prosaic island with a sense of wonder and bemusement. It is no coincidence the imagined worlds of great sea writers, of Melville, Conrad and Golding always found space for madness and obsession, improbable delusions and the strange power of the land.

A century after Anson's voyage, British warships were still calling at Juan Fernández, but improved diet and ready access to Chilean ports left them ill-equipped to fathom the meaning of old accounts. As they coasted the jagged cliffs, dropped anchor in Cumberland Bay and rambled up and down the vertical landscape many wondered why the men of 1741 made simple navigational errors, became oppressed by nostalgia, and obsessed with trifles. Bemused by the inexplicability, fictive and factual versions of the past began to conflate, Crusoe and Selkirk became one, while Anson was credited with secreting a treasure hoard. While Anson buried nothing on the island, other than the tragic victims of a catastrophic voyage, this magical island was capable of anything. The graves are lost, but the delusions live on.

Today the island can be reached in less than a day from almost anywhere on the planet. The journey is a humdrum affair of planes; big ones to Santiago, then a twin-engine Beechcraft to Juan Fernández. Only the open boat ride from la Heradura along the rocky coast to Cumberland Bay and the jetty of San Juan Bautista hints at the very different voyages that brought dying men to an island of wonders, a fitting abode for Prospero. It was a role that Anson, a man of few words, declined to play. By contrast, David Cheap imagined he saw Caliban, and killed him with a pistol.

14

Distant Despair

—◦◦◦—

In the late eighteenth century, the narratives of Selkirk, Crusoe and Anson exerted a powerful grip on British culture, nowhere more than in William Cowper's poem 'Verses, Supposed to be Written by Alexander Selkirk, During his Solitary Abode in the Island of Juan Fernández'. There are two manuscripts of the poem in Cowper's hand; one of them attributes the lines to Robinson Crusoe rather than Selkirk. This conflation of characters would become an increasingly commonplace approach to the core story. Cowper empathised with the Scottish seafarer, catching the despair and anxiety that characterised his early days on the island, and his longing for society. This 'despair' was the result of isolation, which in turn became desolation. Far from delighting in the spectacle of unspoiled nature he was shocked by 'this horrible place'. A voice from the Age of Reason, rather than the Romantic era, Cowper shared Selkirk's solace in revealed religion and was not unfamiliar with more humdrum forms of isolation. Depressive mental illness made human company 'too emotionally demanding', and Cowper lived as a virtual recluse. Convinced God had turned against him he lived on a small private income, gifts and patronage, his poetry was a diversion from despair. His conversion to Evangelical Christianity by former seafarer and slaver John Newton may explain the frequent use of nautical terms, but he read key travel texts, especially those concerning his heroes Cook and Anson.[1] He became a first-rate armchair traveller:

My imagination is so captivated upon these occasions, that I seem to partake with the navigators, in all the dangers they encountered. I lose my anchor; my main-sail is rent into shreds; I kill a shark, and by signs converse with a Patagonian, and all this without moving from the fire-side.[2]

Cowper's isolation from public life demonstrates just how deep the island stories had penetrated into British culture, his literary wanderings enabled him to conjure up the isolation of Juan Fernández and the terrors of the Cape Horn. Although inspired by a love of travel narratives, inner themes of 'Selkirk', imprisonment and despair, reference Cowper's own condition. Both men long for society, but Cowper's contrast between Selkirk's physical isolation with his own 'spiritual self-exile'[3] provided the piece with elemental force. It was a fitting requiem for a very English author who took a South Sea island into the poetical repertoire.

In 'The Task' (1785) Cowper recorded the pleasure of a traveller's tales:

> He travels, and I too. I tread his deck,
> Ascend his topmast, through his peering eyes
> Discover countries, with a kindred heart
> Suffer his woes, and share in his escapes;
> While fancy, like the finger of a clock,
> Runs the great circuit, and is still at home.

He also developed his South Sea references; including a strikingly Selkirkian line about climbing 'ev'ry morn' to the mountain top to look for ships from England. His discussion of Omai, the Tahitian youth who captivated London was paired with apocalyptic visions of drowning sailors, an earthquake and a tidal wave that signalled the end of the world. He was equally acute on the diseases of the ocean, examining calenture through a potent contrast between the fatal grassy dreams of sick seafarers and pleasant reality of his own rural wanderings.[4]

'The Cast-away' picked up the story of the scurvied seaman who fell from the rigging as the *Centurion* staggered round Cape Horn, combining shock, horror and religious sensibility. His influence on Coleridge's 'Ancient Mariner', another epic of despair, set against the towering backdrop of the vast ocean waves of Cape Horn is obvious. Cowper closed his imaginative life with telling lines:

> When snatched from all effectual aid,
> We perish'd, each alone:
> But I beneath a rougher sea,
> And whelm'd in deeper gulfs than he.

He died on 25 April 1800 in the Norfolk market town of East Dereham.[5]

Verses, Supposed to be Written by Alexander Selkirk, during his Solitary Abode in the Island of Juan Fernández

> I am monarch of all I survey,
> My right there is none to dispute,
> From the centre all round to the sea,
> I am lord of the fowl and the brute.
> Oh solitude! where are the charms
> That sages have seen in thy face?
> Better dwell in the midst of alarms,
> Than reign in this horrible place.
>
> I am out of humanity's reach,
> I must finish my journey alone,
> Never hear the sweet music of speech,
> I start at the sound of my own.
> The beasts that roam over the plain,
> My form with indifference see,
> They are so unacquainted with man,
> Their tameness is shocking to me.
>
> Society, friendship, and love,
> Divinely bestow'd upon man,
> Oh had I the wings of a dove,
> My sorrows I then might assuage
> In the ways of religion and truth,
> Might learn from the wisdom of age,
> And be cheer'd by the sallies of youth.

Religion! what treasure untold
Resides in that heav'nly word!
More precious than silver and gold,
Or all that this earth can afford.
But the sound of the church-going bell
These vallies and rocks never heard,
Ne'er sigh'd at the sound of a knell,
Or smil'd when a sabbath appear'd.

Ye winds that have made me your sport,
Convey to this desolate shore
Some cordial endearing report
Of a land I shall visit no more.
My friends do they now and then send
A wish or a thought after me?
O tell me I yet have a friend,
Though a friend I am never to see.

How fleet is a glance of the mind!
Compar'd with the speed of its flight,
The tempest itself lags behind,
And the swift-winged arrows of light.
When I think of my own native land,
In a moment I seem to be there;
But alas! recollection at hand
Soon hurries me back to despair.

But the sea fowl is gone to her nest,
The beast is laid down in his lair,
Ev'n here is a season of rest,
And I to my cabbin repair.
There is mercy in ev'ry place,
And mercy, encouraging thought!
Gives even affliction a grace,
And reconciles man to his lot.

Whaling and the South Pacific

─══❧══─

By the 1780s it seemed Juan Fernández had slipped out of the British world view. Not only had Cook's first voyage opened a new continent, but the dispatch of the First Fleet to Botany Bay provided an alternative, British depot for ships making the interminable voyage into the Pacific, for trade, exploration or war. After Cook most Pacific voyagers entered the Pacific via the Cape of Good Hope. When William Bligh attempted to round Cape Horn in the *Bounty* he was blown back. Cook had switched the axis of British Pacific voyaging, settling New South Wales, opening New Zealand, and completing a new Indian Ocean nexus of trade and power, one that occasionally used Cape Horn as a route home, but had little need for a way station off Valparaiso. When Spain declared war in 1779 the British, hard pressed at sea by the American rebels, the French and Spanish, had nothing left for the South Pacific.[1] After the American war British projects to attack Spanish South America were based at Sydney, rather than Juan Fernández, where the petty bastion commanding Cumberland Bay indicated the need for some serious fighting. Most accounts imply Juan Fernández, deprived of its central place as a strategic nexus and navigational way station in the British world view, was left to the avarice of lethal extractive industries, the intermittent attentions of a new South American political system and the musings of romantic Robinsonians. Yet the reality was very different: British ships continued to call at Juan Fernández, seeking refreshment, intelligence and profit.

After the American Revolution Britain, France and Spain shifted their focus to the imperfectly understood spaces of the Pacific. Cook's heroic voyaging outlined the ocean, and emphasised its material riches. Inspired by avarice, and informed by science, a new breed of men planned voyages to the other side of the world, in search of otter pelts, seal skins and whale oil. They would be aided and abetted by imperial visionaries, economic theorists and national governments seeking an edge in the ultimate competition. In the process new books would be written, and new discoveries made. Britain also faced new competition from the former American colonies. While American merchants surged into the Pacific to exploit the latest British discoveries, the bitter experience of losing the continental empire in America revitalised British oceanic insight. In 1780, with the outcome of the war hanging in the balance India expert Sir John Dalrymple observed: 'England might very well put up with the loss of America, for she would then exchange an empire of dominion which is very difficult to be kept for an empire of trade which keeps itself.'[2] Having failed as a Continental power, Britain should return to its true vocation, linking dominion of the seas with the expansion of trade. Dalrymple advised entering the Pacific via the Cape of Good Hope, the 'easy' route, using the Galápagos and Tahiti as bases to raid Spanish America.

After two centuries of intermittent raiding, Britain broke Spanish dominion in the South Pacific in a single decade, the 1780s, and it did so with merchant ships. That the key to success proved to be oil and smuggling, rather than war and violence, reflected the profound change that the British Empire underwent in the late eighteenth century. At first glance the change might appear to be a response to the shock of losing America, but the process began earlier, and was far more coherent. The 'Second' British Empire was a conscious return to the Tudor vision: 'an "empire" of ocean trade routes, protected by naval bases and nourished by commercial depots or factories, received a new impetus with the growth of British seapower and industrial productivity'.[3] These ideas found expression in contemporary literature on trade, security and history. The need to find markets for burgeoning export industries, combined with naval dominance saw the government force British shipping into the

Pacific over the wreckage of Spanish *imperium*. Prime Minister William Pitt the Younger recognised that access to global markets depended on seapower. The Bourbon powers were desperately trying to hang on to their imperial assets in the face of a rapidly expanding and commercially dynamic state in the first flush of industrialisation, propelled by a democratic political system that empowered merchants and bankers.

After 1782 British interest in the South Pacific shifted to whaling, a trade linked to the settlement of New South Wales, and opportunities for trans-Pacific trade with Spanish America. Sperm whale oil had become a critical resource for industrialisation: the clean, odour-free oil lubricated the spinning and weaving machinery of Britain's burgeoning cloth factories, and lit the street lamps that made cities safe. Before 1776 Britain had relied on a heavily subsidised Greenland whaling fleet and New England whalers, based in Boston and the Quaker community on Nantucket Island. The American whaling trade was devastated by war, while British whalers saw their bounties increased, and the trade boomed. With owners receiving a subsidy of £2 per ton for each ship that sailed, the British trade was essentially artificial, and uncompetitive. Furthermore, this Arctic industry produced low-grade black oil.

In 1783 the government imposed an import tariff equal to the current market price, to teach the Americans that the cost of independence was exclusion from the economic and strategic benefits of Empire. British ministers moved to generate a larger, more efficient domestic industry focused on sperm whale oil. Following the collapse of their market several Nantucket whalers moved to Nova Scotia and, when this opportunity was closed by legislation, to Britain. Fearing Nantucket men based in Nova Scotia would collude with Boston merchants to avoid British Customs London brought the industry under metropolitan supervision. The new Board of Trade of 1784, headed by neo-mercantilist economist Charles Jenkinson, established the bureaucratic power base for a systematic assault on the South Pacific. Cook's voyages had done much to reveal the natural riches of the Pacific, and although the explosive growth of the trade in sea otter pelts between British Columbia and China has attracted much attention, not least because it sparked the Nootka Sound Crisis of 1790, whaling was the real motor of Pacific expansion. Whaling was a far bigger industry, and whaleship owners had far more political clout than fur traders.

Americans began to exploit sperm whale fishing grounds off Brazil and into the South Atlantic in the 1770s. Voyagers reported the prized whales were abundant beyond the Cape of Good Hope, and Cape Horn. Jenkinson recognised that where the whalers led other British commerce would follow. In 1775, whaler Samuel Enderby shifted his base from Boston to London, his main market. In the same year the British government encouraged the South Atlantic trade, offering a prize for the five largest cargoes brought in each year by British built and owned ships, and cut the flat rate subsidy of Greenland trade. Enderby's ships were given British registration, and in 1776 he and other American owners began sending their newly 'British' ships south. As the trade expanded the owners formed a political lobby group, the Southern Whale Fishery Committee, to press the government for financial support and access to the Indian Ocean and South Pacific. British navigation in these seas had long been restricted by the charters of East India and South Seas Companies. Both objected to the removal of exclusive rights, but the government disagreed. It promoted the new industry, both to make Britain self-sufficient in a key commodity, and recruit ships and men from a declining American industry. Critically, the policy was backed by the Board of Trade, while senior naval officers recognised the strategic benefits of increased access and knowledge.[4]

South Pacific whaling would spearhead a trade offensive, expanding the sea-based British commercial empire. Although there would be no new colonies, Britain would acquire 'new spheres and the sinews of power were strengthened without incurring onerous commitments'. This made whalers 'an appropriate instrument for this mission'.[5] The claims of the South Sea

Company were dismissed as 'baseless': the Company had long been a City financial enterprise, with no commercial activity. In June 1786 the Pitt administration passed an Act for the Encouragement of the Southern Whale Fishery, allowing whalers to operate south of the Equator, and up to 500 miles west from the Coast of Spanish South America. The Juan Fernández Islands lay at the epicentre of the newly defined region. In 1788 the Whale Fishery Act was amended to allow fishing in the Southeast Pacific as far as 180° west.[6]

The whalers were enmeshed in a global system. Samuel Enderby and others carried convicts and supplies to the new penal settlement at Botany Bay, via the Cape of Good Hope and the Indian Ocean, before sailing on for the whaling grounds. Facing a two-pronged British assault on an ill-defended *mare clausum*, a handful of Spanish warships and coastguards found British merchant ships on the desolate shores of Patagonia, in the far south of Chile, and at uninhabited offshore island sealing grounds; there were simply too many of these ambitious interlopers to hold the line. Spanish patrols were little more than a face-saving device. The British argued that under international law Spain could not claim possession of unoccupied space, giving them a perfect right to use waters and land 'where as yet no settlements have been made', as long as they did not attempt to trade in violation of Spanish law.[7]

In 1790 British policy was tested. Spanish warships removed a British trade post dealing in sea otter pelts from Nootka Sound on the shores of modern British Columbia just as Spanish opposition to South Pacific whaling and sealing reached a head. John Dalrymple had published further thoughts on the region the year before, following discussions with Sir Joseph Banks and Spanish Minister Count Floridablanca. While Floridablanca warned of the danger posed to Spanish dominion and British trade by citizens of the new American Republic, who would ignore the old world treaties and rules, Dalrymple planned another smash and grab raid on the Pacific, using Juan Fernández to refresh.[8] There was no enthusiasm for significant land operations, this was a truly global maritime strategy. At the height of the crisis in November 1790 the *Times* reported a rumour that Juan Fernández was uninhabited, and about to become British. Instead Pitt exploited the Crisis to secure unrestricted access to the Pacific and the trade with China, as objects of national policy. Forced to back down by an overwhelming naval mobilisation Madrid accepted that British ships 'shall not be disturbed or molested either in navigating or carrying on their fisheries in the Pacific Ocean, or the South Seas, or in landing on the coasts of those seas, in places not already occupied, for the purpose of carrying on their commerce with the natives of those countries.'[9] After 200 years of intermittent raiding, charting and trading the Pacific had been opened to British enterprise by a few oily barques and a battle fleet at Spithead. Fear that Britain would open imperial markets and seize continental resources drove Bourbon Spain to ally with the regicide French Republic in 1796.

British whalers quickly exploited their new freedom to roam the South Pacific, becoming the 'principal instrument of the government's policy of trade expansion in the North Pacific'.[10] In 1792, fifty-nine British ships brought home Pacific cargoes of oil, seal skins, ambergris and whale bone worth more than £189,000, doubling the quantity of the previous year with catches that exceeded domestic demand. Enderby and the 'Whale Fishery' lobby demanded government support: the Board of Trade recommended sending a naval vessel to survey the southwest coast of America and the adjacent islands, to find a suitable base for the whalers. Ultimately they would look to Sydney. The new base enabled whalers, traders and smugglers to range out into the Great South Sea. Barred by occupation and artillery, Más a Tierra occupied a greatly reduced place in this new navigational system, Más Afuera remained a useful watering place, and an attractive sealing ground, but the last years of the eighteenth century reduced the magical islands to a matter of fact way station for pelagic hunters.

The 1788 Fishery Act prompted Samuel Enderby to prepare his first South Pacific voyage. In August he consulted Sir Joseph

Banks, now President of the Royal Society, a key adviser of government on global economic opportunities, imperial resources and grand strategy. Botany Bay was his idea. Could Banks:

inform us if Juan Fernández is settled? If settled, whether there would be any Risk of our ship being seized if she should go to that Place through Distress, or to refresh the crew in case of Scurvy? Or if there are any other Places where she might derive benefit without those Risks?[11]

He also enquired about charts, and reports of sperm whales. In return he promised his ships would conduct research for Banks. Such exchanges propelled eighteenth-century oceanic science, and Banks was happy to oblige. Suitably informed Enderby sent a reconnaissance mission around Cape Horn, the *Emilia* returned to London in 1790 with a full cargo of oil. Enderby sent two more ships in 1791: *Britannia* and *William*. *Britannia* carried convicts and stores to Botany Bay, before heading across the Pacific to fish but *William* sailed direct round Cape Horn, commanded by half-pay naval officer John Moss.

Moss was a protégé of Captain Lord Mulgrave, naval officer, arctic explorer, member of the Board of Trade, and above all a friend and neighbour of Banks.[12] He visited the Juan Fernández Islands twice, collecting material for a substantial report. On his initial approach, in January 1792, he observed a one-gun battery and a watch post at Puerto Inglese. There was an anchorage at around 14 fathoms, but it was dangerously exposed. Rounding the point into Cumberland Bay, Moss observed two ramshackle forts covering the village and landing. One consisted of a dry stone wall; the other was incomplete. When the governor refused permission to obtain wood or water, Moss demonstrated the impotence of the Spanish position by anchoring just out of range of the guns, and quietly fishing. While Moss had little to fear (the governor commanded a mere six soldiers, forty settlers and a rowing boat), this was a disappointing reception; the prospect of goats, fresh food and water was enough to make his scorbutic crew salivate. Their symptoms 'would have been speedily arrested by the fresh venison, fish and vegetables to be obtained there'.[13]

On 15 November 1792 Moss returned, persuading Governor Don Juan Calvo de la Canteza to let him land and cut wood. His sickly crew greatly appreciated 'a large quantity of vegetables', 'a loaf of sugar, four fine sheep and as much craw fish as he wanted'. Moss visited the village, finding a welcome and a cup of Maté at every door, the whole village 'swarmed with children.' The vegetable plots were poor, which the governor attributed to the ravages of a 'grub'. In return for his hospitality Moss gave the governor 'a dozen of wine, a dozen of plates, two dishes, half a dozen of wine glasses, a small pot of pickles and a pair of new boots'. The exchange revealed just how isolated the islands were, far beyond the continental concerns of Spanish imperium. Departing Cumberland Bay, Moss sailed 110 miles to Más Afuera, where his men landed to collect water, goat meat and seal skins. While the other island provided 'all the refreshments that can reasonably be wished', the exposed position meant 'nothing but great distress can warrant anchorage here'. To hold station off Más Afuera a ship had to remain in the lee of the island, which required constant attention as the wind shifted frequently. Moss advised bringing strongly built boats, his had been stove while landing: even so the crew loaded 2,100 seal skins in a few days, no mean feat. Finally Moss put Enderby's Cove on the map. He returned home to find another war had broken out, and rejoined the Royal Navy, serving with distinction until his death in 1799. A decade later, as the attention of the British state turned once more to the South Pacific his notes appeared in the *Naval Chronicle*, as a supplement to Carteret's account.[14]

Predictably the new fishery provided cover for large scale smuggling. Wealthy Chileans and Peruvians, starved of European and Asian luxury goods by the Spanish monopoly, happily bought from long-distance fishermen. The occasional port visit for alleged 'repairs' or refreshment provided ample opportunity to breach the customs regulations, while unoccupied offshore islands offered a useful rendezvous for smugglers, especially Más Afuera and the more distant and difficult island of San Ambrosio.

After Nootka the British government dispatched another voyage to survey the coasts and anchorages needed by the whaling fleet, only to redirect it to the contentious North Pacific, delay sailing while the crisis raged, finally sailing after the Spanish climb-down. The command fell to George Vancouver, who had sailed on two of Cook's voyages.[15] In a sign of the changing strategic picture Vancouver's two ships, *Discovery* and *Chatham* entered the Pacific via the Cape of Good Hope and only reached the South Pacific as they headed home, when Vancouver called at several Pacific Islands, 'for the purposes of watering and surveying'. Expecting a polite welcome he set a rendezvous at Juan Fernández, but the appearance of scurvy, a sprung mainmast and a chance encounter with his consort at sea led him to cancel the visit, sailing past both islands in March 1795. The scurvy responded well to the fresh victuals of Valparaiso, where the Spanish authorities, temporarily allies, proved unusually accommodating.[16]

Vancouver's would be the best-known of several voyages that extended British strategic and commercial activity in the South Pacific and along the west coast of the Americas after 1782, reflecting a growing awareness that these seas were the final link in a global trade network connecting Britain with India, Botany Bay, the Americas and China. It was, perhaps, no coincidence that this vision had been set out by John Campbell some fifty years before.[17] Juan Fernández may have been the ideal base for such projects, but the islands would remain in Spanish hands while peace prevailed. Plans to seize the obvious South Pacific staging post were thwarted by the small garrison, so the British began to examine alternative, uninhabited archipelagos, even though none possessed the vital combination of a secure anchorage, ample water and fresh food. When Vancouver's expedition was redirected to the Pacific Northwest the whaleship owners pressed the Admiralty to locate the 'necessary places of refreshment and security to refit' further south, stopovers that were essential for longer, more profitable voyages. With South Pacific cruises often lasting more than two years the need for fresh food, refit and relaxation was obvious. The economic benefits of prolonged voyages were overwhelming. The government took advice from Banks, and prepared HMS *Rattler* for a combined survey and whaling voyage in 1792. Delayed by the outbreak of another war Captain James Colnett sailed in January 1793.[18]

The *Rattler* voyage was explicitly linked to Vancouver's mission, to which Colnett had contributed his prior knowledge of the Pacific Northwest, and which he was at pains to avoid duplicating – and that of John Moss.[19] The availability of a Spanish manuscript chart which included the isolated San Ambrosio–San Félix archipelago was a great help. The filthy, torn document was worked long and hard, inked over and then soaked when Colnett's cabin was washed out near the end of the voyage.[20] Colnett had served with Cook, sailing to the Pacific Northwest and China, he was the senior man seized in Nootka Sound, before resuming his naval career with a voyage that combined gathering economic intelligence on whaling harbours and stations with strategic reconnaissance. Among his textual sources none was used more frequently than Lionel Wafer's voyage. Colnett provided useful charts of the Galápagos Islands and the San Félix–San Ambrosio archipelago, along with policy recommendations.

Having seen the rich harvest of whales, seals and elephant seals to be made in the far south Colnett favoured establishing a whaling station at Staten Island close by Cape Horn. On the passage south Colnett and his crew had a predictable encounter with the scurvy, cured by two oranges a day and the use of a lime sauce, probably a form of cordial. Colnett had planned to call at Juan Fernández, but he feared Britain and Spain might be at war, so he shifted his attention to the Saint Felix and Saint Ambrose Isles, where he expected to find the same 'refreshments' as Más Afuera, trusting Moss had obtained all the necessary information.[21] He did not mention his fear of being thrown into a Peruvian prison, for a second time. He took care to avoid the Spanish throughout the voyage, which limited the value of his work. He examined the isolated, unoccupied San Félix islands, a largely barren landscape without fresh water. He charted the islands, but the lack of water would be a major drawback for any visitors other than whalers, who filled their barrels with drinking water until they had oil to load. In a pioneering vision of terra-forming he suggested a water tank might be constructed, to be filled by passing ships, while 'a few butts of earth might be landed, 'and several kinds of herbs' raised. Suitably transformed the islands would be habitable, and could be defended. He dismissed the idea that there were any islands further west and concluded with an accurate navigational position, vital in this vast ocean, where islands were easily misplaced.[22] He did not stop to consider the feelings of a small garrison left in such a desolate place. Colnett's account of the San Félix group did not lead to any immediate action, but it was not forgotten.

Reaching the Galápagos Islands, which had been specifically mentioned in his orders, Colnett named islands for Lord Chatham and Admiral Lord Hood, the First Lord and First Naval Lord of the Admiralty. He also stopped at Isla de la Plata, where Drake divided his plunder, and buccaneers refreshed on good water, goats and turtles. There was a good anchorage, close to water: 'In a war with Spain this island would form an excellent station, as well as a place to look out and accommodate the sick, as it lies four leagues from the nearest main land, which is Cape Lorenzo.' Not only could ships lie on the seaward side of the island without being seen from the mainland, but with a chain of longboats they could link up with the Galápagos, commanding the route north and south, as ships were not known to pass further out. British control of the sea lanes would cut off the Spanish from the northwest, and secure the whale fishery.[23]

The whaling side of the venture proving less successful, Colnett headed back to San Félix to salt down seal skins. A stop at the Galápagos cured his men of boils, and they stocked up on fresh turtle. Naming a bay for Sir Joseph Banks reflected the strategic/economic genesis of the expedition; and the critical role of the great man in all contemporary Pacific projects. Colnett's report brought the Galápagos and the Saints into the British world view, as poor substitutes for the one true island destination. His voyage stressed the vital role of importance of 'convenient places for refitting and refreshment' in the Pacific on the eve of the nineteenth century.[24]

Colnett's cautious approach to Spanish settlements was not without justification. Well aware of growing British interest in 'their' ocean, but lacking naval power, the Spanish were only dangerous to those ashore. When Britain and Spain went to war in 1796 the whalers took privateer licences, to make war on men as well as cetaceans.[25] As the Falkland Islands Crisis of 1770 had demonstrated, Spanish attempts to close the loopholes in their imperial carapace were futile in the face of British naval power. On that occasion the British did not press their advantage, but thirty years later the situation had changed.

In an attempt at economy, the Spanish authorities put the Juan Fernández garrison on double duty in 1760, turning the island into a prison camp. While Cumberland Bay remained a guard post against British ships the governor focused on preventing rebellion and escape. Fort Santa Barbara had been rebuilt in stone, the San Francisco Xavier battery covered the beach, while outlying forts in Bahía Pangal and Puerto Inglese also watched for British interlopers. For thirty years the islands slumbered, even Alejandro Malaspina's voyage of discovery did not land. Passing both islands in March 1790 Malaspina was content with Anson's description, and the charts of Carteret, covering Más Afuera, and Ulloa dealing with Bahía Cumberland. Ulloa's description led him to fear losing an anchor. Instead he provided accurate locations for the islands.[26] This information was kept secret, but such threadbare precautions did little to reduce imperial overstretch, dragging the old Empire down to ruin. To secure a vast, thinly populated continental empire which lay exposed to British incursions at almost all points Spain required a powerful navy. Without it Spain could only look to local defences.

Little wonder that Jenkinson, in retirement in 1802, took pride in the success of the fishery he had done so much to foster. It was, in his opinion, worth far more than a continental empire.

Receipts exceeded half a million pounds. British South Pacific whaling endured into the 1830s, when coal gas reduced domestic demand. American whalers persisted because their home market was far slower to adopt gas. As the trade declined, Samuel Enderby's grandson made a grander claim: the trade opened by the whalers 'eventually brought about the independence of such states as Peru and Chili'.[27]

16

The End of an Era

In 1793 Spain and Britain became allies against the French Revolution, opening Peruvian and Chilean ports to British trade.[1] The growth of Australian and Indian commerce into the South Pacific, linking South America with China, increased opportunities for smuggling. Spain changed sides in 1796, reviving interest in South American strategic and commercial opportunities. The government turned to Colnett for advice on South Pacific strategy and welcomed South American revolutionaries, their schemes made doubly attractive by the imperative need to expand the frontiers of commerce, both to sustain the costs of war and to replace the increasingly constricted European markets. Most projects proved abortive, the few that were attempted, notably at Buenos Aires, were spectacular failures. In 1805–6 the Grenville administration adopted Captain Home Popham's plans to seize Valparaiso, only to redirect the resources to reinforce Popham's disastrous attempt to occupy Buenos Aires.[2] Despite all the ambition and energy put into planning for war in the South Pacific Britain rarely had the luxury of focusing on the region in an age of total war, and lacked the resources to operate there on a sustained basis, while Juan Fernández, even if it had been available, was no longer an adequate base. Then, with startling suddenness, the Spanish insurrection against Napoleon changed everything.

Prostrated by war, Spain was unable to defend the American empire against local independence movements, leaving the British to open the trade of Chile and Peru by less dramatic measures. Smuggling, loans and technical support to the revolutionary movements broke the last remnants of Spanish commercial exclusion. Commercial actors created an 'informal' empire, both to avoid expense and remove the temptation to create costly government posts.[3] Naval power would sustain commercial access. Yet as Spain faded into Pacific history, Britain faced a new competitor.

American merchant ships trading to the Columbia River settlement began calling at Juan Fernández in the 1790s, initially for food and water, then to harvest sandalwood from the island and elsewhere to carry to China, along with Pacific sea otter pelts. American whaleships also used the islands to refresh. In a last twitch of the old imperial system, the Viceroy of Peru, Ambrosio O'Higgins, disciplined the governor of Juan Fernández for allowing an American ship to repair in Cumberland Bay. Meanwhile British and American sealers, whalers, smugglers and privateers used Más Afuera as a base and watering station.[4] In the process they annihilated the seal population. New York sealing ship *Eliza* reached Más Afuera in 1792, taking 38,000 skins to Canton. In 1798 seven more arrived. The Spanish removed the sealers from the island in 1801 and again in 1804–5, but the Americans just kept coming back, in ever greater numbers. A short-lived bonanza saw large, if transient populations ashore, with huts and gardens, even celebrating the Fourth of July. One sealer estimated around three million pelts were taken to China in seven years. The pelagic populations were annihilated, and by 1815 there was little to see on Más Afuera but ruined huts and a tragic jumble of bleached bones. Once the seals had been wiped out the sealers stopped coming, but the island continued to suffer. The indigenous flora had been devastated by two invasive species: fecund and ever-hungry goats, whose only virtue was a prodigious appetite that held back the all-embracing, strangling maquis shrub.

An island of life and beauty had been turned into a wasteland by human greed and carelessness; it is unlikely the damage can be undone. Between 1797 and 1809 some 226 American ships called in Chilean ports, of which only 12 were condemned as smugglers. Illicit trade and new ideas broke the monopolist policy of metropolitan Spain. South American independence was essential for economic development.[5] Chilean patriots took control in 1813. Later that year the Royal Navy returned to Juan Fernández.

In 1812 the United States declared war on Britain, invading Canada and attacking British shipping. Captain David Porter's American frigate USS *Essex* ventured into the South Pacific, where he captured a dozen British whaleships off the Galápagos, using information from Colnett's book. A British squadron sent to seize the American fur trade post at Astoria on the Pacific Coast near the Canadian border used the island as a rendezvous. The frigate HMS *Phoebe*, Captain James Hillyar, and the ship sloops HMS *Racoon* and HMS *Cherub* arrived on 11 September 1813, without the transport ship. When they departed on the 18th the *Racoon* sailed north for Astoria, but *Phoebe* and *Cherub* headed east to hunt the *Essex*.[6] The British warships arrived in far better condition than Anson's shattered squadron, but they made good use of island to refit damaged rigging, refill their water casks, gather firewood and fresh food. Edging into Cumberland Bay *Phoebe* had fired a signal gun, summoning a pilot to help the ships work up into the anchorage. Cattle, vegetables and fish improved the health of the crew while the boats were ashore for several days obtaining wood and water. The officers also compiled a fresh set of coastal perspectives.[7] After searching the Galápagos and calling at Callao *Phoebe* and *Cherub* set course for Valparaiso, via Más Afuera. The importance of the islands as navigational markers was obvious. *Phoebe* captured the *Essex* at Valparaiso, while most of the British whalers were recaptured. In November HMS *Racoon* stopped off at the island on passage between British Columbia and Rio. The restored Spanish administration of Chile had begun sending political prisoners to the island, living a squalid life in a newly dug cave overlooking Cumberland Bay.[8]

Royal Marine Lieutenant John Shillibeer provided the next account of the island, serving on the frigate HMS *Briton*. Sent to deal with the *Essex*, *Briton* became the first British warship to visit Pitcairn Island, last refuge of the *Bounty* mutineers, and the Marquesas islands. These exotic locations gave Shillibeer ample opportunity to indulge his literary and artist talents. His romantic affinities were obvious, this was a book compiled in the wake of Coleridge, Byron and Wordsworth. *Briton* arrived on 22 January 1815. Like any well-read traveller, Shillibeer sought the island of Anson and 'the ingenious pen of Daniel De Foe', but he was looking with modern eyes. In contrast to his scorbutic precursors Shillibeer's descriptions were qualified, and slightly lukewarm: 'notwithstanding we did not find it that earthly paradise described by Lord Anson, it is exceedingly beautiful and capable of every improvement'. He sympathised with the Chilean Patriots, appalled by the situation of men of quality and standing 'reduced to the lowest ebb of misery, and the very point of starvation'. Shillibeer reported Cumberland Bay to be 'neither commodious, nor safe'; the island was 'excessively mountainous and romantically picturesque, possessing several crystalline streams of water, and a soil of great fertility'. Sitting on a rocky headland between San Juan and Bahía Pangal, he contemplated 'the most romantic, strange, and incomprehensible scenery which can be found in the formation of the universe', while executing a workmanlike sketch of the bay and the headland. He encountered wild descendants of Anson's plants, Juan Fernández's goats, the loose soil that made any such venture hazardous, and the thieving habits of the Spanish troops. Some ill-disciplined soldiers assaulted the nightwatchmen and stole tools left ashore overnight, prompting Shillibeer to reflect on the long history of Spanish larceny. Having completed her wood and water *Briton* was back at Valparaiso by 19 February, and set course for Plymouth.[9]

At the same time the officers of another British frigate, HMS *Tagus,* produced an excellent coloured view of Cumberland Bay, indicating the watering and wooding locations. Wood came from Bahía Pangal, the lower slopes around the village had been clear felled, including Lord Anson's Valley. Both *Phoebe* and *Tagus* produced charts of the island, featuring Cumberland Bay. All three British frigates collected Spanish chart material, exploiting the chaos to secure hitherto 'secret' manuscripts and printed cartography to inform a new British chart.[10]

Chile emerged as an independent country in 1818, ruled by the landed elite. De facto head of state Bernardo O'Higgins, the illegitimate son of a Irish born Spanish governor of Peru, paid an American merchant ship to liberate the patriot prisoners from Juan Fernández, then abandoned the island. In 1820 Antonio Jose de Irisarri, Chilean representative in Europe proposed ceding Juan Fernández or Valdivia to Britain in return for guaranteeing Chile against Spanish reconquest. O'Higgins rejected any sacrifice of territory. He had been less scrupulous in 1817, proposing to discharge Chile's debts to mercenary naval genius Lord Cochrane by transferring the very same islands![11] The British government expressed no interest, consistently opposing the additional expense of uneconomic territories, Cochrane preferred cash. After leaving Chilean service he visited the island, to refill his ship's water butts.

Maria Graham, a passenger on the flagship, portrayed Cochrane and his officers as overgrown schoolboys, rambling about the romantic island of Robinson Crusoe. Her own participation was limited more by decorum and dress than any lack of interest. Maria knew Selkirk, Crusoe and Cowper. Having fixed their position off Más Afuera on 22 January 1823, Cochrane's ships spent most of the 24th working into Cumberland Bay, anchoring just before sunset, giving Maria ample opportunity to take in the scenery: 'the most picturesque I ever saw, being composed of high perpendicular rocks wooded nearly to the top, with beautiful valleys; and the ruins of the little town in the largest of these heighten the effect'.[12] This was a place of wild beauty, where the intermittent impact of roving mankind had taken the edge off the appalling loneliness that Selkirk had endured.

Going ashore early the next day, Cochrane left the sailors to sweat over the water supply while the officers climbed the mountain, trying to reach the obvious notch in the mountain range, later named 'Selkirk's Mirador'. Maria remained near the beach, inspecting the ruined town. At the foot of the flagstaff in the mouldering fort lay a bronze cannon cast in 1614. Old iron guns were in use as mooring posts: they are still there. Water, piped to boats alongside the small jetty, was excellent. Maria also reflected on the 1821 insurrection, when the prisoners tried to escape on the American whaler *Persia*.[13] She believed the Chilean authorities had blocked any attempt to make the island self-sufficient and abandoned the prison settlement, maintaining sovereignty by a proclamation banning settlement or the taking of cattle and wood. The senior British naval officer on the station advised merchant ships not to call: it is unlikely the advice was heeded.

Although the officers returned frustrated from the climb Cochrane brought an interesting rock sample to discuss. There were always amateur geologists ready to speculate on the volcanic origins of the island. The party selected a suitable spot by a stream for a picnic, using fig leaf tablecloths for a meal of ship's provisions and under-ripe fruit. After dinner Maria and Cochrane wandered into 'Lord Anson's Park', complete with European shrubs and herbs, which prompted a quote from Oliver Goldsmith's 'The Deserted Village'. Indeed, 'Lord Anson has not exaggerated the beauty of the place, or the delights of the climate.'

On 26 January Maria again accompanied the officers ashore, but while they set off for the high ground, to see the other side, she wandered the shore, looking for a good spot for sketching. She chose the beach close by the modern cemetery, almost directly opposite Shillibeer's seat. Bored by her own company, after a few hours Maria began reciting Cowper's gloomy and lowering 'Verses, Supposed to be Written by Alexander Selkirk', repeating the line 'Than reign in this horrible place'. Fortunately Cochrane returned, reporting the officers had reached the notch, and the others had pressed on down the other side. That evening a Chilean man appeared, one of four on the island butchering cattle, curing meat and hides, and boiling down the remains for the tallow. The next day proved rather blustery, so the gentlemen fell to fishing for cod and crayfish, and sailed on 28 January. Their thoughts turned to ownership, discussing the value of the island 'to any nation that takes possession of it as a harbour'. That she meant Britain was clear, 'our whalers resort thither continually'. Characteristically her last word on the subject was 'beautiful'.[14] The assumptions and insights of British visitors implied occupation and possession were more than possible; this little island had almost everything, above all a superb strategic position.

The following year David Douglas, a young Scottish botanist working for the Royal Society, visited the island while on passage to British Columbia. Reflecting the inevitable combination of state and economic interests that propelled scientists into the unknown, Douglas sailed on the Hudson's Bay Company ship *William & Ann*. Close links to leading men of science including botanist William Hooker, together with a successful North American expedition, made him an obvious choice to record new flora, and the first trained botanist to visit Juan Fernández.

Like most sailing ships heading north from Cape Horn, the *William & Ann* used Más Afuera as a navigational beacon, the island was spotted on 14 December 1824. At a distance it appeared 'like a conical black rock' before the ship closed to within two or three miles. Although short of water Captain Hanwell decided the surge on the beach was too severe to attempt a landing. Close in the island seemed to be moderately covered with herbage, supporting a healthy population of goats. Approaching Más a Tierra the following day Douglas hastily penned his impressions: 'the whole island is very mountainous, volcanic, and beautifully covered with woods to the summit of the hills, tops of which are rarely seen, being enveloped in the clouds'.[15]

A day later, with the ship securely anchored in Cumberland Bay, Douglas managed to get into the first boat: 'As we approached the shore we were surprised to see a small vessel at anchor, and on the beach a hut with smoke rising from it.' An English voice then 'directed us in to a sheltered creek'. Walking up the beach, Douglas, ship's doctor John Scouler and the boat crew met

Whitechapel sailor William Clark. Working out of Coquimbo, he was the boat keeper for a party of Spanish (Chilean) hunters, on the other side of the island, slaughtering and skinning wild cattle and seals. Although Clark lived in a small hut with few comforts Douglas was impressed by the cultural attainments of this latter-day Selkirk:

a man of some information; his library amounted to seventeen volumes – Bible and Book of Common Prayer, which he had to keep [in] a secret place when his Spanish friends were there; and odd volume of *Tales of My Landlord* and *Old Mortality*, some of the voyages and Cowper's poems. He has the one by heart addressed to Alexander Selkirk; but what is still more worthy to be noticed, a fine bound copy of Crusoe's adventures, who himself was the latest and most complete edition.[16]

After their strange encounter Douglas and Scouler left the sailors to fill the water butts and wandered into the ruined village. 'Here a few years ago the Spaniards formed a colony; but it is now abandoned, all the houses are destroyed, and the fort, on which were some very large guns. Twenty-six cannons lay on the shore just below.' Amid the general air of decay he was struck by the remains of a church consecrated in 1811, and 'a circular oven of brick, seven feet within, marked on it 1741; probably built by Anson during his residence, it is now occupied by a small species of blue pigeon as their cote'. Abandoned, overrun gardens rich with peaches, quinces, apples, berries and vines were harvested. The only edible vegetable on offer was the radish, which grew to a large size.[17] The sight of a garden, however ruinous, prompted Douglas to sow some of the seeds he had brought, and give some to Clark. In exchange for a tot of rum and few old clothes his Robinsonian friend handed over a young goat. After a second day botanising Douglas had hardly regained the deck when a storm blew up and the ship stood out of the bay.

Like most educated British visitors in the romantic era Douglas knew Anson, Cowper and Crusoe, he was equally certain of his fellow Scot Selkirk. That an itinerant sailor, working on the other side of the world, had Cowper's lines by heart, and a copy of

Crusoe, demonstrates just how deeply this curious place had penetrated into the fluid core of Britishness. As Douglas, Scouler and Clark discussed the various texts that imposed Britishness on Juan Fernández the mythic and the romantic collided. Ruined houses, a fort, a church and even an old oven heightened Douglas's sense of wonder, while the feral gardens of long departed Spanish soldiers, and an unfortunate descendant of Juan Fernández's goats, provided material comforts for scorbutic scientists. Douglas and Scouler even settled on a location for Crusoe's cave. When he came to compile his impressions, Douglas melded the sickly obsessions of Richard Walter with the precise terminology demanded by his patrons, using the Latin taxonomy acquired in William Hooker's botanical lectures at Glasgow University:

No pen can correctly depict the rural enchanting appearance of this island, and the numerous rills descending through the valleys shaded by rich luxuriant verdure emanating in the dark recesses of rocky dells, while the feathery fronds of *Lomaria, Aspidium and Polypodium* several species of which are new and truly princely – form a denseness to the forests.[18]

His list of 78 species collected, most of them unknown variants, took up more space than the discussion of the visit. It was no mean feat, earning the applause of Carl Skottsberg, the master of island botany. Captain Hanwell set course for the Galápagos, where he hoped to complete watering. William Clark's goat was served up a week later, on Christmas Day.

After the final defeat of the Spanish Empire in the South Pacific, British attitudes towards Juan Fernández subtly shifted. What had once been a prize beyond price became a quiet backwater. Even so, the pages of the *Times* suggest the British maintained a serious interest in Juan Fernández and the other Chilean islands. They turned up regularly, in connection with Defoesque romance, maritime disaster, the occasional convict outrage and naval visits. While Juan Fernández had long been a staple of popular culture, comments on the San Félix–San Ambrosio island group reinforced the strategic logic of British commercial interest.

That interest was expanding rapidly, now the closed markets of Imperial Spain had given way to the open ports of newly independent nations anxious for trade. Even the mines of Potosi needed British capital, technology and miners. Trade links with Chile were especially good. Released from Spanish and Peruvian domination Chile was drawn into Britain's informal empire by seapower, money and commercial expertise. Chile's astute leadership recognised that opening their markets to Britain would pay diplomatic dividends. They were happy to see the British at Valparaiso; many thought the port was British, while Santiago, a hundred miles inland, had only a tenth as many Britons.

The Chilean market was dominated by British and American merchants, and linked to global trade patterns, often involving a circumnavigation of the globe. Ships from Britain and the American east coast brought manufactures and luxuries to Chile. There they loaded gold, silver and copper for China, where bullion was turned into tea, silks and spices for shipment home via the Cape of Good Hope. Valparaiso became the biggest port on the west coast of South America, thickly populated with British commercial houses and residents, and glutted with British imports.[19] The value of trade with Chile, Peru, Mexico and the intervening states, together with the endemic instability of the region, made a British squadron essential.[20] The South American Station, formally established in 1826 to monitor the Wars of Independence, evolved into the Pacific Station in 1837. By the 1840s the squadron, based at Valparaiso where a British depot ship was moored, followed a well-practised routine. Harnessing oceanic winds and currents warships called at South Pacific and Northwest Coast locations as occasion demanded. French land grabs in Tahiti and the Marquesas Islands, American claims on the Oregon territory and local wars stressed the vast size of the ocean, and the paucity of resources. British merchants quickly learned the annual routine, they could summon the Navy relatively quickly, and local authorities knew as much. Britain might not possess any formal empire in the area, but the Royal Navy easily upheld the national interest.

The British diplomatic establishment in Chile, led by the Consul, was equally closely linked to commercial interests. Vice Consuls at the main ports acted as agents for British steamship companies and for Marine Insurers Lloyds of London. Chilean copper, guano and nitrates became major exports to the United Kingdom, making the collection of commercial intelligence a core activity for British representatives. The Consuls also ensured the British naval hospital was open to destitute Britons, and British seafarers without ships were sent home. Britain appointed a commercial Consul to Valparaiso in 1823, pre-dating official recognition of the state; he would be exercised by recurring anxieties of a Spanish invasion, or a French attempt to secure a naval base.[21] While the Foreign Office pressed the Consul to calm down, and stop seeing danger in every twist and turn of local politics, the underlying threat was clear. Fortunately for British interests Chile became stable, and the revolution of 1830 temporarily halted Paris's Pacific ambitions.[22] The complex interweaving of local instability, burgeoning commercial interests and concerns that France might secure a strategic base in the South Pacific made the late 1820s a period of heightened tension. The government's self-denying declaration precluded a British move for Juan Fernández, or the strategic southern island of Chiloe, even when they were offered up on a plate. Instead the Royal Navy maintained a watching brief on both places, checking the garrison and the charts. It was equally interested in the unoccupied island groups Colnett had charted in the 1790s, tacking them on to the economically driven *Adventure/Beagle* survey of the Cape Horn region, and other charting missions for the next half century. While the British never occupied Juan Fernández, or any other Chilean island, the possibility was rarely off the table for long, as first France and then the United States challenged British commercial interests and naval hegemony.

Britain had the power to seize and hold any Pacific island; that it chose to occupy none is deeply significant. With access to the markets and port facilities of Valparaiso and Callao British merchants and capitalists replaced older dreams of colonial conquest with the economic dominion of free trade. The naval stores hulk *Nereus* at Valparaiso and the floating coal depot at Callao had little fight left in them, but their presence symbolised the latent power of the dominant fleet, normally superior to any rival squadron, drawing strength from the two power standard that underpinned the British global position. These old hulks carried a flag and a signal gun, enough to summon a force that could bankrupt a South American state in a matter of weeks. Although humble, deeply unromantic depot ships replaced the island paradise at the heart of British South Pacific strategy in the nineteenth century, British squadrons continued to call at Juan Fernández, checking the charts and updating their remark books, just in case they had to come back in earnest.

Unlike the South Atlantic, where Britain seized the vacant Falkland Islands in 1833, there was no need to act in the Pacific, because relations with Chile were always far better than those with Argentina. The Falklands were about as far as the Empire cared to reach; the logistical demands of a base on Juan Fernández were simply unacceptable in peace time, and there was little reason to suspect Chile would close their harbours to the British in war. Instead Juan Fernández became naval picnic ground, a cultural highlight on the annual station tour, allowing the younger officers to stretch their legs, and think themselves well read. Steam-powered printing presses enabled every ship to carry a library, many that came to the South Pacific were equipped with Crusoe, Anson and more arcane literature. Where scorbutic privateers and the living dead of Anson's squadron once staggered ashore to find food and water, imagining themselves in paradise, nineteenth-century voyagers generally arrived in good health, seeking sensation and spectacle. Frustrated by their inability to comprehend what had inspired men to compile prosy rhapsodies only a century before, modern visitors, troubled by the humdrum realities of a perfectly pleasant little island, were quick to invent sensation, wrapping it up in the startlingly vertical landscape of mountain, forest, rocks and ocean.

If Juan Fernández was not an Edenic paradise then it must be a place of human wonder, a Robinsonian dreamscape of imagined romances, caves, castaways, cannibals and redemption. Although the island offered little by way of remains, and only a handful of recognisable features for those fortunate enough to have Anson's *Voyage* with the plates, this made it suitably opaque – meaning could be imposed on every layer of the past. The ruins of Spanish and Chilean occupation, subtly evolved into Selkirk's residence, along with a 'cave' that did not appear in any account of his sojourn, while a Spanish shed halfway up to the 'Lookout', another building his rescuers managed to miss, became Selkirk's house. This suspension of disbelief was aided by enterprising locals happy to tell inquisitive, credulous visitors whatever they wanted to hear, in exchange for cash, supplies or booze. Finally the marks of Defoe's colonial project were written onto Selkirk's Juan Fernández, for an anglophone audience predisposed to assume an air of superiority, and entitled to impose themselves on foreign soil. That this was an island, a quintessentially English island, made the process that much easier. Both British and American visitors read the island as an imperial possession, and assumed they had proprietory rights, founded on literary association and a half-remembered history. The British had ended their interest in an island base, but with America bent on a 'Manifest Destiny' that included other people's land there was always a danger that something untoward might occur. The occasional visit by the Royal Navy was enough to impose a degree of reality on American dreams, invading Mexico was one thing, seizing Juan Fernández quite another.

Yet beneath the surface glitter of occasional visits and literary wandering amid the trees the old British project to set up a base remained active, indeed most Royal Navy visits to Chilean islands were precise, purposeful and portentous. The Hydrographer of the Navy systematically collected charts and sailing directions – just in case – sending his best men to check the San Ambrosio, San Félix islands and Ecuadorean Galápagos Islands as possible bases. The word 'establishment' seemed to hover in the margins of every discussion, waiting for a suitable opportunity. Instead new technology changed the strategic geography of the Imperial problem. To service the communications of a global empire the British state took a keen interest in steam ships, subsidising mail steamship companies to provide the regular and reliable conveyance of official mail. The Pacific Steam Navigation Company, starting in the early 1840s, not only improved links with London, but also provided the coal stocks and machine shops needed to maintain naval steamers in the Pacific.

Nineteenth-century British interest reflected the reality that the islands remained a vital link in the commercial sailing ship route to Mexico, California and British Columbia. The rapid growth of South Pacific trades, dominated by British and American shipping made the location ever more significant. It was the first port of call for sickly crews and damaged ships after rounding Cape Horn. Then in 1849 a gold rush in California prompted an explosion of American shipping. Although the British had access to the ports of Chile and Peru, neither was especially stable, so it was wise to have a fallback position to protect trade. The creation of a permanent naval station reflected a growing American economic challenge, with whalers, traders and a standing naval force. For much of the first half of the nineteenth century the dominant navies in these seas were Anglophone and often at odds. While the Americans won the whaling competition Britain made far more money in other trades, bought oil for their lamps from Nantucket, and read tall Yankee tales about great whales.

Imaginary Voyages

—◦◦◦◦—

Herman Melville was by no means the first to imagine Pacific voyages. For centuries Europeans had been fascinated by the notion of the Antipodes, the weight of an unknown land in the south counterbalancing the land masses of the northern hemisphere, keeping the earth in balance as it rotated. Their literary existence long preceded their discovery, prompting all manner of imaginary writing, which turned speculative geography into the stuff of fiction. Here the link between real and imaginary voyages was ancient, and potent. The mythic antipodes were finally displaced from the map by Captain Cook's second voyage, which proved a negative. He replaced a mega-continent with an alternative geography of island constellations and unknown peoples, which swiftly became subjects of fascination and wonder for European audiences predisposed to see the exotic in this unknown region. Many authors responded to the new discoveries by imagining the next stage of exploration.

Such imaginary voyages have a long history, exploring the frontiers of knowledge, places where different worlds could be imagined. In the twentieth century they were set in outer space, before that the South Pacific had served the same function. These Pacific fictions constitute a distinct literary genre, dominated by colonialist writings from Britain and France. Much attention has been paid to the imperial/colonialist portrayal of indigenous peoples. On uninhabited islands like Juan Fernández men can write their identities without difficulty. There were no indigenous peoples to contest the discoverer's meaning, challenge the naming of places, or resist occupation. There was no need to fight, and no risk that the discoverer could be accused of annihilating local peoples. That said, the twenty-first century has become far more conscious of the devastation wrought by humans on their complex, fragile ecosystems.

The best known of these imaginary voyages, *Robinson Crusoe* and *Gulliver's Travels*, provided a complex mix of agendas and ideologies to contemporary readers. The success of Defoe's book was such that for at least two hundred years the literate world, far from certain what was true and what was not, preferred to engage with the text at a literal level. The quest for 'Crusoe's island' and the 'real' Crusoe, which has continued to this day, is both a testament to Defoe's creative power and a widespread failure of imagination. Defoe wrote in a tradition dating back to Sir John Mandeville and Thomas More, exploiting popular subjects of the day, the survivor/castaway and buccaneer narratives. It was rare that such works were constructed without an agenda.

In one key area the imaginary world was anything but simple. The impact of scurvy on the mind was significant, and unpredictable:

Scurvy was known to result in heightened sensual awareness and made contrasts seem more extreme (such as the difference between pain and pleasure). The disease would leave its victims in unpredictably altered states, often delirious and highly sensitive to visual stimulation, a state of 'scurvied rapture' that also amplified attraction or repulsion.[1]

When scurvy sufferers reached land their condition transformed a fruitful, fertile island into a paradise of mythic proportions. If real travellers, afflicted by a common traveller's disease, were prone to seeing paradise in the prosaic then the field was open to pure imagination, suitably informed by scurvied accounts. More's *Utopia*, disease wracked visions and bookmaking craft offered endless opportunities to reimagine.

The potential for uncertainty was increased by early travel collections, from Hakluyt onward, which included mythic, fabulous and forged texts either from ignorance or an intention to mislead. More set his fable in the part imagined world of

Amerigo Vespucci's second voyage; Defoe exploited a library of different narratives, while Rousseau further muddied the waters by linking Anson and Defoe. In this regard it is essential to stress that uninhabited Juan Fernández was not utopia; it was an earthly paradise where men found goat, cabbage tree and crayfish.

The success of Defoe's book created the 'robinsonade' – stories that followed his model, one that has never lost the power to fascinate, a fact attested by the constant reuse of survivor, castaway and maroon metaphors in contemporary popular culture. The model requires a Juan Fernández-like island, without indigenous peoples. Defoe rarely strayed from reality, because he had a powerful, polemical project in mind, and would not wish to risk it by dabbling in the fantastic. Swift, with more satirical intent, found the fantastic a powerful ally.

For many reasons, seventeenth- and eighteenth-century voyages and travels were closer to fiction than other factual texts, and the space that separated them from fictional alternative could be strikingly small. By the nineteenth century these genres had hardened to the point that such melding of fact and fiction was increasingly contested. Melville's response was unusual, simply bursting the limits, but he did so at a time when audiences were increasingly uneasy about work that blurred the line between fact and fiction. By the 1830s the old-fashioned imaginary voyage had become obsolete, replaced by new, fresh and starkly realistic travel tales. Who could hope to invent anything to compare with John Franklin's arctic cannibal survivor story, or tales of Timbuktu, which opened hitherto mythic spaces to forensic scrutiny. This new literature was organised around scientific voyaging, published in London, and largely propelled by Admiralty Secretary John Barrow.[2]

Such voyages were driven by the quest for useful knowledge, of navigation, terrestrial magnetism, and economic opportunities. In this Barrow followed Sir Joseph Banks, having worked closely with the aging colossus in his last decade at the Royal Society. The emotive power of the genre was reflected in the commercial success of the best narratives, from John Franklin to Charles

Darwin. By the 1840s British audiences demanded their travel tales be true, they did not want any more robinsonades. They wanted a reliable report of proceedings, one that avoided any suspicion of authorial invention. While Leopold von Ranke invested history with an aura of objectivity that transformed it from opinion and argument to 'science', travel texts produced by experienced navigators implied the same detachment, a quality more likely to be found in the straightforward accounts of seamen than the reworked versions of professional scribes. The contrast between Hawkesworth's version of Cook's first voyage and the unvarnished words of the great man from the second provide a compelling case. Yet it cannot be denied that imaginary voyages still shaped the expectations of travellers. Crusoe dominated the mental world of eighteenth and nineteenth century voyagers as they approached Juan Fernández; they went ashore looking for his cave, imposing Defoe's story on the very different reality that they encountered. Those with access to a wider range of texts could add references to Anson, and perhaps Dampier. The wonderment of the Reverend Walter was but little removed from Crusoe, shaped as it had been by a succession of buccaneer narratives themselves clouded by scorbutic rapture. The worlds of fact and fiction were endlessly intertwined.

By the 1820s references to Juan Fernández had become confused, the divergent strains of history and fiction melded and refracted in the minds of passing travellers. In September, HMS *Blonde* ran past the island on her return from Hawaii. Artist and guest Robert Dampier, a distant relative of the old buccaneer, invested the view with a highly developed romantic sensibility:

On Saturday afternoon, still carrying with us our favouring breezes, we made the island of Juan Fernández. The bold, rocky outline of its mountains, which appear very high, has a fine effect from the sea; the vallies & low land seemed uncommonly rich & verdant, calling to mind the beautiful tale of Robinson Crusoe, one gazed on this island with peculiar interest. Goats, which I believe thrive there in great abundance, are now the sole proprietors. Formerly convicts from the Chilean states were banished to this desolate spot.[3]

They had already failed to reach island in February, frustrated by the wind. Dampier joined the ship at Rio de Janeiro, at the invitation of Captain Lord Byron, cousin of the lately deceased poet, and grandson of *Wager* survivor 'Foul Weather Jack' Byron. The Dampier distinction drew between the island's rich natural habitat and desolate location was significant. He read it as a fictive location, an isolated setting for romance and wonder. By contrast Lieutenant George Peard, sailing to the Bering Straits on HMS *Blossom* passed a month later, and observed:

We sailed from Valparaiso on Saturday the 29th with a breeze from the Southward & Westward and kept close to the wind on the Larboard tack in order to fetch the island of Juan Fernández, celebrated for having been for so many years the solitary abode of Alexander Selkirk. But finding this object unattainable, on the 31st we bore WbS [West by South] for Easter Island.[4]

Peard viewed the island as a problem of navigation, ship-handling and weather: it is highly significant that the solitary inhabitant he recalled had been a real mariner. HMS *Blossom* never sighted the island.

The Royal Navy also visited Juan Fernández with scientific purpose. Dispatched in 1826 the survey ship HMS *Adventure*, Captain Philip Parker King and her smaller consort, the soon to be famous HMS *Beagle*, to complete a thorough survey of the Cape Horn region between the River Plate and the strategic island of Chiloe, which had occupied the dreams of English projectors since Charles II's day. Now the object was safe navigation for the growing commercial links with Chile and Peru. Both ships came armed with a battery of chronometers and a library packed with published accounts, charts and manuscript sailing directions. Although the geographical limits of the survey fell far short of Juan Fernández, the wider purpose of improved navigation sustained the age-old link between the island and the passage via Cape Horn or the Straits of Magellan, making it essential to fix the island on the chart and check its condition as a refuge for scorbutic crews.

After completing the west coast survey and visiting Valparaiso to refit and have his chronometers cleaned and rated by the local agent of Liverpool manufacturer Roskell, King included Juan Fernández on the return leg south to Talcahuano and Concepción. *Adventure* arrived in Cumberland Bay on 16 February 1830, five days after leaving the Chilean coast. As the ship approached the island he was struck by the 'remarkable and picturesque view'. Initially only El Yunque registered, 'an abrupt wall of dark-coloured bare rock, eight or nine hundred feet in height, through whose wild ravines, broken by the mountain torrents, views are caught of verdant glade, surrounded by luxuriant woodland'. *Adventure* anchored in *Tryal's* berth, close to Bahía Pangal.[5]

The island had been occupied, rented by Dom Joachim Larrain who left a governor and about forty people to work the seal and cod fisheries for passing trade, and dry fish for the mainland. The seal colony had been greatly reduced by over-fishing. There was no sign of agriculture, a failing which the governor attributed to insect pests; King blamed Chileno indolence. The huts were a good distance away from the old fort at San Juan Bautista, to avoid the harsh winds. The fort was still in tolerable order, having been repaired as recently as 1809, but unarmed; he noted traces of another two batteries. The men quickly set to fishing, both 'cod and crayfish remained plentiful'. So were the goats that fed the buccaneers and saved Lord Anson, but they were hard to catch, remaining high up on the mountains. The lowland areas still belonged to wild dogs descended from packs landed by long forgotten Spanish Viceroys. For the first time a Royal Navy expedition paid close attention to the geology, fauna and botany of the island, linking their findings to samples obtained on Más Afuera. This was a voyage in Anson's wake.

There are few persons who have not read, with much interest, Mr Walter's account of the *Centurion's* voyage, and who are not well acquainted with his description of this island, which we found exceedingly correct. The views of the land, although old-fashioned in execution, are most correctly delineated, and the plan of the bay is quite sufficient for every common purpose of navigation; but as we had an opportunity of fixing its latitude and longitude more correctly, it became desirable to make a more detailed plan than Commodore Anson's.[6]

King also took visual references from Walter's account, noting the link between Anson's 'valley' and the clearances made by earlier Spanish settlers. Some of the junior officers had an opportunity to get beyond the beach, crossing the mountain spine at the pass known as 'Puertozuela' (which had yet to acquire the modern label 'Selkirk's Mirador') and hunt goats on the barren lands beyond. *Adventure* sailed from Cumberland Bay on 22 February.[7] King redrew the charts as part of his global project to record meridional distances to improve accurate navigation. HMS *Beagle* also passed the island, her officers producing some excellent coastal perspectives.[8]

In August 1834 Charles Darwin, in Santiago pursuing his geological researches while the *Beagle* was surveying, met 'a strange genius, a Major Sutcliffe'. A former British officer who had served in the Chilean war of independence, Sutcliffe claimed to have sent a book of old voyages through the Straits of Magellan to Fitzroy. Darwin was sceptical: 'I do not know what to make of him. He is full of marvellous stories; and to the surprise of every one every now & then some of them are proved to be true.'[9] Four months later this mysterious fantasist would be the governor of Juan Fernández, the ideal location for a dramatic collision between English dreams and South American realities – ending in melodrama and exile.

Sutcliffe had been sent to administer the island and the re-established prison settlement. Anxious to bring something of the English improving approach to his new domain Sutcliffe addressed the ramshackle buildings, limited infrastructure and lack of agriculture. Having built a jetty and assessed the commercial opportunities Sutcliffe sent a letter to London *Times* advertising his new domain as a source of wood, water and food. Passing British ships need not bother to anchor, his new jetty made loading easy. Finally he stressed the link to Crusoe and his peculiar position as a British governor, and, quoting Cowper's lines, reckoned himself 'Monarch of all I Survey'.[10]

Sadly, Sutcliffe's dream of Crusoesque dominion proved short-lived. Late on 19 February 1835, only five months after his arrival, he heard a low rumbling, which he thought indicated an earthquake. His officers disagreed, but just before noon the next day Sutcliffe, standing on the wall of Fort Santa Barbara, observed the boats floating in the normally dry boat house, and the mole almost covered with water. As he ordered the boats secured, the sea suddenly disappeared, leaving almost the entire bay between the headlands dry. With the drummer beating to quarters and the church bell ringing the alarm Sutcliffe ordered convicts to carry newly built boats uphill, a task they had hardly begun when a massive earthquake hit the island. Only one boat had been secured, hastily lashed to a fig tree outside the fort. The others were abandoned, and everyone rushed uphill screaming as the ocean, until now quite smooth, suddenly rolled back, like the parting of the Red Sea. No sooner had the people got off the beach than a tsunami surged in, and then out again, taking with it most of the smaller buildings at the water's edge. Sutcliffe recorded four separate waves. High above the bay Felix Baesa was cutting timber; he heard and felt the shock of the earthquake, watched the bay empty and fill, and was lucky not to be hit by rocks falling from El Yunque.

Once the waves subsided Sutcliffe launched the remaining boat and rescued several people from the bay. Two more boats were brought down to pick up furniture, pictures and other items left floating in the eerily calm sea, including Sutcliffe's writing desk and papers, along with a portrait of his great-grandfather John Kay, inventor of the Flying Shuttle. Soon after he 'observed a large column, something like a water spout, ascend in a rapid manner out of the sea … it proved to be smoke, which soon covered the horizon, and eastward point of the Bay, called Punta de Bacalao'. During the night the eruption included flames. Noisy, alarming aftershocks continued until the next morning, interspersed with lightning. Miraculously no one had been killed. 'Had the earthquake happened during the night, scarcely a soul could have escaped.'[11]

With the prison in ruins, and hardly a dry round of ammunition, Sutcliffe had to control 200 convicts, roaming around the wreckage of the village. Lacking the firepower to assert his authority Sutcliffe put on brave front, having his soldiers guard ammunition boxes surreptitiously filled with sand, while his staff recorded every detail of the earthquake and tsunami. The Chileans evinced none of their governor's scientific curiosity, attributing the survival of the chapel and store house to Sutcliffe's recent repair work.

The first ship to arrive after the catastrophe, the American whaler *Cyrus*, provided Sutcliffe with much needed gunpowder and tools. Robert Simpson, commanding the Chilean naval brig *Achilles* arrived on 18 March, with more convicts and three months supplies.[12] She was heading for Talcahuano, which had also been hit by an earthquake. With tools and timber scrounged from passing ships, Sutcliffe set to work to build:

a new town, on the very spot where Commodore Anson had his tents pitched, according to an engraving I had in the history of his voyage round the world, which I called Anson's Town; and to the beautiful and romantic valley in which it was situated I gave the name of Anson's Dale.[13]

Such Elysian visions were swiftly shattered; Sutcliffe observed the island was plagued with rats, despite liberal use of arsenic.

Arsenic played a central role in the next drama to hit the island. Sutcliffe and his military subordinate Lieutenant Saldes, unable to maintain their equilibrium in the febrile atmosphere of the devastated, isolated prison camp, bickered over rank and authority. Saldes resolved the escalating spat by playing the national card, recruiting fellow Chileans, soldiers and the priest. On 1 August a half-hearted convict rebellion resulted in the deposition and expulsion of Governor Sutcliffe, despite his attempt to poison himself, and his persecutors, with some of his ample store. Sent on board a passing ship, he was landed at Talcahuano in late September 1835. The only British government of the island ended in a suitably melodramatic swirl of military punctilio and poison.[14]

Daniel Defoe (right) spun a tale that would capture the imagination of the western world and create a literary genre that wrapped up English identity in tiny islands and oceanic space. The Victorian statue of Alexander Selkirk (left), in his home town of Lower Largo, demonstrates how profoundly his story had melded with that of Crusoe, depicted here as armed and ambitious, not as the nervous castaway.

THE
LIFE
AND
STRANGE SURPRIZING
ADVENTURES
OF
ROBINSON CRUSOE,
Of *YORK,* MARINER:

Who lived Eight and Twenty Years,
all alone in an un-inhabited Island on the
Coast of AMERICA, near the Mouth of
the Great River of OROONOQUE;

Having been caſt on Shore by Shipwreck, wherein all the Men periſhed but himſelf.

WITH
An Account how he was at laſt as ſtrangely deliver'd by PYRATES.

Written by Himſelf.

LONDON;
Printed for W. TAYLOR at the *Ship* in *Pater-Noſter-
Row.* MDCCXIX.

This frontispiece image of Crusoe in the book's first edition (1719) determined the impact of the story before readers had engaged with Defoe's text, but the illustration made it clear that Crusoe's island lay in the Caribbean, off the fabled Orinoco River, the scene of Sir Walter Raleigh's gilded failure.

VTOPIAE INSVLAE FIGVRA

The woodcut that opened Thomas More's *Utopia* of 1516 linked insularity, Englishness and civilisation through the powerful metaphor of the three-masted ship, the vehicle that embodied English imperial ambition.

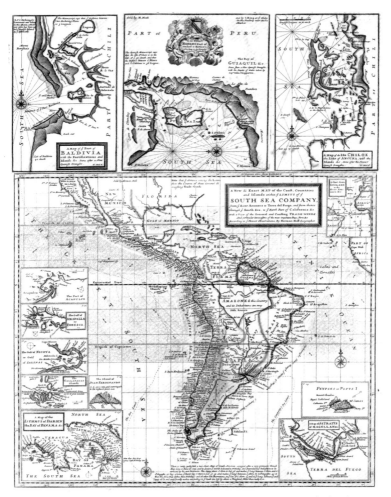

Herman Moll's 'New and Exact Map of the Coast, Countries and Islands within the Limits of the South Sea Company', created to promote the South Sea Company, placed the island of Juan Fernández at the centre of 'the Pacific Sea', and provided a coastal perspective to enable visiting mariners to identify their target.

The coastal perspective taken by the officers of HMS *Tagus* in early 1816 emphasised the majestic verticality of the island. The critical role of the anchorage in Cumberland Bay and the food and watering opportunities of the village at San Juan Bautista are also evident in the seaman's view of Juan Fernández.

The men who put the island into the English lexicon: buccaneer author William Dampier (left), who visited it on four occasions, and George, Lord Anson, who used it to refit his scurvied expedition. Dampier's career ended in humiliation, Anson's with fabulous wealth, political power and naval glory. Their books are still read, and help to shape the way the island is understood.

A View of the COMMODORES TENT on the Island of JUAN FERNANDES.

In the first edition of *A Voyage Round the World in the Years MDCCXL*, Lord Anson chose to have his encampment represented in the midst of an idealised classical landscape; the image distorts the perspective and imposes classical order on the angular hills. This verdant valley remains at the heart of island life today, complete with its own mini-market.

When Lord Anson's men landed, vast breeding herds of majestic elephant seals dominated the beaches. They provided a suitably fantastical element to Anson's book, replacing the sea monsters of medieval cartography with something very real, and equally alarming.

The fabled cave of Alexander Selkirk in Puerto Inglese. As Selkirk did not live in a cave, and Crusoe did not live on the island, the cave demonstrates how easily their stories became intertwined. Today the cave is larger, deepened by treasure hunters seeking equally mythic gold.

In June 1910, *The Times* advertised a pioneering round-the-world tourist voyage for wealthy sportsmen. The RMSS *Atrato* never sailed, and the next English visit had more deadly intent.

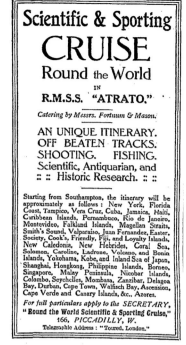

Scientific & Sporting
CRUISE
Round the World
IN
R.M.S.S. "ATRATO."

Catering by Messrs. Fortnum & Mason.

AN UNIQUE ITINERARY.
OFF BEATEN TRACKS.
SHOOTING.   FISHING.
Scientific, Antiquarian, and
:: :: Historic Research. :: ::

Starting from Southampton, the itinerary will be approximately as follows : New York, Florida Coast, Tampico, Vera Cruz, Cuba, Jamaica, Haiti, Caribbean Islands, Pernambuco, Rio de Janeiro, Montevideo, Falkland Islands, Magellan Straits, Smith's Sound, Valparaiso, Juan Fernandez, Easter, Society, Cook's, Friendly, Fiji, and Loyalty Islands, New Caledonia, New Hebrides, Coral Sea, Solomon, Caroline, Ladrone, Volcano, and Bonin Islands, Yokohama, Kobe, and Inland Sea of Japan, Shanghai, Hongkong, Philippine Islands, Borneo, Singapore, Malay Peninsula, Nicobar Islands, Colombo, Seychelles, Mombasa, Zanzibar, Delagoa Bay, Durban, Cape Town, Walfisch Bay, Ascension, Cape Verde and Canary Islands, &c., Azores.

For full particulars apply to the SECRETARY,
"Round the World Scientific & Sporting Cruise,"
166, *PICCADILLY, W.*
Telegraphic Address : "Toured, London."

The wider world finally arrived on the island on 14 March 1915, when a global conflict brought HMS *Kent*, *Glasgow* and *Orama* into Cumberland Bay, where they caught the German light cruiser SMS *Dresden* (below) at anchor. The Germans scuttled their ship, which still lies where she sank, 60 metres below the waves.

A vertical island. High up at 'Selkirk's Mirador' the angularity of El Yunque and the thick vegetation create a distinctive razor's edge on the rim of an ancient volcano.

The sailor's view of Crusoe's domain: heading into Cumberland Bay, the island resembles a natural amphitheatre, clad in green and artfully arranged around the majestic heights of El Yunque. This photograph was taken in late 2010, the year of the most recent tsunami.

Cashiered and sent back to England, Sutcliffe tried to earn a living with his pen, waging a futile campaign to recover back pay and costs from Chile. Piqued by criticism of his government in the *Nautical Magazine* he compiled a pamphlet that combined a serious, if self-serving discussion of the tsunami with a long, rambling, justification of his conduct during the revolt – which takes far longer to read than the events it details merit. In 1843 he published a more substantial text on the story at the heart of the island's enduring fascination: *Crusoiana; or Truth versus Fiction Elucidated in a History of the Islands of Juan Fernández.*

I cannot refrain from mentioning the great eagerness that was displayed by every visitor who arrived there during my government to ramble upon a spot so familiar to their youthful recollections; many an inquirer has asked 'where was Selkirk's residence' or 'what information can you give respecting the Scotch Mariner?'[15]

The book is something of a grab bag, combining published material, personal information and a few useful illustrations. Cowper's poem was given in full, while Sutcliffe traced the idea that Defoe stole Selkirk's journal back to John Entick. His control of the evidence began to slip when he reached Anson's voyage. The eighty-page account is almost entirely edited quotation, with a major digression on the loss of the *Wager*, a ship that never reached the island. He reported the visits of Carteret and Moss, who 'found the colony in a flourishing condition', along with more recent views, including Maria Graham and his own earthquake pamphlet.[16] As a pioneer compilation, *Crusoiana* provided a useful résumé for later authors.

Sutcliffe died in 1849, poverty stricken, mad and quite forgotten, but his pioneering scientific record of the earthquake and tsunami echoed Dampier's curiosity. The centre of his map of Cumberland Bay was occupied by a strikingly original fish, found in a wardrobe that washed ashore after the wave had passed. The map, one of four bold, if not entirely reliable lithographs of the island that illustrated Sutcliffe's pamphlet, was the most substantial addition to island images since Anson. The opening dramatic view shows a heroic Sutcliffe directing the response to the first wave, getting his boat uphill while the priest comforts his flock, and the smoking volcano erupts in the middle distance. A night view of the eruption added immediacy to the phenomenon. The charming view of San Juan Bautista from Cumberland Bay shows another settlement at Bahía Pangal.

While Sutcliffe's text advanced his version of events, and his claim for compensation, his images reflected another agenda. The map applied British names to the island. Anson was awarded a Dale and a Town, Puerto Inglese was renamed Selkirk Dale, with an imaginary Selkirk Town located on the rocks above the site of 'Selkirk's Cave'. It is not clear how far Sutcliffe created the mythic narratives that have dominated perceptions of the island since the 1830s, but his aggressive application of names misled those who followed, much as his play-acting with arsenic misled his rebellious subjects. Soon American visitors were repeating Sutcliffe's names, recasting freshly minted words into ancient facts, upon which they based fresh layers of myth-making and wonder. Sutcliffe's writings, on Juan Fernández and other subjects, contain much misrepresentation and not a little straightforward dishonesty. He cannot be considered a reliable witness for events that reflect on his own conduct, or the career of his illustrious ancestor, but his record of the 1835 tsunami remains a unique record of a momentous event. His 'strange genius' still hovers over the island.[17]

In truth Sutcliffe was well away. The year after he left Chile and Peru were at war; a small Peruvian force captured the island, burnt the town he had so recently erected and then withdrew. The fifty-man garrison, in truth only a prison guard, surrendered without a fight. The Peruvians released the political prisoners, hoping to destabilise Chile, leaving the common criminals and the garrison to buy a passage back to Valparaiso aboard a passing American whaler. Despite rumours that an American lessee would take over, Juan Fernández remained uninhabited for the next five year, slowly crumbling into a romantic ruin. Human habitation made little sense once Chile and Peru opened their ports for business. Whaling vessels from America, Britain and France were frequent visitors, looking for water and fresh food. They traded goods with the garrison, but were equally pleased with an unoccupied island. The French naval expedition of Captain Dumot d'Urville visited in June 1838.[18]

In 1842 Archibald Osborne, another irascible Scot, took up residence, having left a whaleship in the bay after a dispute. His occupation did not end well. A Chilean family with title to the island returned the following year, and Osborne recruited a handful of fellow drifters, leaving the tiny island divided between rough Anglophone seafarers and the Chileans. Anticipating an attack, the Chileans struck first, capturing the sailors. Osborne was wounded in the fracas, and swiftly executed. His 'followers' left soon after. The Chilean Supreme Court acquitted the family of murder. Once again Juan Fernández was empty, seemingly too small for a dozen people to live in amity.

18

An American South Pacific

By the end of the eighteenth century the South Pacific was slowly leaving the realms of magic as British navigators and explorers filled in the blanks, and exploited the whales, seals and sea otters to make their fortunes. After the division of the English-speaking world in 1783 it did not take the Americans long to find the Pacific. As economic opportunities increased America approached the ocean in ways that were shaped by their British heritage, and commercial interests formed under British rule. Soon American whalers and traders were rounding Cape Horn. By this time the British had reduced their South Pacific to order, they no longer needed to dream of power; they were in command. Instead it would be the Americans who developed a new vision of the Pacific, one of old tales, and great whales. For sixty years, years in which the oceans were America's dreamscape, the South Pacific provided an ideal setting for heroics and horror. It was a space where nature fought back.

The American Pacific grew out of the dynamic maritime culture of New England. In the Pacific, American ships were free from the restrictions on trade and navigation imposed by the East India Company; restraints that kept independent English traders out of the Chinese and Indian markets, developing a trade network that produced profits on as many legs of the voyage as possible. These enterprising, literate Yankees raided the library for information about markets and routes. They found a few shelves of useful English language texts, from Exquemelin and Dampier to Anson and Cook, combining solid navigational information about where to stop for water, refreshment and anti-scorbutics, with the location of fur seals, sea otters and whales.

In 1788 the *Columbia* and the *Lady Washington* sailed to Oregon via Cape Horn, linking Northwest Coast sea otter pelts with the Chinese market and a return cargo of luxury goods. They came in the wake of the British, heirs to the knowledge and expertise of centuries, captured in printed texts that were the common heritage of the Anglophone seafaring community. One of the *Columbia*'s junior officers, Robert Haswell, referenced the buccaneer voyages, John Hawkesworth's edition of Cook, Byron and Carteret's account of Más Afuera in his log.[1] In April 1788 the *Columbia* sighted Más Afuera. A 'great many streams' were seen from the ship, cascading down into the sea, but landing was 'excessively dangerous and a dependence on this place for either wood or water will be highly imprudent in any navigator that may hereafter follow our track'. Water ought to be topped up at the Falklands Islands or the Strait of Le Maire, while no well stowed ship should run out of wood before reaching the Northwest Coast. Juan Fernández was the 'proper place' to water. Although it was occupied by about 500 Spaniards and Chileans, 'most of them convicts', water was easy to obtain. Cumberland Bay 'abounds with excellent fish', and there was plenty of 'anti-scorbutic' to restore the health of any of the crew that had begun 'declining'.

Haswell, with a good eye for economic opportunities, suggested Juan Fernández would be an ideal base for 'future adventurers in this very remote clime'. He was equally impressed by fur seals, 'in greater abundance than at any place I ever saw'. That said any visiting mariner should 'be careful not to put himself in the power of the Spaniards. To this end Captain Gray had been ordered to water at Mas Afuera'. While the *Columbia* visited Juan Fernández the ship remained under weigh. Rather than land and risk seizure they moved on to San Ambrosio, where a boat crew landed on 3 May 1788, they 'killed a vast number of seals, and sea lyons, which were incredibly numerous'. The blubber was rendered down for oil, and the skins dried before the ship moved on three days later. San Félix was reported to be more habitable than San Ambrosio, but neither ever attracted a settled population, only raiding gangs of sealers, annihilating animals for profit.[2]

On the *Columbia*'s second voyage Captain Gray landed at Juan Fernández, seeking food, water and an opportunity to repair storm damage incurred rounding the Horn. He met a cordial welcome from the governor, who was promptly sacked by the Viceroy of Peru,[3] making it unlikely any more American ships would call at the prison colony. Instead American voyagers deliberately sought uninhabited islands. The new voyagers were quickly into their stride, generating windfall profits that helped to create the first American millionaires.

Whalers soon followed the fur traders into the South Pacific. Like every American ship rounding the Horn, they needed to stop for food, water and refreshment. The Juan Fernández Islands, which featured in so many familiar British texts, were the obvious place. That Más Afuera also contained a massive seal colony was a bonus. The sustained assault on the seal colony for the Chinese market began in 1793, when the ships of Captain Stewart and Captain Obed Paddock of Nantucket anchored at Más Afuera to harvest Pacific seals. Having filled the ship with dried pelts and seal oil Paddock sailed for Canton where they were highly prized. In January 1798 Captain Edmund Fanning arrived in the *Betsey*, the cargo packed into his 100-ton ship generated a profit of $12,000, after covering the cost of the ship. Little wonder more followed. In 1800 Matthew Folger arrived in the Salem ship *Minerva*, only to encounter fellow American Amasa Delano in the *Perseverance*.

By this time up to a dozen American sealers could be seen anchored off Más Afuera, slowly working their way through a population so dense that in the early days it had been hard to find a footing on the beach. Delano reckoned there had been three million seals, and that his ship alone took 100,000 pelts to China. Delano also visited the San Ambrosio group. Turning the cash into Chinese luxuries, silk, porcelain, spices and tea, ensured a profitable round trip. Like so many of his British and American precursors Delano wrote for the information of other seafarers, describing the anchorages, watering places and food supplies of the Juan Fernández Islands, before shifting to the mechanics of slaughtering seals. Payment per skin ranged from 35 cents to $3.[4] Delano also recounted a horrific tale of mutiny, murder and cannibalism that Herman Melville would develop in *Benito Cereno*. While sealers and whalers made ample use of Más Afuera they tended to avoid Juan Fernández, where the garrison was as likely to seize the ship as offer assistance. This was imperial policy.[5]

In September 1801 the Boston sealing ship *Belle Sauvage* was seized in Cumberland Bay, engaged in smuggling to acquire vital Lima dollars for the China market. Delano visited Más a Tierra twice. In 1800 he landed safely on the western coast, far away from the settlement, and again 1805, when Governor Don Thomas Higgins upheld the law laid down by the Viceroy, his uncle Don Ambrozio, refusing to supply fresh food. Delano knew the Crusoe and Selkirk stories, including Entick's claim that Defoe stole Selkirk's journal. Matthew Folger set off on another Pacific voyage in 1807, commanding the *Topaz*. This time his luck ran out. After discovering John Adams, last of the *Bounty* mutineers and his extended family on long forgotten Pitcairn Island Folger's crew went down with scurvy. Despite the evil reputation of the garrison Folger set course for Juan Fernández. Arriving in Cumberland Bay he requested assistance: this was granted, but no sooner had he reached the shore than the Spaniards opened fire with eight twenty-four pounder cannon, cutting up the rigging and shattering the foretopmast of his ship. The ship was seized and ransacked. A new governor arrived, and sent the Americans back to Valparaiso, where further trials awaited. While in detention Folger managed to pass on the news of Pitcairn to the Royal Navy. Folger finally received compensation for his detention in 1809, including permission to sail the *Topaz* with a cargo for Spain.[6] Soon after that the Spanish regime in Chile was overthrown, opening a new era in South Pacific navigation. Then, in June 1812, America declared war on Britain.

A Literature of Defeat: Reconstructing the Loss of the USS *Essex*

Captain David Porter USN brought the frigate USS *Essex* into the South Pacific to protect American whaleships and attack their British rivals. The influence of whaling voyages on his cruise and his book was obvious.[1] He exploited British texts, local knowledge and American whaling men to seize a dozen British whaleships off the Galápagos Islands. Then he refitted in the Marquesas Islands, taking part in a local war, while his crew savoured the sensuous delights offered by local custom and practice, including the tradition that naked girls swam out to greet incoming ships. Suitably refreshed, the Americans headed back to Valparaiso, where the *Essex* was blockaded and then captured. Porter went home as a prisoner of war on parole. With little else to occupy his time he compiled an extensive account of his voyage, one that made him the hero of his own tale. He had much to explain, having ignored specific orders to avoid combat with enemy warships, and needlessly prolonged the action after defeat had become inevitable, at the cost of many brave men's lives, simply to demonstrate his own courage.

Porter must have been relieved to receive a hero's welcome when he reached New York in July 1814. The public and the press accepted his version of events without demur; public ovations, dinners and other celebrations helped Porter rewrite the meaning of defeat along lines suggested by Navy Secretary William Jones, who claimed Porter and his crew arrived, 'in triumph though captives'.[2] After that Porter spent a frustrating few months unable to get to sea or achieve anything worthy of his celebrity before the war ended.

While he waited at New York, Porter, assisted by old room-mate and drinking buddy Washington Irving (the leading American creative writer of the era), transformed his narrative into a *Journal of a Cruise to the Pacific Ocean by Captain David Porter ... Containing descriptions of the Cape de Verde Islands, Coasts of Brazil, Patagonia, Chile and of the Galápagos Islands* of 1815.[3] This energetic, ambitious, and occasionally unreliable account found a ready audience. Porter used the text to declare himself a hero, claiming he had devastated the British whale fishery, inflicted $2.5 million in damage, and cost the British $6 million to counter his cruise, redeploying ships and men that could have been used to attack the United States. In truth the damage inflicted by his cruise had been negligible; only one prize made it back to the United States, as a cartel, and the British warships that rounded Cape Horn in pursuit of the *Essex* did not come from the North American station. The British had ample reason to reinforce their squadron on the west coast, to protect their trade in the chaotic conditions caused by the Spanish American revolutionary wars. Despite such reservations Porter's book became a central pillar in the mythology of American victory in the War of 1812.

This was something rich and strange, mixing art, literature, history and travelogue. While Porter described his book as a 'Journal' to create the illusion that it was a 'simple' narrative, Pacific voyaging in the wake of Captain Cook, he had many agendas.[4] The most obvious was the conquest of empire, Porter took possession of Nukahiva in the Marquesas Islands, because 'the climate, fertility, local situation, friendly disposition of the natives, and convenience of this island promise to make it at some future day or great importance to the vessels of the United States navigating the Pacific'. His government took a very different view, ignoring his assertion of sovereignty over 'Madison's Island', named for the president.[5]

Porter's self-justificatory travelogue created an American Pacific, revealing an ocean open for trade to American audiences. In his wake sailed Owen Chase, Richard Henry Dana Jr, Herman

Melville and Joshua Slocum. By way of the whaleship *Essex* narrative, Porter's *USS Essex Journal* lies at the heart of *Moby Dick*, the ultimate American novel.

After 1812 American literature consciously strove to create a sense of national identity. The much hyped heroics of the Navy, and the privateers made the sea and the seaman interesting subjects.[6] For the next thirty years America would have a cultural frontier on the ocean, one that waxed and then waned in harmony with the glory days of post-war deep-water commerce, whaling and travel, replaced by a continental vision in the railroad age. While America took up Porter's book, and placed a copy on every American warship, contemporary British reviewers were unimpressed. They lambasted his honour and integrity, while affecting to be outraged by his salacious tale of promiscuous liaisons with the girls of the Marquesas Islands. In fact Porter's more exotic stories were true, providing Pacific literature with its defining metaphors, islands that combined sensual abandon with the cannibal and his feast.

By the early nineteenth century, literacy rates among foremast sailors were increasing rapidly, with New England men leading the way. On long voyages (and there were none longer than a whaling venture to the South Seas), sailors would read and reread their limited supply of books, bringing the illiterate into their world by declaiming the texts. Often they memorised slabs of text, a trait evident in Melville's work. Sailors exchanged books with any ships they met, caring more for novelty than quality or relevance. Seamen were both consumers and producers of literature, while they read they also created and reimagined other stories, stories that melded fact and fiction through their own experience. The construction of commonplace books, transcribed collections of things read or heard, reached its apogee in the entomological section of *Moby Dick*. American seamen were acute critics of popular literature, especially sea writing, condemning James Fenimore Cooper's absurd use of sea terms.[7] By contrast, sea writing was largely conceived as a literal (rather than imaginative) genre, concerned with understanding, navigation, trade and new countries. Nowhere was this more obvious than in the next great Pacific book. The curious career of the USS *Essex* in fact and fiction was followed by a gothic horror that inspired the greatest American work of fiction.

After the British and Americans stopped fighting in the Pacific, the Pacific decided to fight the Americans. In 1819 the Nantucket whaleship *Essex* sailed with a crew of twenty. After a hard five-week passage, battling heavy seas and westerly gales to round Cape Horn, the ship called at St Mary's Island on the coast of Chile, a well-known whaler rendezvous, looking for news and reports. Then they made Más Afuera, 'where we got some wood and fish', before heading onto the whaling grounds in search of prey.[8] Eleven months later the ship was attacked in the middle of the ocean, at a position on the equator some 120° west, by a huge bull sperm whale. The whale rammed the ship twice; her hull smashed open, the *Essex* sank. The crew took to their boats with few provisions, alone on a vast empty sea.

While food soon ran short, water was rarely a problem as the boats encountered frequent drenching storms. They had enough canvas to rig sails and managed to catch fish and birds, even lighting fires to cook them, but they were a very long way from any known inhabited island across the great sweep of the sea. The wind was adverse, and the navigation less than perfect. Three men were left on bare, uninhabited Ducie Island the day after Christmas and a course shaped for Easter Island. A week later the men were beginning to despond; food ran short, and with it hope. On 4 January 1821 the boats were still in company to the south of Easter Island; incapable of beating up into the wind to reach it, they were obliged to set a course for Juan Fernández, 'which lay east-southeast from us some two thousand five hundred miles'.[9]

Second mate Matthew P. Joy died on 10 January, and was buried at sea. On the 12th First Mate Own Chase's boat became separated from the other two. On the 20th Richard Peterson, a black man, died in Chase's boat. He too was buried. By now the remaining men in the boat were becoming delusional. On the

28th Isaac Cole died. He was carved up to feed his friends: they stripped off his flesh and took out his heart, before heaving the bony carcass and remaining offal over the side. They ate him first as raw flesh to satiate their hunger, then roasted over a small fire; finally they trimmed Cole into thin strips that could be dried in the wind for later consumption. By 15 February the boat was, they estimated, about three hundred miles from Juan Fernández, but their provisions were almost out. On the 17th Chase spotted an island which he believed to be Más Afuera, 'and immediately upon this reflection, the life blood began to flow again briskly in my veins'. Early on the following morning a sail was sighted, and they were rescued by the British brig *Indian*, outbound from London. A few hours later they passed Más Afuera, heading for Valparaiso, where they arrived on the 25th.

The other two boats, led by Captain George Pollard Jr, remained in company. While Chase's bald narrative of what transpired lacks the first hand immediacy of his account of life and death on his own boat, the story demands further examination. At its heart is a tale of horror in which twelve men put to sea in two boats, and a month later two were rescued from a single boat. In the process four black crewmen had been eaten by their companions. The first, Lawson Thomas, probably died on 15 January (the record states 25 January, but that seems to be a misprint). Charles Shorter died on the 23rd, and 'his body was shared for food between the crews of the two boats'. On the 27th Isaiah Shepherd died, and on the 28th another black man named Samuel Reed died. As Chase observes; 'the bodies of these men constituted their only food while it lasted'. That four black men, in all probability the only black men in the two boats, should die at convenient intervals after the food ran out is unlikely to have been a coincidence. It is more likely they were selected for execution as less 'important' than their white brethren. The two boats became separated during the night of 28 January, and Chase does not record whether these grim 'provisions' were held equally. The third boat was never seen again. Three days later the Captain's boat had run out food. There were no more black men who could 'die', so Charles Ramsdell shot Owen Coffin, after the usual cannibal excuse of 'drawing lots'. Brazilla Ray 'died' next, Coffin having lasted the party (by now much diminished) a whole ten days. That left the Captain Pollard and Ramsdell to eke out their grisly provisions. On 23 February they were rescued by Nantucket whaleship *Dauphine*, which, in a terrible twist of fate, was commanded by one of Coffin's relatives.[10] Chase's decision to pass swiftly over these events with no more than a bare two-page statement of fact is deeply suggestive. The sheer horror of his tale needed no embroidery; a typhoon of adjectives could not improve his clinical chronicle.

The men left on Ducie Island were luckier, all survived, although they had to wait far longer for rescue. Captain Charles Ridgely of the USS *Constellation* paid the English merchant ship *Surrey* to call at the island, and they were finally picked on 5 April 1821.[11] *The Wreck of the Whaleship Essex, A Narrative by Owen Chase, First Mate* appeared later that year. While it was not a runaway success with squeamish landsmen, the story had great traction among whalers.

The *Essex* was only one among many American vessels operating on the vastness of the South Pacific. Once the War of 1812 had ended American ships returned to the South Pacific in growing numbers, both to pursue the sperm whale, by 1818 at least sixty whalers were in the area, and to trade with both Spanish and rebel provinces as the Wars of Independence raged. These trades were important, and the men who ran them had influence, so from 1817 at least one American warship was on station, protecting American interests. In this the Americans found themselves working closely with the Royal Navy to ensure both sides in the conflict acted lawfully, and did so without undue partiality toward the insurgents. Juan Fernández remained a popular rendezvous and refreshment stop.

In 1822 Commodore Charles Stewart called at the island on his way to Chile, as the rendezvous for his battleship, the USS *Franklin*, the sloop USS *Dolphin*, and three merchant ships that sailed with him from New York. The crew of the *Dolphin*, the first ship to arrive, had five days to enjoy the island, which had a tiny Chilean population, and an abundance of fruit, wild hogs and fresh water. Commander David Connor charted Cumberland Bay while he waited, and piloted the flagship to the anchorage when she arrived. He had already brought the merchant ship *Canton* into the bay. Two of Stewart's midshipmen planned to duel when they reached the island, but the Commodore issued a stern warning, stopping their plans. Midshipman Charles Wilkes recalled an exciting hunt for wild cattle, a lot of fishing, and visited the 'Cave of Selkirk and the other marked objects,' before taking in the 'beautiful foliage, and enduring the frequent showers'. He did not mention Crusoe. After a few days refreshing and watering the American ships headed for Valparaiso, where they picked up the terrifying story of the whaleship *Essex*. In an instant the vision of an island paradise had been swept away by cannibal horror, 'too terrible to be told'.[12]

In January 1823 Stewart landed a party on Juan Fernández, where they built a small schooner for his squadron using a pre-cut frame purchased from the American merchant ship *Pearl* eight months before. The suitably named *Robinson Crusoe* and her sisters *Water-Witch* and *Peruvian* were used as dispatch vessels to keep up communications between the flagship and the Caribbean via Panama. The ship was sold later that year, taking part in the liberation of Peru.[13]

Sea Stories

———

In August 1834, Richard Henry Dana Jr, son of a prosperous Boston family, set out on a sea voyage. He was hoping to recover from ophthalmia, an eye condition that threatened his legal studies. The brig *Pilgrim* was heading for the Mexican province of California, to load a cargo of hides. While learning the ropes of his new profession Dana kept a journal. Returning to Boston in September 1836 he completed his studies and wrote *Two Years Before the Mast*, one of the best known of all sea stories. Dana skilfully engaged his audience of landlubbers by taking them through the stages of the seaman's life – from green landsman, retching over the rail, to finished topman – as a journal of experience. He explained what he learned, what was being done, and dissected the unique and strange world of the square rigged sailing ship, a machine driven by teams of men, and a floating society with its own dynamics, rituals and precedents. It remains a wonderful guide to the life and language of the sea. Despite the prosaic attention to detail Dana was at heart a poet. Rapturous descriptions seemed to burst out of him as he responded to striking seascapes, landfalls and the changing of night to day. His voyage via Cape Horn was viewed from below hatches; neither hero nor leader, Dana follows, watches, learns and develops.

An educated, well-read man, Dana was at once familiar with the latest trends in romantic writing, and the classic story of Robinson Crusoe. These elements shaped his response to Juan Fernández, which he first saw at daybreak on Tuesday 25 November 1834:

it was dead ahead ... rising like a deep blue cloud out of the sea ... so high and so blue did it appear, that I mistook it for a cloud, resting over the island, and looked for the island under it, until it gradually turned to a deader and greener color, and I could mark the inequalities upon its surface. At length we could distinguish trees and rocks; and by the afternoon, this beautiful island lay fairly before us, and we directed our course to the only harbor.[1]

The heightened state of Dana's perception may have reflected the scurvy-inducing fact that when the anchor finally dropped into Cumberland Bay the *Pilgrim* had completed a non-stop 103-day voyage from Boston. He had not recovered his equilibrium, or his vitamin levels when he took the watch, at three o'clock that morning:

I shall never forget the peculiar sensation which I experienced on finding myself once more surrounded by land, feeling the night breeze coming from off shore, and hearing the frogs and crickets. The mountains seemed almost to hang over us.

Eerie noises from the dark, shadowy mountains only heightened his anxiety to see more of this 'romantic, I may almost say, classic island'.

Volunteering to join the boat crews sent to fill the ship's casks Dana managed to get ashore. Delays in clearing the stream anchor gave him time to visit the area around San Juan Bautista. He described the village huts as 'Robinson Crusoe like – of posts and branches of trees', and recalled Lord Anson's fruit tree planting exploits. He was markedly less impressed with the distinctly civilised edifices that accommodated the governor, the church and the barracks. After dawn everything lost a little of the romance of dusk and dark; the lowering mountains appeared less intimidating. 'They seemed to bear off towards the centre of the island, and were green and well-wooded, with some large, and, I am told, exceedingly fertile valleys, with mule-tracks leading to different parts of the island.'

Dana's impressionistic writing reflected a basic problem. As an ordinary seaman he had little chance to walk the ground, and none to discuss the subject with those ashore. He had no Spanish, and Governor Thomas Sutcliffe – the only man on the island who spoke English – was 'out of my walk'. Sutcliffe came aboard for dinner with a padre and a moustachioed junior officer in a dirty uniform. While the governor dined with the captain, New Bedford whaler *Cortes* came into harbour homeward bound, and anxious for east coast news. Dana may have picked up some useful Pacific information from her crew. When Sutcliffe's boat arrived to take him back to the shore it brought local gifts, a pail of milk, a few shells and a block of sandalwood. Having stowed the water casks the *Pilgrim* unmoored shortly before sundown and, after some fiddly work with the two anchors, a fouled hawse and the uncertain flaws of wind, stood out of Cumberland Bay under the stars.

It was bright starlight when we were clear of the bay, and the lofty island lay behind us, in its still beauty, and I gave a parting look, and bid farewell, to the most romantic spot of earth that my eyes had ever seen. I did then, and have ever since, felt an attachment for that island, altogether peculiar. It was partly, no doubt, from its having been the first land that I had seen since leaving home, and still more from the associations which every one has connected with it in their childhood from reading Robinson Crusoe. To this I may add the height and romantic outline of its mountains, the beauty and freshness of its verdure, and the extreme fertility of its soil, and its solitary position in the midst of the wide expanse of the South Pacific, as all concurring to give it its peculiar charm.[2]

By the morning of 27 November the *Pilgrim* was once again all alone on a vast ocean. Although he would never again cast his eyes on the magic island of Defoe and Anson, Dana never forgot Juan Fernández, it fuelled his dreams and reveries, and he would add further reflections to his journal as the voyage progressed. These combined first-hand testimony, discussions with shipmates, additional reading, navigational information gleaned from books, and ship-to-ship conversations or 'gams' like those featured in *Moby Dick*. While his engaging prose brought the island to life, Dana's imaginative response became popular as a prosaic guide. This search for the practical reflected a shift from the romanticism of the 1820s to the age of realism.[3]

Dana's Robinsonian reflections mattered because his book caught the attention of readers at a time when the South Pacific was remote but endlessly fascinating. Within a decade the sea passage to the west coast had become an obsession with gold hungry speculators and adventurers heading for the California Gold fields, many would repeat the *Pilgrim*'s refreshment stop at Juan Fernández and, Dana in hand, set off to impose their own Crusoe on a remarkably reluctant landscape. At least fifty ships called in 1849–50, but visits quickly tailed off as the Gold Rush subsided and the Trans-isthmian railway opened in 1855 to filter off the passenger traffic.[4]

Arriving on the *Anteus* from New York early in 1849, American author John Ross Browne was struck by 'the strange delight with which I gazed upon that isle of romance':

the unfeigned rapture I felt in anticipation of exploring that miniature world in the desert of waters, so fraught with the happiest associations of youth; so remote from all the ordinary realities of life; the actual embodiment of the most absorbing, most fascinating of all the dreams of fancy.[5]

Browne was evidently set on earning a living with his pen in California, and his overloaded adjectives did not abate as his reflections meandered onward, to 'wondrous', 'Utopian', 'dream-like' 'sublimity'. There can be little doubt that while Browne did not record any scorbutic effects, he was retailing the disturbed exoticism of the sick, situated with lines from Shakespeare's *Tempest*, where the magic island is said to

> suffer a sea-change
> into something rich and strange.

Once ashore Browne and his companions quickly found Crusoe's 'rustic castle', which he helpfully illustrated for less well travelled readers. Having paid his respects to the hero of his childhood

Browne was in 'ecstatic bliss'. He went on to complete the tourist trail by visiting Selkirk's cave, which was being hacked about by 20 enthusiastic, heavily armed miner-tourists making a stop on their way to San Francisco. One of the tourists declared it 'the most fascinating spot on the face of the globe ... I hope to see the cave Robinson dug, or the ruins of his little hovel.' Browne recalled how the miners chopped out lumps of Robinsonian souvenir rock, 'every man had literally his pockets full of rocks'. Overwhelmed by the romance of the island, the miner's thoughts quickly turned to gold, and American annexation.[6] Such mismatches between fiction and fact helped to confuse the meaning of the island, which evolved in new and strange directions in the years that followed.

The indolence of anglophone newspapermen ensured American visits to Juan Fernández frequently turned up in British newspapers, especially when they were linked to Crusoe. In July 1859 *The Times* carried a typical piece of second-hand reportage from the *San Francisco Times*, which stressed both continuing British interest, and a remarkably wide access to the global news industry.

A VISIT TO ROBINSON CRUSOE'S ISLAND.

While on board the ship *Golden Rocket*, lying at Greenwich Dock, we were permitted by Captain C. N. Pendleton to examine his log book, in which he gives an account of his visit to the island of Juan Fernández (Robinson Crusoe's island). The ship was on her last passage to this port [San Francisco] from Boston, and had on board 55 passengers (25 of whom were ladies) who intend to make California their future place of residence. Getting short of water Captain Pendleton decide to stop at Juan Fernández for a further supply, and therefore shaped his course thither – the island being nearly in his track. At 6 pm on the evening of the March 24 they doubled the eastern end of the island, and at 7 rounded too off the Bay of St. Joseph [Cumberland Bay], at the head of which the few inhabitants now remaining on the island are located. The facilities for loading water at the island Captain Pendleton reports to be not very good. The casks must be taken on shore and filled, rolled back into the water and parbuckled into the boat. While the crew were at this work the passengers rambled off in different directions to make discoveries. The island is about 25 miles long by about four in breadth [a considerable exaggeration]. The land is very high, rising in ragged, precipitous peaks – one of them called El Yunque 3,500 feet above the level of the sea. The peaks are generally overhung with clouds. The valleys are exceedingly fertile, the grass growing to the height of six or eight feet. Figs, strawberries, peaches, and cherries abound in their season. The *Golden Rocket* was there in the season of peaches, and the valleys and hill sides were full of trees loaded-down with delicious fruit. Captain Pendleton bought four barrels of the inhabitants, and the passengers about as many more. Strawberries flourish best in December and January. There are three remarkable caves in the side of the hill facing the harbour, about 30 feet in length, 25 in width, and about the same in height. The inhabitants now number but 14, of whom Messrs Day and Kirkaldie from Valparaiso are the chief persons, they having been appointed overseers of the island by the Chilian Government. Formerly a penal colony, numbering 500, was located here, and the caves above mentioned were used by them, but the project was found to be impracticable and the convicts were taken back to the mainland. The *Golden Rocket* anchored on the opposite side from that upon which Selkirk lived, and there being a mountain to cross to reach the Robinson Crusoe abode, no one ventured to make the journey. The best landing is on the eastern side, but the water is 20 fathoms deep at the head of the bay, and in some places so bold is the shore that a boat tied by her painter and drifting to her limits would be in 75 fathoms. An immense number of goats are running wild over the island, and an abundance of fish are taken on every cast. The water is obtained from a number of never-failing rivulets trickling down over the rocks from this cloud-capped mountain.[7]

The combination of solid, seamanlike information about water supply, fishing and the anchorage with rhapsodies on the subject of Selkirk/Crusoe, reveal the article began life in *Golden Rocket*'s log book, before falling into the hands of a half educated hack writer needing some copy. Facts and figures artlessly combine with attempts at romantic scenic imagery. By this date the Selkirk cave was well known, while the striking ellipse by which it becomes 'the Robinson Crusoe abode' in the same sentence had many precursors. It would have been interesting to learn if Day and Kirkaldie were English, American or Scottish. The *Times* reprint will have been read by far more people than the original *San Francisco* article, because the London paper had astonishing circulation figures, and the British had never forgotten Crusoe, the fictional embodiment of their imperial achievement.

Poet of the Pacific

⟨≈⟩

Among the great books of the sea, Herman Melville's *Moby-Dick; or, The Whale* of 1851, has few peers. Around the simple narrative of Captain Ahab's obsessive pursuit of the great white whale that had taken his leg, the whale's deliberate destruction of his ship, and the loss of all but one member of the crew, Melville created an epic vision that melded the limitless ocean with the obsessions of a small community, the very real menace of the mighty sperm whale and the emerging American assumption of ownership over the vast Pacific. Melville used his own experience to draw together many strands of the Anglo-American imagination, along with the rich history of a savage trade, into a philosophy of the ocean.

Melville began his seafaring career in 1839 as a crewman bound from New York to Liverpool. He encountered another Yankee intellectual reflecting on his experience as a merchant seaman in Dana's *Two Years before the Mast*, a book that provided a sense of camaraderie, even kinship. How far Dana inspired his whaling voyage to the Pacific is unclear, but the example was fresh and strong. Not that Melville was the only budding author to see the opportunity. By the 1840s, American sea writing in the Dana mould was at its apogee. These stories were generally 'useful', reflecting first-hand experience, with an emphasis on authorial expertise. They recounted voyages in a ship-shape and seaworthy manner, rendering the romantic writings of Cooper and Irving passé. These texts relied on their journals, the inevitable commonplace book of recorded facts and readings. Melville would both play to the new sensibility, and subvert it, using the entomology section in *Moby Dick* to connect, the more effectively to disguise his deeper purpose.[1]

Melville's Pacific was both a familiar and familial ocean. In 1827, when he was only eight, cousin Thomas wrote home from the USS *Vincennes* at the Peruvian port of Callao, anticipating a voyage among the islands. He visited the Marquesas, the islands that dominated Porter's narrative, entering the Typee valley, home of a cannibal tribe. In 1831 his uncle bought the book that recounted these adventures, admittedly through the oft-averted eyes of Chaplain Charles Stewart. These experiences came tumbling in on Melville at an impressionable age: he and his elder brother idolised their cousin, and the impact of such exotic voyaging would become obvious. When he joined the whaleship *Acushnet*, Melville found an ideal environment for reading, listening and reflecting: the voyage would be long, and the library limited.[2]

In May 1841 the whaler may have passed in sight of Juan Fernández, or Más Afuera, but the voyage from Rio had been quick, there was no need to stop for refreshment. Instead Melville listened intently to the tale of the whaleship *Essex*, stove and sunk by a giant sperm whale, as told by Owen Chase's son. This combination of disaster, starvation, cannibalism and the vast, glittering expanse of the Pacific laid the foundations of a great book. Still sailing north, the *Acushnet* met another whaler, and as the crew exchanged tall tales and domestic gossip Melville met Owen Chase's son, borrowed a copy of the whaleship *Essex* narrative and entered a world of sublime imagery: 'The reading of this wondrous story upon the landless sea & close to the very latitude of the shipwreck had a surprising effect on me.' He even imagined that he had seen Owen Chase, albeit at a distance. Later he obtained a copy of Chase's book, which he greatly prized, filling it with annotations and notes.[3]

Sailing across the South Pacific, the *Acushnet*'s crew began to suffer the effects of poor diet. There is little reason to doubt that Melville was already mildly scorbutic when he gave vent to a line about the Marquesas, the first island they stopped at. 'No description can do justice to its beauty' could have been written by Chaplain Richard Walter a century before, wrapping romantic reveries of an island paradise in a suitably scorbutic confession of literary inadequacy. However, this island had something else to offer, something that was not available at Juan Fernández. Sailing into Nukahiva Bay on 23 June 1841, *Acushnet* was boarded by a bevy of naked girls and, as was customary, the rest of the day and the night were given over to an orgy, proving the veracity of David Porter's account. 'Our ship was now wholly given up to every species of riot and debauchery. Not the feeblest barrier was interposed between unholy passions of the crew and their unlimited gratification.' Melville's claims that he stood aside, merely observing were, one suspects, addressed to his mother. They carry little conviction in the light of his subsequent actions.[4]

When it came time to leave paradise, Melville deserted ship, 'living in the garden of Eden before the Fall'. Three weeks later, obviously tiring of paradise, he joined another whaleship, before spending time on Tahiti, Eimeo, Maui and Oahu. Later he would pad out his version of castaway life with suitably modified extracts from Porter's *Journal*, a book he only encountered after returning to the United States, and Chaplain Stewart's altogether more restrained text. In 1842 Melville, sailing between Eimeo and Maui on board the whaler *Charles and Henry*, read an expurgated edition of *Robinson Crusoe*, and it is unlikely he ever went back to the original text. This version provided the basic guide for a white man writing about life among 'savages'; it is likely he was familiar with similar editions from childhood, along with an equally sanitised edition of *Gulliver's Travels*. Much was lost in such editions: violence, death and the exotic. These losses mattered because Melville would become 'the Modern Crusoe'.[5] This was entirely appropriate, for while he became a castaway by choice, in the mould of Alexander Selkirk, Melville was quick to see that the purpose of voyaging was to arrive at strange and exotic places, and take the opportunity to immerse himself in their exoticism. He would be a mariner by necessity, a poet by sensibility and an author by trade.

On 17 August 1843 Melville, tiring of life in a Hawaiian bowling alley, signed on as an ordinary seaman on the frigate USS *United States*. Here he perfected his superlative skills as a story-teller, a raconteur with a rich stock of exotic and alarming tales. He used and improved Dana's *Two Year's Before the Mast*, a text that would serve him throughout his career, along with a good selection of modern English history, travel and fiction. Among them he encountered the four-volume voyage narrative of HM ships *Adventure* and *Beagle*, now best known for the volume written by Charles Darwin, which contained a rich diet of coastal surveying, runs ashore and weirdness, human, animal and vegetable, along with a visit to Juan Fernández. Such shipboard literary adventures provided a running theme throughout Melville's fictionalised narrative *White Jacket*. On the *United States* Melville read not only more than he had recently done, but more deeply than he had ever done before.[6]

On 19 November the *United States* reached the Juan Fernández group, sailing past Más Afuera, and then Más a Tierra. While Melville may or may not have seen one of the Juan Fernández islands from the deck of the *Acushnet* in 1841, he did see them from the deck of the *United States*, the voyage that he reworked in *White Jacket*. The ship did not stop in Cumberland Bay, denying Melville the opportunity to add new layers of detail to his personal robinsonade. Another sailor on the *United States* left a journal in which he waxed lyrical about El Yunque, the 3,000-foot-high mountain, 'an abrupt wall of dark coloured bare rock', and 'caught a view of verdant glades surrounded by luxuriant woodland' and the grassy lower slopes.

The story of Alexander Selkirk was well known to most; the journal keeper paraphrased William Cowper's 'Monarch of all I survey' as they passed 'the famed island of Juan Fernández', and left his own response:

we approached it rapidly and run close in, and I have seldom seen a more remarkable and picturesque view than it presented when seen from a short distance. The mountain of the Anvil, so called from its resemblance to a Blacksmith's Anvil, it appears conspicuously placed in the range of precipitous mountains and is alone an object of interest.[7]

'Profoundly moved by the sight of the island, the emblem of man's isolation from other human beings and his triumphant survival', Melville needed little more to imagine this new world. He already knew both *Crusoe* and *Gulliver*, defining texts of mysterious island life. Fourteen years later he mused on the event, while observing a Greek island: 'Was here again afflicted with the great curse of modern travel – scepticism. Could no more realise that St. John had ever had revelations here, than when off Juan Fernandez, could believe in Robinson Crusoe according to De Foe.' While Hershel Parker observed that Melville was mistaken as to the reality of the story, he may have missed something deeper. It is unlikely Melville was ignorant of the fictional nature of Crusoe, or the real Selkirk. Like so many American voyagers he preferred to compound the stories, and it was this compound that he was unable to place in the landscape. His expurgated Crusoe portrayed a solitary man, living like Selkirk, rather than Defoe's energetic colonial master, liberator of the oppressed and beacon of religious tolerance.[8]

Passing on the great ship anchored at Valparaiso, where news arrived that David Porter had died, in Istanbul of all places. On 27 November the colours were half-masted in respect for the man who imagined an American South Pacific, which reminded Melville that he had yet to read Porter's *Journal*, the founding text of the genre. The voyage ended in October 1844 at Charlestown Navy Yard, Boston. Melville had been in the Pacific for more than three years, visited many islands and the odd mainland city, seen whaling up close, heard many marvellous tales, and developed a fair few of his own. He had enough material for a sea book or two, and in Dana both a model to emulate, and an ideal audience.[9] *Typee*, his first book, was published in London by John Murray, printer and publisher to the Admiralty.

Melville's Pacific books *Typee* and *Omoo* proved popular, but audiences on both sides of the Atlantic were obsessed with literal truth. They wanted Melville to be a simple chronicler of fact, a man lacking in imagination and invention, entirely unaffected by the wider cultural legacies that were the birthright of all Anglophone seafarers. As John Murray (son of Byron's publisher) noted: 'I wish some means could be taken to convince the English public that your Books are not fictitious imitations of Robinson Crusoe. 'Tis the feeling of being tricked which impedes their circulation here ...'[10] Murray needed 'proof' of truth to promote the book to a sceptical audience. While the dramatic reappearance of his companion on the Marquesas did no harm, Melville took a very different view. His next book, *Mardi*, was strikingly different. If his audience doubted the truth of his travelogue he might as well turn to fiction.

By contrast, American reviewers saw Melville as 'the de Foe of the Ocean', although the *Southern Literary Messenger* managed to mangle the analogy, declaring his work 'the most life-like and natural fiction since Robinson's Crusoe's account of life on the island of *Juan Fernández*'. British reviews developed a different line. In February 1850 *The Athenaeum* judged:

Mr Melville stands as far apart from any past or present marine painter in pen and ink as Turner does from the magnificent artist villipended by Mr Ruskin for Turner's sake – Vandevelde. He was the only writer who could convey the poetry of the Ship – her voyages and her crew – in a manner that matched Turner's, with something of the *Rime of the Ancient Mariner* about them, an art higher than the actor's or the scene painters.[11]

Melville had transcended a genre dominated by the literal truth of things recorded. Hitherto contemporary sea stories had varied little, and while the eye-witness travelogues of Charles Darwin and Captain Basil Hall occupied different spaces to the fiction of Fenimore Cooper and Frederick Marryat, Melville's original approach, 'a creation of genius', moulded narrative into poetry, where ships and men were enchanted by the ocean.[12]

One astute English reviewer sensed a shift in the literary balance of power. Melville had given American literature a truly unique voice, one that surpassed the best British models, and older American tales by Washington Irving and Fenimore Cooper, owning a vast, mysterious space that defied categorisation, possession or control. For all his admiration of the Royal Navy, and his cultural links with Britain, Melville was an American author, celebrating the democratic spirit of his nation, the politics of Andrew Jackson and the expansive force propelling his countrymen across the ocean to Hawaii. He read and admired British authors from Shakespeare onwards, but found an essential camaraderie with contemporary Americans. He dedicated *Moby Dick* to Nathaniel Hawthorne because Hawthorne had been a critical sounding board for his ideas, and represented a key facet of his ambition, to be an American author writing about American subjects.[13]

While Melville's adventures in the Pacific were hardly the stuff of heroic literature, his books transformed them into epic fables. Writing *Moby Dick* was another, perhaps more heroic journey, 'the most daring and prolonged aesthetic adventure that had ever been conducted in the hemisphere in the English language'. Melville took the natural world, and the strange tales that surrounded it, as the source material. He then crafted versions that, in seeking the truth, achieved a heightened reality. As a whaler, Melville experienced the world he would explore in print, and heard many tall tales along the way. He soon learned how to tell a tale, his ability to hold an audience was fashioned on the long quiet watches that punctuate Pacific voyages, but unlike the majority of seafaring raconteurs he collected and developed other stories, stories with the narrative power to chill the soul, stories of mutiny and massacre, of cannibalism and disaster, none more compelling that the narratives of the whaleship *Essex* and the mutiny on the *Globe*. These were only too true. Melville's genius lay not in the invention of the story, which was invariably based on his own experiences, or borrowed from another book, but the elemental melding of fact, fiction, and poetry into a new way of seeing.[14] His quality was Shakespearean. *Moby Dick* gave shape and meaning to the American Pacific. Across vast extremes of space, humanity and inhumanity were wrapped up in the slaughter of advanced mammals, a horrific trade that achieved a degree of dignity through the pre-industrial nature of the pursuit – the risks run by the whalemen, and the puny scale of their whaleboat – when set against the might and majesty of a full grown sperm whale. His argument was subversive, the superior intelligence of the mighty whale defeated the obsessive intent of a maniacal, murderous mariner, and the humans paid dearly for his folly.

Melville poured his creative being into *Moby Dick*, it was the summation of his art, but it met with a decidedly lukewarm response. Many reviewers ignored it altogether; a few praised the lively energetic style; others criticised the lack of formal structure, the wild mixture of philosophy, biology, seafaring and unconventional religious opinions. It did not sell, ignored and abused for the rest of the century.

From the start of his career Melville had been supported by London publishers, initially John Murray and then Richard Bentley, the leading houses for naval history. They had an audience for sea stories, and recognised the merit of the new author, but the economic returns on their investment proved less rich than they hoped. This mattered because in the 1840s American literature was not a paying career, only Irving and Cooper made a living from writing, and neither was doing very well. Other authors relied on day jobs, rich wives or family support.[15] After *Moby Dick* Melville accepted that model: he took a post in the New York Customs, writing for pleasure rather than from economic necessity.

In 1854 he compiled a series of sketches of the Galápagos Islands for *Putnam's Monthly Magazine* under their Spanish name 'The Encantadas', or enchanted islands. *Putnam's* was seeking a new American voice, and Melville duly obliged: blending his own distinctly limited experience of the islands with a rich haul of readings to mould an American literature of the sea, an imaginative reworking of reality. While their location in a vast empty ocean made the Galápagos obvious landfalls and refreshment stops, the sheer strangeness of the tortoise and iguana, the combination of the weird and the prosaic, made them ideal settings. As Melville observed: 'for slight is the difference between good fiction and a well told fact, especially when either lies in the atmosphere of the great western ocean'. He used the 'distance of the Pacific from the seat of America's leading literary periodicals' to invest the islands with 'fantastic qualities'.[16]

In 1858 Melville gave a public lecture on the 'South Seas', a term he greatly preferred to the 'Pacific, evoking the ancient, oak panelled rooms of the moribund South Sea Company, the 'South Sea Bubble', William Dampier and Harris's voyages, the lexicon of early English South Pacific voyaging. He recognised that the acquisition of California in the late 1840s, and the almost immediate discovery of gold in 1848 'first opened the Pacific as a thoroughfare for American ships', that the underlying vision, dominated by land and gold, linked American voyagers to their Spanish forebears: he made them, rather than the English, the true descendants of Juan Fernández. It was equally predictable that the Americans shifted their attention to a shorter route for the movement of men and gold. The Panama Railway, linking Aspinwall (modern Colón) and Panama across the Isthmus in 1855, ended the age of heroic voyaging. The press of progress had no sooner opened an American Pacific than it was closed down by superior communications, leaving the Polynesian islands as 'the last provocative to those jaded tourists to whom even Europe has become hackneyed, and who look upon the Parthenon and the Pyramids with a yawn'. Deeply enamoured of the native peoples, Melville condemned missionary interference and punitive vengeance by 'civilised sorts'.[17]

Melville's pre-contact, pre-industrial Pacific was in terminal decline: continental attractions, new sources of oil and a dramatic change in methods of travel emptied the ocean of observers, whether armed with harpoons or pens. In Melville's Pacific Juan Fernández had been a useful rendezvous; providing inbound shipping with fresh water and provisions, while those outbound could pick up news from home. Within a decade the whaling trade had shifted north, the overland rail link tapped the passenger traffic, while the idyllic island of castaway mariners subsided into the quiescent sloth of an isolated backwater. In less than a decade America would forget the South Pacific altogether, finding a new identity in the bitter legacy of internal conflict, a state ripped apart by a bitter bloody Civil War had no need of Pacific Oceans, external frontiers or sailor heroes.

After 1855 the Pacific slowly ebbed out of the American world view, the overland rail link replaced the passage round Cape Horn, while American deep water merchant shipping was largely foreign manned. When the Americans finally returned to the ocean they were heading for China, not the South Seas. The old whaling days were done, and although Latin American Republics were occasionally reminded that a heavy-handed Uncle Sam was in charge, to their abiding annoyance, the ocean has lost its allure. Soon Melville's Nantucket whalers, who had owned the Pacific 'as emperors own their empires', were gone.[18] The last Nantucket whaleship sailed for the Pacific in 1869, the year that a deranged, food-hoarding Owen Chase, narrator of the ultimate cannibal boat trip died. That last ship did not return. The explosive growth of mineral oil extraction collapsed an iconic industry, leaving the American Pacific silent and still.

When Melville died in 1891 the South Seas he had inherited from David Porter and Richard Henry Dana, and his own unique vision of life and death on a limitless sea, was done. America had lost contact with the sea; it became a continent, and the Wild West replaced the shimmering ocean. As Haskell Springer observed, the western frontier became 'a hoary cliché', while the ocean, the permanent enduring and very real American frontier 'hardly registers today in our cultural consciousness as setting, theme, metaphor, symbol, or powerful shaper of literary history'.[19] After six frenetic decades the Americans departed, leaving the stage to the descendants of Drake, Dampier, Defoe and Anson. The British remembered Melville and his ocean; the sea was still at the heart of their culture, and their ships ruled the Pacific. American commercial shipping collapsed as iron and steam replaced wood and canvas, unable to compete with the economic opportunities opened up by trans-continental expansion, industry and railroads.

A British Base in the Pacific

⸺⟆⟆⟆⸺

While passing American sailors dreamed of Crusoe's island, the British incorporated it into larger narratives of power and empire. The assumed ownership of the eighteenth century, recently revived by Thomas Sutcliffe, gained quasi-official status. The process began with a book: prompted by King William IV (1830–37), friend of Nelson and an enthusiastic if undiscriminating consumer of naval history, Admiralty Secretary John Barrow compiled the first biography of Anson. The treatment of Juan Fernández reflected a lifelong interest in geography and exploration, linking the great circumnavigator to Selkirk, and more recent voyagers like John Byron and Basil Hall. Barrow attributed Anson's undying fame to his demonstration of all the qualities requisite in a great naval commander, above all moral courage and equanimity in the face of disaster. He used the loss of the *Wager* and subsequent mutinies, along with references to the chaos that followed the sack of Paita to stress Anson's attention to discipline as a critical stage in the creation of the modern navy. He made Anson the exemplary naval leader, and a model of leadership for the rising generation.

Barrow began the process of totemising the horrific expedition; after a century the sheer scale of human misery could be quietly set aside, reclaiming the voyage for a very Whiggish version of the Royal Navy's history, one in which the present happy position of global pre-eminence flowed from centuries of heroic endeavour. By reducing six hundred scorbutic dead to necessary sacrifices to the cause Barrow made Anson's voyage a fit subject for trophies, memorials and antiquities. Indeed he wrote a great deal more about the figurehead of the old *Centurion* than he did about her suffering crew. When the famous ship was broken up King George III gave the 16-foot-tall figurehead, a lion rampant, to the Duke of Richmond, who placed it on a pedestal at Goodwood. Years later William IV 'recovered' the trophy, installing it in a commanding position at Windsor Castle. Eventually Queen Adelaide persuaded the old sea captain that it belonged in the Anson Ward at the Royal Naval Hospital, Greenwich.[1] By no coincidence Barrow's biography found its way into the ward rooms of most British warships, including those sailing to the Pacific.

After two decades of relative calm, the South Pacific returned to the centre of British interest in the early 1840s, when France and the United States pushed into the vast informal empire of trade and communication run from London. In April 1842 Rear Admiral Richard Thomas, commanding the Pacific Station, reported the arrival of a French frigate at Valparaiso, commanded by an Admiral with Pacific experience, carrying a governor, 130 troops and all the apparatus of a colony. Then the French headed off into the wide ocean, destination unknown. Three more ships were expected, and more troops. 'Rumours assign different destinations to this expedition', Thomas wrote. He discounted an attempt to settle part of New Zealand, favouring 'some of the islands in the Pacific, or some part of the coast of Upper California'.[2] Soon after, he learned the French had seized Tahiti. Elsewhere the Americans were consolidating their hold on Hawaii and attempting to filibuster Mexican California. These unwelcome developments suggested the next commander in chief should be a man of decision, well-connected to the ministry, and backed by a larger force.

When Rear Admiral Sir George Seymour left the Admiralty Board in May 1844 for the Pacific command he had effectively written his own orders. Furthermore he was strikingly well connected with the higher echelons of aristocratic society and the Tory party, and his social pretensions were backed by professional merit. His station was bounded by Cape Horn, the Antarctic Circle, the Bering Straits and the 170th degree west.[3] Given the vast distances that would separate the flagship from London, his orders were necessarily expansive and advisory. Expected to use his judgement on most questions short of declaring war, his tasks were to uphold British interests across the region, calling at the many islands and harbours where British traders might be found, and above all promote British commerce.

Seymour's command would be punctuated by a dispute about the American–Canadian border in the northwest – the Oregon Crisis, the French annexation of Tahiti and the Mexican–American War, events that focused British attention on the region. While the diplomatic exchanges have been studied, the strategic assessments produced by Seymour and the Admiralty, which included a base at Juan Fernández, have been largely ignored.

As a competent professional, Seymour read himself into the new job on the outbound voyage, consulting Vancouver's narrative, along with recent accounts of the Oregon country, American naval preparations and their turbulent, grandstanding political process. He quickly realised the Royal Navy had no reason to leave Valparaiso for Juan Fernández, or any other insular location, at least not in peace time. Valparaiso, the most important commercial port on the west coast of South America, had ample supplies of food, coal and regular steam communications back to London. The attention he paid to offshore islands reflected a desire to be prepared, rather than any ambition to seize. While the French and Americans kept out of Chile, and avoided the very narrow list of vital British interests, there was every prospect that the islands would slumber on, with little more than the occasional visit to betray the deeper thoughts of the Admiralty. Rumours that the United States planned to seize an island base on the south coast of Chile prompted a flurry of interest late in 1847, but proved groundless.[4] Although the Oregon Crisis would be resolved by forceful diplomacy, Seymour decided to check out a key location, just in case.

The Admiral's Picnic

—⟨⟨⟨⟨⟩⟩⟩⟩—

On 5 December 1847, Seymour's flagship, the eighty-gun *Collingwood*, arrived off Juan Fernández. The most powerful British ship to have graced those waters for a century dropped anchor in Cumberland Bay that evening, having made a few short tacks to fetch the anchorage. Not for her the smashed beak-head, frayed rigging and ill-set sails that marked the *Centurion*'s wretched approach. Where the *Centurion* had staggered in, reeking and foul, dead men laying in their own filth, rats everywhere, Sir George expected the flagship to match his own spotless style: the *Collingwood* was a thing of beauty. Even the crew had to be handsome: two ugly midshipmen had been dispatched to other vessels.[1]

Collingwood was both Sir George's flagship and his home. His wife and three daughters lived on board for large parts of the commission. Such domesticity provided a major element in the floating theatre of British Empire. While the British had no possessions closer than New Zealand they exerted enormous influence, essentially an informal empire, over the newly independent states of South America. While Juan Fernández had no significance for British regional trade or investment, and precious few people, the admiral was curious. A diversion to the magical island of Crusoe and Lord Anson would be a pleasant change from the endless round of civic functionaries, pushy consuls and grasping merchants. He could dispense with formalities and enjoy himself. He brought the family along, as any good *paterfamilias* would, to enjoy the view.

From his elevated position on the quarter deck Commander Philip Somerville, struck by the 'bold' scenery, reflected the island was 'remarkable for Lord Anson's having put in when scurvy attacked and carried off so many of his men'. The British battleship found the Chilean brig *Janequeo* at anchor, the two ships having raced across from Valparaiso. Having moored and furled sails the large kedge anchor was laid out to secure the ship against Shelvocke's storm. The following day the pinnace went ashore to begin watering, the British were astonished when the tenuous local community demanded payment. On 8 December one watch of sailors were allowed ashore to wash their clothes and hammocks, exploiting the water supply at source. Once the Chilean ship had departed British attitudes subtly shifted, from visit to occupation: they began by conducting great gun exercise, firing at a mark set up on shore. On the 10th the second watch took their turn ashore to wash and mend while the upper deck batteries were exercised before lunch. The 11th saw the men turn to and clean the lower deck. Sunday 12th was devoted to divine service. On the 14th the Royal Marines and small arm men from the ship's company went ashore to exercise firing at a mark, while the midshipmen were given a chance to practise with the ship's six-pounder field gun. All of this occurred on the sovereign territory of a foreign power. The following morning more gun drill was followed by the normal ritual of departure, weighing the kedge, shortening the cable, crossing the royal topgallant yards and hosting in the boats. At 2.30 on 15 December, having left ample time for the men to eat, the anchor was raised and the *Collingwood* sailed out of the bay on a light south-southeasterly breeze, the prevailing wind in those quarters.[2]

On the first day at anchor a party of junior officers had gone ashore to ramble; one of them did not return. Among the handsome, well-connected boys that graced the admiral's quarter-deck, fourteen-year-old James Graham Goodenough was on his first voyage.[3] Scrambling through the dense undergrowth Goodenough had fallen into a ravine. Despite a sprained wrist and other injuries he managed to yell a warning to his friend Clements Markham. With night coming on Markham rushed back to the ship to get help, leaving Goodenough on a ledge half way down the ravine.[4] The next morning Goodenough, battered and bruised, crawled out and met Admiral Seymour, who had come ashore to search for one of his prized young men. Goodenough recovered from his ordeal, rising to prominence in the Victorian Navy.[5] Thirty years later he made another ill-advised run ashore on a Pacific Island. He landed on Santa Cruz, as Commodore of the Australian Station, on 11 August 1875. The locals had a bad reputation, and they did not disappoint. Goodenough was hit in the side by a 'poisoned' arrow, six others were similarly wounded. Tetanus set in, and he died on 20 August. Two seamen shared his fate. While the Victorians deified Goodenough as an exemplary Christian Martyr, that identity has come under increasing scrutiny from Pacific historians more concerned with the other side of encounter.[6] Ownership and possession were complex issues; they had a nasty habit of biting the unwary. Goodenough was unusual only in finding this out on more than one occasion. His companion on the earlier ill-starred ramble ashore, Clements Markham, long outlived him, becoming a historian of Spanish exploration in the Pacific, before sending Captain Scott to another kind of heroic death.

The casual use of Chilean territory to resupply the water tanks may have violated Chilean sovereignty, as did literally bombarding the shores of Cumberland Bay with shot and shell, and then landing a small army to occupy the ground and continue firing, it but it was entirely consistent with time-honoured British attitudes. Despite the Chilean flag, and Chilean inhabitants, Juan Fernández remained defiantly 'British', a tiny green speck amid a vast British ocean, located at the heart of the defining sea-culture of a world power, one small part of a vast 'informal empire' that fuelled the explosive expansion of British trade and prosperity at the mid-century. Global power, cemented by victory over Napoleon, may have changed British attitudes, but Juan Fernández had been 'British' for close on two hundred years, a location that connected the Victorians to their heroic, not to mention piratical precursors. The island occupied a privileged place in their mental world, a world in which

Crusoe was familiar to every literate Briton, while anyone with a smattering of education could pick up the stories of Selkirk and Anson.

Philip Somerville recorded his reading habits, reflecting a serious attempt to master the island's fascinating history. His ardent evangelical faith and Freemasonry, Anglo-Irish identity and introspection made him a curious witness to the more exotic aspects of Pacific life. While lamenting the licentious behaviour of native women Somerville never described what he had seen, or the all too human feelings that such sights excited. Recourse to a stiff lecture on self-improvement the following morning at least had the quality of consistency. While the ship's library may have been exiguous, and individual officer's collections somewhat restricted by lack of space, Admiral Seymour had the money and shelves for a superior reference collection. Somerville, his constant companion over the chess board during the long, slow evenings of Pacific voyaging under sail, had ample opportunity to borrow.[7] He read Pacific voyages by Fitzroy and Darwin, Wallis, Cook, and Anson. Nor was he the only officer keeping a journal.

While Somerville wrote for private reflection, his friend and shipmate Lieutenant Frederick Walpole was altogether more ambitious. Walpole came from distinguished stock, a younger son of Horatio, third Earl of Orford and a descendant of Sir Robert Walpole, the first prime minister. These political connections may have secured him a berth on Seymour's Tory ship. It would be his last sea service; he ended his days as a member of Parliament.[8] He had sailed with Somerville half a decade before, when the older man mentored him through a difficult period.

Walpole did not record what he read, but we can safely assume that he shared texts and discussed the distant lands they visited, from San Francisco to Hawaii by way of Tahiti, Mazatlan and Lima with Somerville. 'Fredk Walpole came in while I was writing this [his journal] and had a chat. He is a nice young fellow and a great favourite of mine', and 'a host in himself'.[9] These discussions shaped the way they responded to the Pacific, and the island. They help to explain not only what they reported, but also the complete omission of routine activities. Similarly, Somerville's influence may explain the absence of salacious detail from Walpole's record of the cruise.

Among the many Juan Fernández texts that Somerville read, the most recent, and among the most effusive, was Richard Henry Dana's *Two Years Before the Mast*.[10] He was equally familiar with Carteret's voyage, which he read for information on the hot topic of Tahiti, while taking occasional detours for a literary encounter with other regions, including a European grand tour taking in Germany, Austria, Belgium and northern France, and another exploring Egypt and Nubia. Naval voyage narratives were staple fare; recent examples with local connections included those by Philip Parker King, Robert Fitzroy, Edmund Belcher, and Frederick Beechey, along with Thomas Sutcliffe's pamphlets. Taken with a solid diet of improving evangelical tracts and texts on the emerging Tahitian imbroglio, such books shaped the way they responded to the voyage.

Walpole's *Four Years in the Pacific*, published in 1849, included a lyrical chapter on the island. Having come unwillingly from the fleshpots, clubs and excursions of Valparaiso, the ship's officers were not disposed to enjoy their offshore venture, and found little to lift their spirits when they first caught sight of the 'poor barren rock'. Unlike Anson's men, they were in fine health, well fed and definitely not scorbutic; consequently Juan Fernández took a little time to work its magic. As they came closer the 'fine, bold appearance' and then the 'verdant valleys' offered a more pleasing prospect, while a 'clear, sparkling' waterfall 'positively made me long to explore'.[11] Even the ruins of the last prison settlement were scenic.

Returning to his books, Walpole quickly situated himself in the history of this strange place, getting his bearings by retrieving those of Selkirk, Anson, Defoe and Dampier. The island of mystery and romance gripped Walpole's imagination, mixing personal observations with things recorded, or merely 'said to be'. Officers and men went ashore, with various agendas: to take in the scenery, fish, forage for fresh food, or simply wash their clothes in fresh water.[12] Soon the island echoed with English voices. The Chilean occupants, a single extended family, scratched out an existence raising cattle, apparently too idle to cultivate the soil.[13] Walpole also found an American Crusoe, 'left by some ship for reasons probably not creditable enough to be related truly'. He expressed himself contented with his lot, and said he made money by selling firewood and goat's flesh to the whalers, and by guiding them on their shooting excursions. Hunting goats with a pack of dogs was 'one of the things necessary to be done on the island'. Used to well-bred packs of fox-hounds, Walpole was distinctly unimpressed by the canine assets on offer, and set off alone. Soon he was lost in rapture, amid 'scenery of the wildest beauty' and 'vegetation of the most vigorous growth':

Here you rambled in the cool shade, a stream of purest water by your side – there banks of the sweetest thyme invited to response, while vistas, glen, and peak, seemed placed but to be admired. Flowers clustered round you, and the humming-bird, darting from bush to bush, his varied plumage sparkling in the sun, enlivened the whole. Our noble ship in the bay spoke highly for the ingenuity of man, but the eye turned with delight to the freshness and beauty of nature.[14]

Older buccaneer romances about an edible world had been replaced by the reveries of a well-fed tourist. While Walpole praised the usual culinary delights of fish and flesh, echoing lines on the singular ease of fishing, he doubted the old story about Selkirk goats with slit ears. *Collingwood*'s officers enjoyed goat flesh with mint sauce, 'eaten as lamb'. Suitably rested and restored by the time the flagship sailed, the ship's company had taken a good harvest of local fish. The resourceful Somerville stowed some live crayfish for his friends in Valparaiso.[15]

Inspired by the wonders of nature, the isolation of the island or the realisation that his audience would expect comprehensive coverage of Robinson Crusoe's residence, Walpole rambled across many a page, describing the beauty and abundance of Juan Fernández. He left the story suitably opaque, reviving an old debate about the real author of *Crusoe*, indulging the suitably aristocratic notion that no mere hack journalist could have written it; with Robert Harley, Lord Oxford, promoter of the 'South Sea Bubble', as his preferred candidate. Whoever wrote it, 'the work is so truthful, it were worse than sceptical to doubt it'.[16]

On 14 December 1847, the day before departure, the admiral, his wife and three daughters 'gave a delightful picnic in West (or English) Bay' (i.e. Puerto Inglese). The officers dined in tents, spread among the myrtle trees, and then took a wander through an idyllic landscape of low trees and rivulets, smoking Raleigh's 'fragrant weed', a necessary occasion, the admiral having banned such filthy habits from the flagship. Strolling through this delightful scene, wreathed in smoke, Walpole affected to be reminded of the 'hardy adventurers' of older days, and recognised with becoming humility the very different nature of his own voyage to this paradise for scorbutic mariners. Such reveries concluded with a knowing paragraph that placed the island and the diffuse memories it evoked firmly in the Victorian imagination:

After a delightful stay we went back to comparatively civilized places, townships, traffics, and all the paraphernalia of this money-making world. I must not forget to mention, to the credit of the moderns, that one of our number petitioned our chief for leave to remain on the island: emulous of Selkirk, or wishing to verify Defoe's account of Robinson Crusoe, he seriously begged to be left behind. It is needless to say his request was not granted.[17]

By leaving the inspiration that prompted this new Selkirk unclear, Walpole adroitly enlisted the lure of Robinsonian residence and Selkirkian survival as familiar signposts for readers grappling with prosy descriptions of the vistas and visions he had experienced. While hardly in the ranks of Darwin and other Humboldtian scientific travellers, Walpole reflected the mental world of the 1840s, just before Melville's *Typee* reinvented the Pacific island story. Walpole's publisher had no doubt Juan Fernández would attract readers, much as it had in the days of Dampier and Woodes

Rogers 150 years before. Walpole's cultured observations mark a turning point in discussions of Juan Fernández. It was published by Richard Bentley. Two years later Bentley published Melville's mighty whale book. While Walpole's slight, charming Pacific memoir required a second edition, and opportunistic Parisian publishing maestro Galignani knocked off a pirate edition, *Moby Dick* foundered.

Seymour enjoyed the book. He may have noticed a passage, hidden in the historical introduction to Walpole's travelogue, which reflected British interest in the island as a naval station. In a secret report Seymour accepted Chile was unlikely to give up the island, but he hoped to secure effective control through a contractor.

If this island was obtainable it would be desirable to secure it. The anchorage is exposed to the North and the depth of water too great for improvement by breakwater, but it is better than St Helena and Ascension as I am told for anchorage and very superior garden cultivation and climate.[18]

There was no need to act; the Pacific soon calmed down. Walpole sought to undermine Chilean sovereignty, focusing on the Spanish 'lust of dominion', Chilean idleness and the endless disasters, both natural and man-made, that afflicted the island under Hispanic rule, a theme that culminated with the declaration that it had been 'abandoned' to nature. His words hinted at the notion of '*terra nullius*', an island free for occupation, as the Falkland Islands had been only a decade and a half before. Anxious to provide good title, Walpole even looked for the signs of earlier British occupation; he found Anson's camp with ease, but not the graves of the expedition. Instead he noted the fruit trees that his Lordship had introduced.[19] Tasty as their fruits might be, they were a poor substitute as indicators of title to some solid grave markers.

Occupation, Possession, Ownership and Title

———✦———

Legal title to Juan Fernández and Más Afuera was never in doubt. They belonged to Spain, which first discovered and occupied the uninhabited islands, and then to Chile, as successor to the defunct Spanish Empire. However, the value of that legal title had been challenged, in fact if not in law. They had been left vacant for close on 200 years, with Dutch, English, British, American and finally Peruvian occupation undermining any continuity of title. Furthermore, the occupants of Juan Fernández had no means of controlling Cumberland Bay, let alone the rest of the island, Santa Clara or Más Afuera. The steady accumulation of cartographic and text information in other countries, first Holland and then Britain, meant that by the 1740s the islands were wide open to hostile occupation: the Spanish were obliged to occupy Juan Fernández. Occupation worked, blocking a British take-over, short of war, until the end of the Empire in South America. Combining a fort with legal title provided a solid basis for possession.

While the Spanish retained some of Anson's place names, such as Cumberland Bay, they seem to have taken a more thorough approach to removing land markers, notably those of burial. No corner of this foreign field would be 'for ever England'; indeed the cemetery at San Juan Bautista is dominated by a memorial to German sailors.

The island that Somerville and Walpole enjoyed was fast becoming the romantic ruin of the southern seas, a curiosity to be seen, examined, and tasted. The Chilean government had no interest in the place; in December 1847 Captain Benjamin

Munoz Gamero, who had been to Juan Fernández a decade earlier, concluded the abandoned settlement was rapidly decaying, and would soon disappear altogether 'if steps are not quickly taken to remedy its condition'. Not only were the goats eating the island bare, but visiting ships and the few inhabitants were wasteful and destructive. The Royal Navy continued to picnic on the idyllic islands and inlets of Chile. The battleship HMS *Asia* called in 1848; two years later HMS *Portland* visited San Ambrosio and San Félix, to check their suitability as naval bases.[1] The 1849 California Gold Rush created a sudden upsurge in traffic, many American ships stopped off to visit the romantic sites, a few Americans even speculated on the possibility of seizing the islands for the United States. Suitably alarmed, the Chilean authorities sent out two more penal colonies; both ended in revolt, escape and disaster. Finally the steamship made Juan Fernández a backwater.

The island had been on the track used by sailing ships heading north and south, but steamers hugged the coast 300 miles to the east, rarely troubling the islands without good reason. Good reasons to visit an island so far away, and so nearly empty, were few and far between. In 1854 a boat load of survivors from the Boston ship *Townsend*, destroyed by fire after rounding the Horn, fetched up at Más Afuera, and then limped into Cumberland Bay, where they found food, shelter, and ship to the mainland.[2] Another American ship sank at sea nearby in 1860, this time the entire crew managed to reach the island.[3] Such occasional disasters aside, Juan Fernández drifted out of mind. Spanish warships visited briefly in 1865–6 during a naval war with Chile. British and American warships stopped more often, to make maps and relax.

In February 1865 HMS *Clio* called; midshipman Lord Charles Beresford led a party of seamen ashore to hunt goats, only to discover three Robinson Crusoes, living on a diet of crayfish.[4] Action man Charlie added to the repertoire of hunting techniques; diving to recover goats that fell into the sea after being shot by sportsmen on the ship. In 1868 Commodore Powell and the officers of HMS *Topaze*, flagship of the Pacific Squadron, had a large iron plaque specially cast in Valparaiso to commemorate Selkirk, it was then carried up to the newly imagined 'Lookout', by a squad of perspiring matelots, then hammered into the mountain:

In Memory

of

Alexander Selkirk,

Mariner

A native of Largo in the County of Fife, Scotland, who lived on this island in complete solitude for four years and four months, he was landed from the *Cinque Ports* galley, 96 tons, 18 guns, AD 1704, and was taken off in the *Duke*, privateer, 12th February, 1709. He died Lieutenant of H.M.S. *Weymouth* , AD 1723, aged 47. This tablet is erected near Selkirk's lookout, by Commodore Powell and the officers of HMS *Topaze*, AD 1868.[5]

For all the apparent innocence of modern sailors marking their sense of a heroic precursor, the plaque could equally well be read as an indication of ownership, a very solid piece of engineering that helped build a British title. It remains where Powell left it, commanding the pass over the island's mountainous spine, surrounded by innumerable maritime graffito carved into the rock to remind visitors of the enduring bond of sailors, and their love of a run ashore. Close by, an incongruous viewing platform has been erected, in case visitors miss the scenic majesty of 'Selkirk's Mirador', the most romantic spot on the island. Commodore Powell also reported Juan Fernández had been hit by a tidal wave after a major earthquake on the South American coast.[6] This time there were no casualties.

In February 1872 the sloop HMS *Reindeer* stopped at Juan Fernández, Captain William Kennedy being 'desirous of visiting the spot associated with the story of 'Robinson Crusoe'. He found HMS *Scylla* already there, with orders cancelling his return to England round the Horn. He profited from the news by remaining for a few days:

hunting the wild goats and thoroughly enjoying ourselves. The day before our departure some of our sportsmen accidentally set fire to the brushwood and destroyed a quantity of stacked timber. A claim was made against me for 2000 dollars for the damage done.

Nothing came of the claim. While Kennedy reported the affair in his usual breezy offhand way, the damage was significant, about a square mile of standing trees were destroyed. This naval carelessness led to a belated but essential Chilean ban on further logging, to preserve the soil and island resources.[7] Predictably, the order was ineffective.

British concepts of ownership took on a new character when HMS *Challenger* arrived in Cumberland Bay on 13 November 1875, anchoring with scientific precision at exactly 6.30 pm. The *Challenger* was nearing the end of a pioneering oceanographic circumnavigation of 68,690 miles, inspired by the strange and disturbing things that had emerged from the primordial slime at the bottom of the deep ocean. This weird new world had come to the light during naval surveys of the ocean floor, undertaken to ensure the fast expanding network of privately funded British submarine telegraph cables was laid on suitably flat terrain. So compelling was the Royal Society's case that notoriously stingy Prime Minister William Gladstone sanctioned the cost. The expedition sailed in the wake of other scientific navigators, of Cook, Flinders and Franklin, men who gave the British possession of vast swathes of the littoral by charting the seas, and naming the headlands, inlets and rivers. These scientific navigators worked at the meeting point of astronomy and terrestrial magnetism, where heavenly bodies and magnetic fields contributed to safe oceanic passage making.

Stripped of cannon, the ship had been fitted out as a mobile laboratory for the scientists, a strong supporting cast of officers and seamen would get them to their many destinations, operating dredges, grabs, sweeps and trawls to collect natural wonders that ranged from the beautiful to the downright bizarre.[8] *Challenger* supplemented the existing British possessory catalogue of books and charts with a library of data; the *Report of the Scientific Results of the Exploring Voyage of HMS Challenger*[9] implied British dominion over the ocean, the deep sea trenches, fisheries and any number of well-catalogued islands. That Juan Fernández, the 'natural habitat' of British castaways and maroons, would be among those rocky outposts was never in doubt. Consequently when the *Times* reviewed the text it was more concerned to link the island to Anson, Defoe and Selkirk than trouble its readers with scientific issues.[10]

While the *Challenger* narrative tried to explain the world that had been observed, the voyagers, doubtless driven into the ship's library by the long, tedious days spent on open ocean passages, were heavily influenced by the past.[11] Their version of Dampier, Defoe and Darwin was the one that would be taken up by their successors. They provided a check list of reasons why the island should be seen in a British setting, one that had been created on the forty day passage from Tahiti. With twelve of those days spent totally becalmed, and many more under easy sail, the scientists had ample opportunity to catch up on their reading. Furthermore deep sea sounding and sampling on this passage had been largely unrewarding. Henry Moseley read Woodes Rogers, Dampier, Funnel, Shelvocke, Anson and many more.[12] He would not have been alone in taking such a liberal survey of Britain's long relationship with the island. This was no ordinary stop; it had a uniquely British history and romance. 'It was with the liveliest interest that we approached the scene of Alexander Selkirk's life of seclusion and hardship.' The very existence of Juan Fernández was the main reason why most of his scientific colleagues had undertaken the voyage in the first place:

The study of *Robinson Crusoe* certainly first gave me a desire to go to sea and Darwin's *Journal* settled the matter. Defoe was obliged to lay the scene of his romance in the West Indies in order to bring in the Carib man Friday. He thus gained the parrot, but he lost the sea-elephants and fur seals of Juan Fernández, one of the latter would have made a capital pet for Robinson Crusoe.

After reading Philip Parker King's account, Mosely concluded, 'no doubt the general appearance of the vegetation is very different now from what it was when the island was first visited'.[13]

Selkirk's tale had an obvious resonance with the large number of Scots officers and scientists. Midshipman Lord George Campbell, son of statesman-scientist the eighth Duke of Argyll, maintained a detached perspective in his 'log-letters', a running commentary published soon after his return to Britain. He was neither blinded by mythology, nor deluded by scurvy. While Moseley recognised a landscape of devastated nature Campbell believed, a single house and a few cattle aside, the island was unchanged since the buccaneers, Selkirk, Anson and his diseased crew had departed:

Certainly until I saw Juan Fernández I had never sufficiently pitied Selkirk, for I had dreamed that the real island must be like Defoe's ideal island, a pretty, pleasant little spot, with tree clad hillocks rising here and there from low undulating land, forming a foreground to more distant crags and rocks among which he learned to catch the goats – rivalling them in speed and activity among the rocky fastnesses. But all that imaginary foreground exists not at all, for Juan Fernández is all steep hill and mountain.

The scenery is grand; gloomy and wild-looking enough on the dull stormy day on which we arrived, clouds driving past and enveloping the highest ridge of the mountain, a dark-coloured sea fretting against the steep cliffs and shore, and clouds of sea-birds swaying in great 'flocks, to and fro, over the water; but cheerful and beautiful on the bright sunny morning which followed – so beautiful that I thought 'this beats Tahiti'. Our anchorage is in Cumberland Bay: shallow in form, but disagreeably deep in depth close up to the shore, from which rises a semicircle of high land, forming bold headlands on right and left, and sweeping brokenly up thence to the highest ridge – a square-shaped, craggy, precipitous mass of rock, with trees clinging to its sides to near the summit. The spurs of these hills are covered with coarse grass or moss, and in the ravines are woods of myrtle and small tree-shrubs. The soil beneath these trees is singularly loose, and where they grow, as they do, on exceedingly steep slopes, it is dangerous to trust to them for help, as the roots easily give way, and down you go, carrying tree after tree with you in your descent.

Half a mile from the ship there was splendid, but laborious, cod-fishing; laborious on account of sharks playing with the bait, and treating your stout fishing-line as though 'twere made of single gut; also on account of the forty-fathom depth these cod-fish lived in. From beneath the ship's keel we hauled up cray-fish and conger-eels in lobster-pots by dozens; and round about her sides flashed shoals of fish –cavalli – only requiring a hook with a piece of worsted tied roughly on, and swished over the surface, to be caught one after another, giving splendid play on a rod.

And on shore, too, there was something to be seen and done. There was Selkirk's 'look-out' to clamber up the hill-side to – the spot where tradition says he watched day after day for a passing sail, and from whence he could look down on both sides of his island home, over the wooded slopes, down to the cliff-fringed shore, on to the deserted ocean's expanse.

Down the beds of the small ravines run burns, overgrown by dock-leaves of enormous size, and the banks are clothed with a rich vegetation of dark-leaved myrtle, bignonia, and winter-bark, tree-shrubs, with tall grass, ferns, and flowering plants. And as you lie there humming-birds come darting and thrumming within reach of your stick, flitting from flower to flower which dot blue and white 'the foliage of bignonias and myrtles. And on the steep grassy slopes above the sea-cliffs herds of wild goats are seen quietly browsing, quietly, that is, till they scent you, when they are off – as wild as chamois.

These humming-birds – ruby-throated, and one other kind – are peculiar to the island, and in great numbers. A wild kid was shot, and we thought that we had never tasted better meat.[14]

When the ship came to anchor in Anson's Cumberland Bay the weather was windy and dull, thick scudding clouds obscured El Yunque. The next morning was calm and sunny. Once they reached the shore the visitors found the island but lightly held. Campbell reported a Chilean entrepreneur was raising cattle to sell to passing shipping, and harvesting the seals for pelts. The business was failing, and the owner seemed intent on annihilating the seal population, by now restricted to Santa Clara.[15] Despite his initial scepticism, Campbell had fallen under the spell of the island. He bought the romantic 'lookout' story, enjoyed some sport with the rod, noted the flora, the hummingbirds, and like Moseley waxed lyrical about the flavour of a Juan Fernández goat. Campbell even explained Mr Goodenough's fall, his access to scientific expertise and sharp naval eye provided a fine introduction to the island.

Moseley recorded the trees had been clear felled to around 700 feet above sea level, but he pushed on into the fields of *Gunnera chilensis*, the immense leaves of which spread above his head like natural marquees. In this paradise of biodiversity Moseley was another convert to Commodore Powell's 'Lookout':

Selkirk's monument is placed on the crest of a short, sharp ridge in a gap in the mountains at a height of about 1,800 feet above the sea. From this a steep descent leads down on either side to the shore. Here Selkirk sat and watched the sea on both sides of the island in long-deferred hope of sighting a sail.

Here we rested for some time, enjoying the view. Juan Fernández is only ten miles in length, and 20 square miles in area, and from this elevated point nearly the whole extent of the island can be overlooked. Yet this tiny spot of land contains birds, land shells, trees and ferns which occur nowhere else in the vast expanse of the universe.

Having cut down and eaten a cabbage palm, and sampled the goats, Moseley was especially pleased with the crayfish *Palinurus frontalis* (now known as the Juan Fernández rock lobster, *Jasus frontalis*), as good to eat as it was to study. 'The soil is good wheat ground, the stones about the spot are of lava, and the hills at the back contain basalt.'[16] The navigators took terrestrial magnetic readings every day with Fox dip circles, and recorded the weather as very humid, with temperatures of 57–60° Fahrenheit. The ship's officers also took sights to fix the location:

Latitude 33° 37' 36'' south
Longitude 78° 53' 0'' west.

Juan Fernández gave the scientists and the officers an opportunity to ramble ashore, eat some fresh food, and enjoy the historical links of this little fragment of the English imagination, defiantly located in a great ocean named by a Portuguese Captain in Spanish service, whose rich fisheries were sustained by a major ocean current from the far south, named for Alexander von Humboldt, the Prussian demi-god of the observational sciences they pursued. Humboldt's travels in the Americas had inspired Darwin, and revolutionised scientific methodology. The distractions of the past, and the dining table, help to explain the bucolic flavour of the resulting texts.

Challenger's anchor was raised at precisely 6.30 pm on 15 November, a mere 48 hours after it had been dropped, and the ship headed for Valparaiso. Here Campbell took his leave, following promotion to lieutenant. The scientists had taken on board a kid, 'a direct descendant of Alexander Selkirk's goats'; in a sign of changing times it became part of the shipboard family, rather than Christmas dinner.[17]

The *Challenger* expedition transformed oceanography, earth sciences and marine biology, a pioneering achievement honoured by an ill-fated American space shuttle, one of three to be named for Royal Navy survey vessels. It also influenced British imperial policy. Lord George Campbell's father was in no doubt about the value of science to the Imperial project, or of Pacific Islands to the British economy. In 1888 *Challenger* veteran Sir John Murray recommended annexing Christmas Island, to exploit the rich deposits of phosphates. Argyll agreed, and Prime Minister Gladstone acted.[18]

Settlers

It was now too late for the British to occupy Juan Fernández. Modern settlement began in 1877 when former Austrian army officer Alfred de Rodt proposed a fresh settlement to the Chilean authorities. He offered to take sixty people and a thousand head of cattle to the island, to produce charcoal, export native palms and sell food to passing ships. Basking in the suitably pointless title Inspector of Colonisation de Rodt recruited settlers from Spain, France, Germany, Mexico and Switzerland, and their names still dominate the island: Gonzalez, Charpentier, Camacho, Recabarren, Lopez and Schiller. Despite the harsh economic realities of island life, and limited opportunities for trade, the population slowly increased. However de Rodt, bankrupted by his project, began systematic forestry to keep his little colony alive. By 1900 the accessible parts of the island had been clear felled. When the timber supply failed crayfish exports took over, a German cannery operated in the 1890s, replaced by a French service running live langosta to Valparaiso. Tourism began in the 1890s. When de Rodt died in 1905 there were 122 souls in residence, and they considered themselves the masters of the island, exploiting the natural resources untroubled by modern concerns for biodiversity, unique species, or the stability of the thin soil clinging precariously to the mountainside.[1]

By the 1890s Dampier, Selkirk, Anson and Malaspina were but dim memories, treasured by dusty historians and the odd romantic traveller. The brief moment in time when the interaction of politics, geography, ocean currents and disease had turned Juan Fernández into a little English heaven amid the epic vastness of the South Pacific were done. Few ships visited, and the inhabitants were annihilating the forests to make charcoal. Ecological devastation and new patterns of oceanic voyaging had reduced the place to irrelevance; isolation and otherness took over. The only vessels that passed the island were large sailing ships carrying bulk cargoes of grain, guano and coal around the globe. These ships were larger, faster and more seaworthy, while improved food preservation and anti-scorbutics extended their port to port range. They had no need to stop for food or water.[2] Those that did sought refuge rather than a run ashore.

One such was the full-rigged sailing ship *Rappahannock*, a large 'Down Easter' that arrived in Cumberland Bay in November 1891. Built at Bath (Maine) a little more than a year earlier, this mighty wooden ship carried an enormous spread of canvas, including three sets of sky sails to catch every hint of breeze. The crew christened their strikingly beautiful vessel 'the big bird'. Vessels of this size and power operated in truly global trading patterns, carrying bulky cargo over vast distances, distances and oceans that remained uneconomic for contemporary steam ships. Her maiden voyage began at Philadelphia, loading 120,000 cases of kerosene for Japan. The next leg of the voyage carried 4,400 tons of Japanese coal to San Francisco. Wheat from Port Costa was hauled round to Liverpool, where another coal cargo for San Francisco was loaded on 27 July 1891. The voyage south was slow, taking an excruciating 44 days to round Cape Horn. Shortly after rounding the Horn, Captain Wiley Rogers Dickerson discovered the coal in the forward hold had caught fire. He set course for the nearest land, Juan Fernández. Two days later, on 11 November, Dickerson brought the ship into Cumberland Bay and moored her head and stern over a sand bank, with the bow pointing inshore, trying to keep the wind blowing from astern, to limit the spread of the fire. Unable to put out the blaze Dickerson tried to scuttle the ship, but the conflagration deep in the hold was already out of control. He ordered the crew to abandon ship with whatever they could save of the ship's stores. Around midnight the forward hold exploded. Dickerson observed the deck seams open, revealing a raging inferno at the heart of the tightly packed cargo. The 'big bird' sank in six fathoms at the bow and four at the stern. By the following evening the mighty ship was little more than smouldering wreck. Dickerson, his wife, two daughters and twenty-seven crewmen were marooned. De Rodt's loggers did not have a fishing boat, let alone a ship.

To make matters worse, the Chilean Civil War meant the normal supply ship had not arrived, obliging the loggers and their unexpected guests to exist on the old Selkirkian diet of goats and fish. Then there was the language problem. The Americans had no Spanish; fortunately, one of the Portuguese loggers knew enough English to liaise. The next task was to get off the island. Dickerson observed:

We established a lookout on Crusoe's mountain and kept two men on duty there at all times. Several times the men on watch saw sails and signals were made, to no effect. Once the men tried to row off to a passing ship, but she got away without noticing us.[3]

Finally a small Chilean barque took the mate back to Valparaiso, carrying a letter to the American Consul. At this time relations between Chile and the United States were strained, but on 29 November the Chilean naval vessel *Huemal* (deer) arrived and took the shipwrecked party back to the mainland. They returned to America on the warship USS *Baltimore*, which had been stationed at Valparaiso during the Chilean Civil War.[4]

The spontaneous combustion of coal on long voyages was not uncommon. All four of the ships that loaded at the same coal jetty as the *Rappahannock* were lost in the same way, which suggests the coal had been loaded wet. Today *Rappahannock*'s mighty iron capstan sits in the surf, between the tides at San Juan Bautista, just across the bay from the jetty, mute testimony to a long forgotten disaster. A century and more in the sea, constantly grinding against the smooth steely rocks of the foreshore have left it worn and weather-beaten, almost indistinguishable from its surroundings. Another crew was reported to be at Juan Fernández that year, from the British ship *Carpathian*. HMS *Melpomene* was detached to check. Although the brief visit to the two islands did not turn up any shipwrecked sailors her captain produced a useful report on Más Afuera and Juan Fernández.[5]

Herman Melville died in 1891. Five years later fellow American Joshua Slocum began a single-handed circumnavigation, a faint echo of earlier glory, reducing the great unknown to a pond that could be crossed by a single man in a decked boat. Where Porter, Dana and Melville went to sea on voyages of war, whaling and trade, Slocum's voyage had been designed from the outset as a literary adventure. He set off with a book deal in his reefer jacket. *Sailing Alone Around the World* recorded a 46,000-mile voyage that took three years to complete. With Slocum's story the Pacific moved from the age of endeavour to the age of leisure.

For all his hard-won seafaring expertise, Slocum was at heart a romantic. Sighting the island in the far distance on 26 April 1895, he wrote that 'a thousand emotions thrilled me'. After a long day's sail, hovering off the rocky coast overnight he got a tow into Cumberland Bay the next morning. Here he met the 'king' of the island, long-time resident Manuel Carroza, an Azorean seaman who had come ashore at this isolated spot after many years serving on New Bedford whalers. He also heard about the absent 'governor' Alfred de Rodt. Slocum fried up some donuts and served them with coffee, taking payment in 'ancient and curious coins … some from the wreck of a galleon sunk in the bay no one knows when'. In all probability they came from Shelvocke's *Speedwell*.[6]

Like any deep-sea mariner, Slocum delighted in a run ashore. His description of the island provides lyrical flourishes similar to those of his scorbutic precursors. It was 'a lovely spot', he wrote: 'The hills are well wooded, the valleys fertile, and pouring down through many ravines are steams of pure water.' There were goats, and perhaps a wild dog or two, but no serpents marred this Pacific Eden. (Descriptions of rambling in the undergrowth with beautiful children take on a sinister twist in the light of his 1906 trial for raping a minor.) The graveyard on the point already contained a fair few burials, of seamen and settlers alike. He heard the sad story of the *Rappahannock*, which he turned to literary effect, noting how the islanders recovered her timbers and utilised them in the construction of houses, which naturally enough presented a ship-like appearance. He made the by now obligatory pilgrimage to the Lookout, and recorded the text of Commodore Powell's plaque. His oft-quoted admonition, 'Blessed Island of Juan Fernández! Why Alexander Selkirk ever left you was more than I could make out', needs to be read in context; Slocum, unlike Selkirk, was enjoying the society of the islanders. Having had his fill of the solitary Selkirk, Slocum took a boat trip to Puerto Inglese (which now rejoiced in the name of Robinson Crusoe Bay), to the hero's cave, which he found 'dry and inhabitable', and well located to avoid the wind. Slocum sailed on 5 May, after a ten-day 'visit to the home and to the very cave of Robinson Crusoe', and wrote the island back into world literature.

Yet nothing on the island is ever quite what it seems. A week later Slocum discovered his 'friend' Manuel Carroza had bilked him out of his potatoes, exchanging a sack full of rotting tubers for his sound vegetables.[7] To his credit Slocum left his initial, favourable, impressions of the Azorean vegetable bandit in the text.

Slocum's romantic sentiments came easily to an old man sailing round the world in a wooden boat: they would become increasingly fashionable as twentieth-century humanity worked ever harder to seek out the last refuges of imagination and eccentricity, isolated places where it was still possible for lost souls to hide. British attention had long been focused elsewhere. American and French naval challenges collapsed in the 1850s, leaving the South Pacific under British imperial dominion. British ships just kept on coming back. In late February 1902 the flagship of the Pacific Station, HMS *Warspite* added her name to an unwritten visitor's book. Rear Admiral Bickford reported:

On the 19th of February I left Valparaiso in the *Warspite*, and arrived off Juan Fernández Island on the morning of the 21st February. Part of the Quarterly Target Practice was carried out that forenoon, and the ship anchored in Cumberland Bay in the afternoon. General leave was given by watches, which appeared to be much appreciate (judging by the numbers who availed themselves of the opportunity) and fresh beef of very good quality was obtained for the crew.[8]

After firing her four 9.2-inch guns at a floating target, the elderly armoured cruiser, limping home to pay off, spent the afternoon of 21 February and all of the following day cleaning the ship, washing clothes and giving the crew leave. They obtained 812 pounds of fresh beef. Having mustered the crew at quarters, to ensure none of them harboured Selkirkian ambitions, the anchor was raised at 8.55 pm, beginning a stately passage to Coquimbo at no more than eight knots, the same cruising speed as Anson's *Centurion*. Bickford forgot to mention that Able Seaman John Walter had been lost overboard while hoisting out the target, despite a rapid reversal of course and launching a boat. The old connections of the island persisted, it was a place where sailors died, where ships found fresh food and water, and guns were fired. It is likely some of the *Warspite*'s officers scratched their names into the rocky walls of the lookout, joining the growing collection that surrounded Commodore Powell's ferrous testament.

Warspite's visit, entirely routine for ships on the Pacific Station spoke eloquently of the close relationship between Britain and Chile. The British were in Chile for many reasons, but most revolved around commercial opportunities, with shipping and mining high on the list. Chile was closely integrated into the 'informal' British empire of capital, trade and naval protection. This was a relationship of mutual benefit. Both parties made money, Chile acquired a powerful patron, and Britain had access to the best harbour on the coast. After 1830 the country was an attractive place to live and do business, political stability ensured by an oligarchic political system dominated by landowners. British merchants dominated business at Valparaiso, and by 1850 Chilean imports and exports, each worth £4 million. The British held the keys to the Chilean economy, and they outnumbered other foreign merchants by a factor of two or three. By the 1870s there were around 4,000 Britons in Chile, mostly engaged in commerce and mining. British trade surpassed that of France, Germany and the United States combined. British global shipping networks linked supplier to market, enabling both the Californian and Australian gold rushes to be fed with Chilean grain.

The presence of the Royal Navy at Valparaiso, where most of the British community lived, was a useful (if largely latent) source of support. To many observers it seemed that Valparaiso 'was little more than an English colony'. The Navy 'remained off the coast, a silent but potent demonstration of British authority'. It upheld law and order at a time when civil wars and instability were not uncommon, reassured the business community, and reduced the risks of regional trade. In large part this was self-interest. British companies dominated Chilean coastal shipping. Later, British submarine telegraph cable companies secured a commanding position on key routes to and through Chile.[9] Down to 1879 copper had been Chile's main export, most ships heading to Swansea for smelting, and a return cargo of Welsh coal. As copper production slowed, the explosive growth of nitrate exports absorbed even more sailing ships. The acquisition of the arid, nitrate rich Atacama region from Peru and Bolivia in the Pacific War of 1879–1881 suited British capitalists. Fearing Peru meant to nationalise their holdings, they funded and supplied the Chilean military. The dominance of extractive industries ensured Chilean industry and transport networks developed to service mining and farming.

While Anglo-Chilean trade largely ignored Juan Fernández, the island was soon back in the headlines. Early in the twentieth century the pursuit of the unusual and romantic saw it join a long list of places hitherto visited only by seamen, castaways and lunatics of many different types among the headline destinations of an oceanic cruise. In 1912 the 'Round the World Scientific and Sporting Cruise' company offered passages on the elderly Royal Mail Steam Packet *Atrato*, a small two-funnelled ship of ancient profile that had served out her time on the West Indies route. The outline itinerary suggested a mammoth undertaking, stopping at any island, port or coast that had some pretension to fame. Juan Fernández followed the Straits of Magellan and Valparaiso, and was in turn followed by Easter Island in a mighty catalogue of wonders suitable for those undertaking 'off beaten tracks' shooting, fishing, scientific, antiquarian and historic research. 'Catering by Messrs Fortnum & Mason' would ensure there was little danger of scurvy. Despite the fanfare, the cruise never departed.[10]

The Battle of Cumberland Bay

—〜〜〜—

By 1914 it seemed Juan Fernández was no longer of any interest: a small fishing settlement with no commerce, steamships rarely visited. Yet two centuries of intermittent occupation, charting, picnics and assumed ownership left a potent legacy. In the British world view Juan Fernández remained an informal possession, a place to be used. When the First World War broke out Britain's global network of sea control, oceanic communications markets and supplies had to be secured.

British strategy was primarily economic and imperial, and focused on the need to protect a network of shipping routes, dominated by British ships, and others insured in London, and linked into the British commercial system. France, Russia and the United States no longer threatened British oceanic communications: the new threat came from Imperial Germany, which had far fewer ships and bases outside Europe. In August 1914 the German threat in the Pacific was limited to a handful of regular cruisers, the East Asia squadron of Vice Admiral Maximilian Graf von Spee. This did not constitute a significant danger, and there was no need for a global convoy system to deal with it. Good intelligence, communications dominance and control of the coal supply would suffice. The Germans could only operate as fugitives, hiding in the distant spaces of the broad ocean. While the Pacific coastline of Chile and Peru appeared distant and unimportant in 1914, nothing could be further from the truth. If the British Empire was going to win the war it would need Chilean nitrates, Argentine beef, Australian grain and global communications. Any break in the world shipping system was potentially fatal. Britain relied on communications dominance to keep track on the German ships, but the system was imperfect, especially in the South Pacific, between Tahiti and Juan Fernández, where there were few telegraph cables or wireless relays, and most merchant ships still relied on sails.

The vast range of oceanic trade explained why the British were relatively confident about the security of their shipping – steam had become essential for modern warships, and only Britain had the facilities to operate steam warships in the South Pacific. In the sailing ship era the threat had been more substantial; the British planned to secure a Pacific pair for the Falkland Islands, occupying Juan Fernández or one of the San Félix group further north. These islands had been secretly visited, surveyed and assessed. Although very much part of British strategic planning, they were never mentioned in public. The telegraph cable, steam navigation and the local naval dominance of Chile reduced the risk just as exports of nitrates began to rocket, making Chile an essential economic partner, and boosting the demand for large sailing ships to bring the noisome cargoes home to Britain. By 1900 this vital trade seemed secure, and the Pacific Station was greatly reduced. After the construction of an imperial dry dock at Esquimalt in British Columbia in the late 1880s, to service modern warships, it had been hoped that Canada would pick up some of the burden. When Canada took over the dockyard in 1905 the British stood down the Pacific Station, and assets were withdrawn to face the Germans in European waters. This left a gaping hole in the British global trade defence system.

In 1914 Admiral von Spee moved into that vast, empty space. Like Anson he set out to disrupt and damage a global imperial system that he could not hope to destroy. The German Admiral would have to operate on oceans dominated by British ships, communications and coal. His force, two armoured and one light cruiser, with supporting colliers, left the German colonies around Samoa, moving east to attack French Tahiti on 22 September. Although von Spee forced the British and their Japanese allies to concentrate their heavy units, he was comprehensively outclassed by the newer, faster and substantially more powerful battlecruiser

HMAS *Australia*. Having failed to score any decisive blows in the region, and well aware that he faced a superior force von Spee set a course for Chile.

The British had several options. Rear Admiral Patey, commanding the Royal Australian Navy, anticipated Spee's move and favoured pursuit. His superiors in London preferred to secure Australian sea lanes while troop convoys were sent to seize German Pacific Colonies and to reinforce the European theatre. They kept Patey and the *Australia* patrolling round Fiji, Samoa and New Caledonia while von Spee set course for South America. Using radio von Spee rendezvoused with two more light cruisers at Easter Island, and summoned vital colliers to Más Afuera, fearing the residents of Juan Fernández had a working radio. In reality they did not. The coal came from commercial stocks in Chile. Later it transpired the colliers were ex-German merchant ships, lately transferred to Chilean owners. Although they flew the Chilean flag, officers, crew and cargo were German. Under international law belligerent merchant vessels could not change their ownership and registration, but the British Foreign Office, without consulting the Admiralty, allowed Chileans to 'buy' 25 ships, complete with German crew. They would refuel von Spee.[1]

There was a certain irony in the indignant *Times* headline of 23 November, 'Juan Fernández as a Base', but only because the base was 'Coaling German Warships'. The Chileans had tracked the Kosmos Company steamers *Negada* and *Luxor* but failed to stop them clearing port. These two ships, along with the newly American registered *Sacramento*, which had been allowed to proceed from San Francisco, supplied von Spee. The *Sacramento*'s owners claimed to have 'sold' the coal to the Germans, but they brought the crew of the French barque *Valentine*, sunk by the German cruiser *Dresden* off Más Afuera. Confronted with clear evidence of German malpractice and local weakness Chile promised to uphold its neutrality, quickly dispatching the armed training ship *General Baquedano* to check the islands for any residual German presence.[2]

News that von Spee was heading for the Chilean port of Coronel, which had a large German community and commercial interests, prompted Admiral Sir Christopher Cradock, hurriedly dispatched from the Atlantic, to arrange the rendezvous for his colliers at Juan Fernández. Hurrying north to locate the enemy before he could damage British commerce Cradock left his battleship, HMS *Canopus,* to escort the colliers. They never arrived. Cradock encountered von Spee off Coronel late on 1 November 1914. Neither admiral had expected to meet the other in full force. Cradock considered his orders were to fight to the end, despite being heavily outnumbered. Von Spee had more ships and heavy guns, the advantage of light and well-trained crews. Cradock's flagship HMS *Good Hope* and the armoured cruiser HMS *Monmouth* blew up; there were no survivors. The light cruiser HMS *Glasgow* and the Armed Merchant Cruiser *Otranto* escaped. Although they won the Germans had used half their ammunition, which was impossible to replace.

Stunned by the defeat and galvanised by the return to office of Admiral Lord Fisher, the Admiralty despatched a suitable force to resolve the situation. On 4 November their Lordships directed a pincer movement of battlecruisers, ships built with the speed and firepower to destroy armoured cruisers. *Princess Royal* went to the Caribbean entrance of the Panama Canal, *Invincible* and *Inflexible* set out for Cape Horn, and *Australia* was belatedly ordered to the west coast of Central America, to check the Panama Canal and then sweep south. *Australia* left Suva on 14 November, and arrived on the Mexican coast twelve days later. Admiral Patey had orders to visit the coasts and islands of Central and South America: he began by searching the Galápagos archipelago between 4 and 6 December. The islands were clear, so he headed northeast to inspect the Gulf of Panama and follow the coast south to Guayaquil.

These movements were interrupted on 10 December, just as the *Australia* entered the Bay of Panama, by news that von Spee's force had been almost entirely destroyed by *Invincible, Inflexible* and other ships of Vice Admiral Sir Doveton Sturdee's force off the

Falkland Islands two days earlier. With both German armoured cruisers sunk there was no need for British battlecruisers in the Pacific, the South Atlantic or the Caribbean. Only the fugitive light cruiser *Dresden* remained at large, with a few transports and the armed merchant ship *Prinz Eitel Friedrich*. Surplus to requirements Patey was directed to take his flagship through the Canal, but the Canal had been closed to heavy traffic and new orders were sent on 12 December to make the long passage south through the Straits of Magellan. The route took in three locations where German ships had called, or were expected to call: Callao, San Félix and Valparaiso. At Valparaiso *Australia* was to rendezvous with two ships from Sturdee's force, the armoured cruiser HMS *Kent* and the armed merchant cruiser HMS *Orama,* which were working up the coast. Between calling at Callao on 18 December and reaching Valparaiso on the 26th, *Australia* stopped at San Félix. The inspection reflected more than a century of interest in these islands, dating back to James Colnett's visit. With *Australia* heading south the Admiralty recalled Admiral Sturdee's battlecruisers, just as HMS *Inflexible* set a course for the Juan Fernández, 'which the Germans had been using so freely as a rendezvous'.[3]

After making a powerful impression on those who retained any lingering German sympathies, *Australia* left Valparaiso on the 27th, stopped off Coronel to lay a wreath at the battle-field the following day, and entered the Straits of Magellan on 31 December. After coaling at the Falklands, *Australia* captured the 5,000-ton German supply ship *Eleonore Woermann*, which had been attempting to link up with the *Dresden* on the 6 December. Superior force, communication dominance and good cruiser work had dismantled German plans for a war on trade.

By December 1914 both Chile and Peru, recognising how blatantly Germany had abused their neutrality, had interned the German colliers, forcing *Prinz Eitel Friedrich*, waiting for supplies at isolated Easter Island, to leave the Pacific.[4] That left the last of von Spee's warships, the light cruiser *Dresden* hiding in the maze of inlets around the Straits of Magellan and Tierra del Fuego, violating the rights of belligerent warships to stop for 24 hours in neutral harbours. By this time the British were intercepting German radio traffic, enabling the armoured cruiser HMS *Kent* to catch *Dresden* at the rendezvous she had set for her colliers on 7 March. Once again *Dresden* escaped, only to limp into Cumberland Bay on 8 March, her boilers almost burnt out by sustained high speed running, desperately short of coal, effectively out of ammunition, short of most stores and without any spare boiler tubes. The German ship was barely operational. Under International Law the Germans had 24 hours to complete their repairs and provisions before leaving, alternatively they could accept internment. Captain Ludecke ignored the Chilean authorities on the island, the lighthouse keeper, because the Chileans had no means of enforcing their neutrality. He pressed on with boiler repairs, hoping to reach the Chilean naval base at Talcahuano before interning his ship.

Once again *Dresden* was betrayed by coded signals requesting a collier to rendezvous in the Bay sent on 9 March. The message was intercepted by the British light cruiser *Glasgow*, and decoded by her signals officer. Captain John Luce headed for Juan Fernández with *Kent* and the Armed Merchant Cruiser *Orama*. On the morning of 14 March *Glasgow* approached Cumberland from the west; the more powerful *Kent* came round the eastern end of the island. They found *Dresden* still flying German colours, and getting up steam ready to sail, forewarned by lookouts on the mountain ridge. Anxious to complete his mission, Captain Luce steamed into the Bay, carefully placing the *Glasgow* in a position that ensured any shells that missed the German cruiser would not land on San Juan Bautista. Opening fire at 8,400 yards, *Glasgow* hit the stationary ship with the first salvo, *Kent* followed and within three minutes the Germans had hauled down their colours, claiming they were already interned, detonated the forward magazine and scrambled ashore. The Armed Merchant Cruiser *Orama* joined in just as the ceasefire was ordered. Not all the British shells hit the target; half a dozen unexploded six-inch rounds remain buried in the hills behind the *Dresden*'s position. Eight Germans died and sixteen were wounded; the latter were treated on board the *Orama*, which carried them to Valparaiso. *Dresden* sank an hour later. Her remains lie 200 feet down at the western end of the Bay. Captain Luce settled local claims for damages with the lighthouse keeper and departed: 'leaving the islands to the age long loneliness from which they had been so rudely awakened by the limitless spread of the war'.[5] Any loneliness had always been more apparent than real.

Chile protested the violation of her neutrality by both Britain and Germany. Britain explained that the German ships using Juan Fernández as a base between September 1914 and March 1915 had sunk British merchant ships, and that in the absence of any Chilean authorities on shore able to uphold their neutrality the Royal Navy had a right to enter Chilean waters and destroy the enemy. This argument was accepted by Chile. The Germans ignored the complaint for six months, fatally damaging their case. The German crew were interned on the mainland for the rest of the war, although Wilhelm Canaris, head of the Abwehr spy organisation in the Second World War, escaped. After the war the German community in Chile erected a memorial to the men who died in the battle; they lie in a plot that overlooks the last anchorage of the *Dresden*, only a few hundred yards from the place where they died. After the war Hugo Wever, a survivor of the ship, came back to live up in the hills above Lord Anson Valley, a solitary existence that earned him the title of the German Crusoe.

The South Pacific may have seemed to be no more than a minor backwater, briefly fought over – but the reality was very different. Once the last German ships had been destroyed Chilean nitrates flowed to Britain, enabling the allies to make fertiliser and high explosive. The continued functioning of the entire global trading system was a matter of the utmost importance; Britain could not risk the loss of any single segment of that system. Despite the setback at Coronel, the British global system worked; the German cruisers had been hunted down and destroyed, allowing the Empire to concentrate heavy naval units at home, and control the oceanic trade routes. The worldwide phase of the war was over, but it was not forgotten. In 1918 the Admiralty and the Foreign Office returned to the South Pacific.

From the *Challenger* to the Admiralty Handbook

As the official summary of scientific results confidently predicted, the *Challenger* expedition 'opened out a new era in the study of Oceanography', while the novelty and richness of the results attracted the attention of many leading scientists and geographers. The voyage had 'opened new doors to the geographer', while oceanography became 'a favoured scientific study', a discipline around which all manner of scientific, anthropological, geological and historical studies could coalesce.[1] The relevance of such studies to the needs of a unique global empire was understood by the academic empire builders of late Victorian Britain. This research, like so much of the British project, would enhance imperial strategic power through knowledge rather than strength. Maritime powers need to be better informed, more intelligent and supremely adept if they were going to compete with larger and more populous continental powers. Victorian Britain exemplified those qualities.

During the First World War, the Naval Intelligence Division commissioned handbooks on fifty nations of strategic, economic or political interest. It was no accident that the general editor, Henry Newton Dickson (professor of geography at Reading University), had worked on the *Challenger* data. This may explain the strikingly fulsome treatment of Juan Fernández in the final text. Dickson's pre-war career in commercial geography placed him at the heart of the growing link between academic research and strategic needs of the state. His interest in the global distribution of key commodities like wheat and oil, together with means to move them, dovetailed perfectly with Admiralty thinking. Dickson had worked with imperial geographical thinker Sir Halford Mackinder.[2] These connections harnessed the scientific foundations laid by the *Challenger* to the contemporary political/strategic imperatives of empire.

The project began in July 1915, with the battle of Cumberland Bay still fresh in the memory of its creator, director of naval intelligence Admiral Reginald 'Blinker' Hall. The project was based at the Royal Geographical Society in Kensington, revealing the hitherto discrete role of the state in a major intelligence organisation that had operated for 80 years conveniently disguised as mere amateurish curiosity. The handbooks, incisive resumes of topography, communications, populations and trade, would facilitate 'the discussion of naval, military, and political problems, as distinct from the examination of the problems themselves.'[3] The *Confidential Handbook on the Juan Fernández and San Ambrosio–San Félix Islands* was printed in time for the Paris Peace Conference.

Pairing the Juan Fernández Islands with San Félix and San Ambrosio was significant.[4] Long-term British interest, the specifics of the *Dresden* affair, and an enduring concern to record and assess every potential oceanic base in a vast ocean, obvious from pre-war research, visits and instructions, gave these isolated fragments a significance far beyond their negligible economic utility. The Admiralty was well aware, even if the printed text did not mention the fact, that von Spee had rendezvoused at Más Afuera, while Admiral Cradock had planned to base his colliers at Más a Tierra. These islands were critical to coal powered strategy in the South Pacific.

Despite four hundred years of unchallenged title, the Foreign Office handbook dismissed Chilean sovereignty over the Juan Fernández group as little more than sentiment, preferring to stress their misgovernment by the Spanish, and the Chileans:

Chilean satisfaction at the possession of these islands would probably be found, if analysed, to be mainly due to national sentiment, which in its turn is derived from their geographical propinquity and their transition from Spanish sovereignty to the dominion of the Republic at the time when its independence was achieved. Más a Fuera is practically valueless to Chile, It has never been permanently colonised, and is still (1918) without a single inhabitant ... The island has no harbour; there is not even a bay or roadstead where a vessel can anchor in security; but, being more than 6,000 ft in altitude it is visible from a great distance in clear weather and serves the navigator as an unerring guide to his position ... . Más a Tierra also serves as a sea-mark.[5]

Despite the implication that the islands were badly run and valueless to Chile, the Foreign Office stressed that 'the most natural, just and expedient status' would be for them to remain Chilean. However, the handbook made a clear distinction between these islands and 'San Félix and San Ambrosio', which 'are not specifically mentioned in the first article of the Chilean Constitution, in which the boundaries of the Republic are broadly defined. The islands are still without inhabitants, and are rarely visited even by fishermen.' Furthermore, while these islands were isolated and secluded in peacetime, the handbook noted:

It may well be otherwise in time of war, when the belligerents are naval powers. The roadstead of San Félix affords in some respects better anchorage than any at the Juan Fernández Islands. The holding ground is none of the best at either place, but at San Félix the bottom is more level and the depth more convenient.[6]

Peruvian warships had refuelled at San Félix in 1865, while the possible establishment of a radio transmitter at Más Afuera, von Spee's rendezvous, made the advantage of the more distant islands absolute.

The history of the Juan Fernández group was largely drawn from Vicuña Mackenna's 1883 account *Juan Fernández: historia verdadera*, backed by a useful bibliography of British, American and more recent Chilean publications, among which the discreet mention of volume III of the Admiralty's own *South American Pilot* should not be missed.[7] It sat somewhat incongruously alongside the first English publication by Swedish botanist Carl

Skottsberg, the great scientific analyst of the island's unique ecosystem.[8] Clearly the libraries of the Royal Geographical Society and the Admiralty Hydrographic Office were well equipped. The authors of the *Confidential Handbook* questioned Mackenna's assertion that Juan Fernández had any strategic value for the Chilean Navy:

Even if Chile should go to the expense of fortifying Más-á-Tierra – which is not in the least likely – this would not hinder an enemy ship from coaling at San Félix, though the latter affords no fresh water or provisions.

The threat that the Admiralty envisaged became clear as the text wound to a conclusion. Maximilian von Spee's coal-hungry cruisers were things of the past, the new danger came from large diesel-powered U-boats, stretching around the world to attack the shipping lanes linking Britain to Australasia:

San Félix is also excellently adapted for a temporary base or depot for submarine vessels' stores – petrol, provisions, tanks or barrels of fresh water, even projectiles. Petrol and few light stores might be landed at San Ambrosio in fine weather, and would be less easy of discovery by an enemy searcher than at San Félix.[9]

The published version of 1920 studiously avoided the vexed issues of sovereignty and title, simply reprinting the relevant passage of the Chilean Constitution, in Spanish and English, and despite an editorial claim to be 'substantially as they were issued' for official use, San Félix and San Ambrosio had been excised. While these two barren specks of land were commercially irrelevant, the cut had a deeper purpose. The Admiralty was remarkably well informed about this group of barren islands, and the many uses to which they had been put. Passages deprecating the merits of Spanish and Chilean rule remained, although without the link to questions of sovereignty.

To emphasise the distinct objectives of the two texts, the San Ambrosio group was only mentioned once in the published edition, as the only other place where the otherwise unique Juan

Fernández rock lobster could be found.[10] The quality of realism was emphasised by the conspicuous passage dealing with the sinking of the *Dresden*. While His Majesty's Government made a full and unreserved apology for breaching Chilean neutrality there was another meaning to be drawn from the insertion of a Foreign Office form of words. A British naval officer facing a similar dilemma in future should act first, leaving the Foreign Office to clear up any diplomatic fallout later.

The Admiralty Handbook was the first truly objective piece of British writing about the islands, a far cry from the romance and wonder of Selkirk and Defoe, the scorbutic musings of Walter or the narrowly technical reports of Philip Parker King. Exploiting a wide range of sources it addressed the practical concerns of naval officers and diplomats; location, utility, sovereignty and resources, peeling away layers of mystery. No longer would Royal Navy warships arrive in Cumberland Bay in thrall to Crusoe and Anson, stumbling into ravines as they searched for non-existent caves and graves. The next visitors knew that the island was Chilean territory and dirt poor; there were few resources, apart from fish.

Not that the British ever entirely left the island at the end of the earth. In 1926 another cruise touching at Juan Fernández was offered to readers of the *Times*. The Pacific Steam Navigation Company's ten-year-old liner *Orduna* would host the 'Cruise of the Season' around South America; the visit to 'Robinson Crusoe's Island Juan Fernández' was the highlight. Departure was set for 6 January 1927. This time we can be sure the *Orduna* reached the island. A picture of her lying in Cumberland Bay, smoke rising from her single funnel, was reproduced in the Second World War Admiralty Handbook on the Pacific Islands.[11]

British commercial interests in Chile peaked in 1914, dominated by nitrate exports. At least 30 per cent of Chilean trade was in British hands and this trade had been essential to the British war effort, an ample reward for the long-term effort to control both the Chilean economy and the South Pacific. After 1918 Britain's commanding position slowly ebbed away. The loss of British capital in the World War, the Great Depression and the Second World War destroyed that influence. Unable to lend large sums to developing economies like Chile Britain lost market share to the United States, an industrial heavyweight and hemispheric power. British governments offered little support when market conditions turned against British interests.[12] By contrast the Royal Navy has retained a major presence in Chile, fully half the modern Chilean Navy consists of second-hand British frigates, while Chilean Naval officers pride themselves on their British connections, and handle their ships with seamanship and skill reflecting two centuries of contact.

Between the wars the Royal Navy made further visits to the isolated, curious islands of Juan Fernández. In June 1929 the light cruiser HMS *Caradoc* arrived after a rough three-day passage from Coronel and anchored off the mole in Cumberland Bay. The officers knew the romantic history of the island, making the now obligatory visit to 'Selkirk's Cave', the lookout, complete with Commodore Powell's iron plaque, and the prisoner's caves at San Juan Bautista. At this point the village had around three hundred inhabitants, 'who live in log huts and obtain their living by fishing'. Crayfish were the key export, kept alive in the bay to await the steamer. To complete the idyllic scene the ship was visited by an exiled Scotsman, who proclaimed himself 'King of the Island'. The cruise journal included a picture of the island showing the hills behind the village remained strikingly bare, doubtless because 'Sheep and goats were seen grazing on the pastures covering the upper slopes of the mountains, whilst cattle grazed contentedly in the peaceful surroundings of the farmsteads in the valley.' The mid-winter weather was generally atrocious, lashing rain storms limiting the opportunities for runs ashore. Instead the crew set about fishing, hauling in vast catches. A paper chase, opportunities to buy local wooden curios and the disappearance of ship's dog ('Bonzo') completed the ten-day visit – the last event suggesting that the lure of island life extended beyond solitary humans.[13] Bonzo joined the descendants of eighteenth-century canine castaways, sent to stop the English using the island.

The Admiralty Handbook remained a useful, if outmoded guide when a second global conflict erupted in 1939, but the Director of Naval Intelligence, Admiral John Godfrey, called for something more detailed and up to date: 'The work of fighting and Government Departments is facilitated if countries of strategic importance are covered by handbooks which deal in a convenient and easily digested form, with their geography, ethnology, administration, and resources.'[14] The significant place accorded to Juan Fernández and its near neighbours suggests little change in British thinking across time. The islands featured in the four-volume compendium *The Pacific Islands*, rather than the cancelled Chilean volume.

Once again Juan Fernández and other isolated specks of Chilean sovereignty that punctuated the vast Southern Ocean were accorded a thorough treatment that belied their territorial insignificance. The sheer scale of the ocean, when compared with the minute specks of land that were under discussion, stressed the point that this volume was about sea lanes; maps and charts stressed the direction and value of trade passing through the Panama canal and heading for Australasia.[15]

The importance of Juan Fernández and the San Ambrosio group, clearly stated in 1919, was left implicit. The descriptions of the four islands were solid, with good diagrams and coastal perspectives of the two Juan Fernández Islands. The history was altogether more succinct, ignoring Anson while adding in a few new errors of fact. Further confusion was created by renaming Selkirk's Mirador as 'Robinson Crusoe's Lookout'. This time there was a radio station in Cumberland Bay. The value of Carl Skottsberg's extensive work on flora, fauna and climate was acknowledged. Ignoring the sovereignty question that had been so prominent in 1919 suggests the authors were well aware that the islands were off the beaten track of this global war. Even the submarine telegraph cables that criss-crossed the globe in the half-century between 1870 and 1920 passed without stopping at Juan Fernández.

Although the Second World War did not reach the islands, the Chilean government took steps to prevent a second *Dresden* incident, removing Hugo Wever as a security risk and landing some second-hand artillery to uphold their neutrality. A pair of Armstrong six-inch guns and some 57-millimetre Krupp weapons in small turrets provided a suitable gesture.[16] In the event, Juan Fernández escaped the twentieth century's second global conflict; it was about as far from the fighting as any place on earth, but the hasty construction of defences to meet the last threat, all too reminiscent of the 1740s, added yet another layer of mystery to an already confused island. The big guns were British, manufactured at Newcastle in 1896 for the cruiser *Esmeralda*, named in honour of Lord Cochrane's greatest exploit as commander in chief of the Chilean Navy. Today the guns stand silent and forlorn at the edge of Cumberland Bay, gaunt reminders of another age. One of them had a children's playground built around it after the 2010 tsunami. Together they stand guard over Lord Anson's valley, and the local store. Grey-green with the patina of age and neglect, the old guns reflect abandoned ideas and ancient things, slowly being drawn into an older landscape, two more uncertain indications of British possession. Their corroded breeches still carry the maker's name and serial numbers, proudly stamped at Elswick-on-Tyne, when Britain ruled the world and Chile was secure behind her strategic aegis. They have joined the rusty shells of eighteenth-century Bourbon cannon, relics of long-forgotten alarms, futile, broken symbols of power pointing out over a harbour more often troubled by natural terrors than human violence.

At least the big guns remained defiantly planted through the latest natural disaster, but the same cannot be said for the 57-millimetre armoured pill boxes. Built to be moved around on wheeled carriages, these pint-sized coastal defence batteries, effectively horse-drawn tanks, were caught out in the open by the tsunami, and redeployed across the two-acre debris field, pathetic upturned monuments to the real power on this island.

28

Making Robinson's Island

—◦◦◦—

In 1935 Juan Fernández became a National Park, largely as a result of a sustained public campaign by Swedish botanist Carl Skottsberg, who embarrassed the Chilean government into action by highlighting the ecological devastation wrought by years of occupation and mismanagement. Sadly, the change of status did not stop the appalling degradation of a unique, fragile ecosystem.

Skottsberg had ample ammunition for his campaign, having visited the islands in 1908 and 1917. In 1956 he published *The Natural History of Juan Fernández*, a three-volume compendium on the unique biosystems of the Juan Fernández group and Easter Island. His detailed study recorded the devastating impact of human activity, slowly building up to a sustained explosion of disgust, blasting the reckless destruction of the island. He did not believe the 'National Park' had made any difference because, as he wryly noted, Mr Otto Rieggel had celebrated its creation by introducing six pairs of rabbits, 'which, as everywhere else, will take what the sheep leave'. The island was now 'being transformed into a cattle and sheep farm, a new and strange type of national park'. He hoped that a moderate increase in tourism to Robinson Crusoe's island would encourage the islanders to abandon destructive attempts to raise cattle and sheep. Instead he wanted to impress visitors with unique flora and fauna, and repair the path up the mountain, because 'everybody will want to see Selkirk's Lookout, ... read the memorial tablet and behold the grand views. And there is no point within easy reach where the endemic flora and fauna was, at least in 1917, – better displayed.' In a savage, sardonic summary, Skottsberg pointed an accusing finger at the Chilean government: 'If the responsible authorities do not change their attitude, Juan Fernández will become a ... disgrace to an enlightened world.'[1] His words bore fruit; Chile finally took the island in hand.

The ongoing battle to 'save' the island's unique ecosystem provides a striking study of the law of unforeseen consequences. Spanish visitors introduced the hardy Pyrenean goat to provide food for hungry mariners, no one stopped to consider the impact these alien creatures might have on an island where all succulent plants were vulnerable to voracious herbivores. Spanish attempts to eradicate the goats failed, leaving them, along with cattle, horses and even rabbits, to reshape the landscape. Modern efforts to restore the island to a pre-contact condition have been thwarted by the local population, who think that their interests take priority over the ecosystem. Notions of an Edenic Paradise remain flawed.

Both Eden and Paradise are Middle Eastern concepts, filled with verdant spaces, trees and an ideal climate: the search for them was a key element in romanticism. The connection with gardens, the Edenic unspoiled version, or Paradise, the skilfully constructed man-made variety, should not be taken too literally. These places are about internal calm, not external vision. Gardens, and garden-like islands, may be used to represent Paradise, but the keys to paradise lie inside each human being.[2] No sooner had the Europeans located 'paradise' in the Americas than they discovered how fragile such places were, how the very things they sought, mineral wealth, timber resources and agricultural land were destroying these unique locations. Soon the new colonial rulers were obliged to think about the impact they were having, and attempt to reconstruct the ecosystem.

In many respects the isolated oceanic island, like the frail ships which carried scientific circumnavigators in the seventeenth and eighteenth centuries, stimulated the emergence of a detached, critical, self-conscious view of European origins and behaviour, of the kind dramatically prefigured by Daniel Defoe in *Robinson Crusoe*. As Darwin had demonstrated on the Galápagos, islands were ideal laboratories for full-scale experimentation and data gathering to check the impact of human activity on plants and animals, soil and climate. English/British critiques of Spanish and Chilean rule over Juan Fernández were invariably a question of inefficient resource management.

Alexander von Humboldt linked these concerns with Indian holist philosophies, stressing the interdependence of man and the natural world. Humboldt's great expedition to South America and his impact on Darwin provide an essential linkage between observation, philosophy and theory. Because uninhabited off-shore islands were less risky to European invaders than the continent, lacking hostile peoples and lethal diseases, they were among the first places to be colonised, studied and ruined. Much early writing was produced by mariners and travellers, largely practical in approach, and impacted by the mental debilities that accompany scurvy. Sir Francis Drake gave the English a taste for oceanic exploits, which prompted a rapid expansion of print culture. These texts invested islands with Edenic qualities of fruitfulness, which were soon linked to Renaissance botanical gardens, man-made versions of Paradise. A century later islands were equally capable of becoming utopias, promised lands distant from the disorders of the old world, including the English Civil War. John Milton's *Paradise Lost* was not unconnected with these precious, distant refuges, which took a prominent place in the escapist literature of the age. As literacy rates rose, the scale and variety of publications expanded, and took greater notice of market trends. Publishing crazes, already in full swing by the end of the seventeenth century, saw travel literature become the most widely consumed genre.[3]

While islands were invested with quasi-religious significance international law emphasised that colonial annexation was only legitimate if the colonisers cleared and worked, or 'improved' the land. Man must dominate nature to earn title; if they left the land unused the colonists had no legal right to ownership. Introducing European livestock devastated semi-arid landscapes, the destruction of the grass and low scrub prompting extensive soil erosion. As the soil slipped into the sea paradise became desert. The British response began when Sir Joseph Banks pressed the government to enact forest legislation to reverse the tide, like his French contemporaries Banks's particular focus was the potential of tropical forests for shipbuilding. It soon became clear that deforestation and soil erosion reduced rainfall, especially on mountain areas, and that the key to regeneration was the restoration of high level tree cover. Scientific insight collided with the romantic cult of the tropical island when Rousseau developed Crusoe and Anson into the idea that an island of untamed nature would be an ideal redemptive space for Europeans. Natural gardens would help to restore virtue to modern society. Crusoe's redemption through hard work, faith and good deeds, physical, rather than intellectual exercise, made him the ideal romantic hero. Rousseau himself came no closer to Crusoe than a two month occupation of the Swiss island of St Pierre on Lake Bienne, in the autumn of 1765, but that left him in raptures. This melding of paradise and utopia into an ideal society, prompted by islands of the South Pacific, took root in Britain almost as soon as it appeared.[4] Island life was attractive to French and German readers, restricted to the European continent by wars and upheaval in an age of revolution and chaos, not least because Anglo-French conflicts made such places impossible to reach. The series of wars that raged across Europe between 1778 and 1815 made the Pacific an unattainable dreamscape for continental readers. That they chose to travel with Crusoe as well as Cook only emphasised the fact that all journeys combine exploration and imagination.

Rousseau's Pacific built on an older perception of this vast empty space, and the tiny islands that gave it scale and meaning. From the early sixteenth century, travellers' tales such as those of Hawkins, Schouten and Le Maire provided utopian and paradisiacal dreams with a suitably exotic locus, a development that accelerated as Enlightenment science shifted man from the centre of the picture. The island became an ideal laboratory in which to examine the nature of society, the impact of difference, and of alternative societies but little removed from More's *Utopia* or Bacon's *New Atlantis*. The boundaries between purely imagined tales, invented scenarios set on real islands, often, like Gulliver, with real people in them, and apparently simple accounts of castaway existence blurred, refracting reality into a myriad of shapes and colours. The explosion of buccaneer literature around 1700 took Juan Fernández into the heart of this fluid mental world. The genre of island life carried potent religious, cultural, and moral meaning, the well-being of the island acquiring a moral dimension.[5] Crusoe's improving stewardship was rewarded by dominion over man and beast. In the late twentieth century Chile tried to combine environmental restoration of indigenous species with tourist opportunities.

In the spring of 1965 American academic Ralph Woodward led a party of students to the island, still a serious expedition at that date, requiring a boat journey from the mainland, and lengthy, complex bureaucratic procedures. 'Our principal desire was to see Selkirk's cave', he observed, paying a dutiful visit to Puerto Inglese, where cattle, goats and sheep were being raised, to see the much-frequented shrine of misguided American Robinsoniana. The expedition camped out at San Juan Bautista, climbed 'Selkirk's Mirador', visited Blanca Luz Brum (the Uruguayan painter and hostel owner), and got to know the locals. Woodward was struck by the sincere and genuine hospitality of a community with limited resources. There were around 580 people living on the island, while a small, strikingly eccentric trickle of visitors came to search for things that did not exist. Woodward followed up the visit, recovering much of the history of the island from Spanish, English and American sources.[6] Coincidentally, Blanca Luz petitioned the Chilean authorities to change the island's name from Más a Tierra to Robinson Crusoe, with an eye on the emerging tourist industry. In 1966 Chile acted, renaming Más Afuera for Alexander Selkirk at the same time ('Alejandro Selkirk Island'), forestalling a Venezuelan project to name an island in memory of Defoe's hero. The irony that neither Crusoe nor Selkirk ever set foot on the islands named for them was overlooked, completing the bizarre collusion of fiction and fact that has dominated perceptions of the islands for centuries. While mass tourism has yet to hit the distinctly cool beaches of Cumberland Bay, the new names ensured no one need wonder where these great stories had taken place, or where to go to fulfil a childhood fantasy. Selkirk and Crusoe had made islands into places of magic and wonder, rather than the setting for grim, lonely death. They became places of redemption, utopian escapes from the world and all its wickedness.

Three decades later, American travel writer Thurston Clarke arrived, seeking Crusoe and other castaways. Juan Fernández was only the first of many islands that became the subject of Clarke's *Islomania*, a theme drawn from Richard Henry Dana's richly interleaved vision of a childhood possession, a Robinsonian space rendered sacred by memory and lush, aromatic, fruitfulness. Characterising Juan Fernández as 'King Kong's Island married to a finger of Lawrence of Arabia's Desert' reflected the impact of technicolour cinemascope on travel writing. Clarke did not travel alone; indeed, his fellow travellers proved a particularly rich literary resource, as they drank in beachfront bars plastered with news cuttings about Hugo Wever. Clarke claimed he had seen Crusoe's cave, although it was evidently the same place Woodward had attributed to Selkirk, and followed John Ross Brown's account in *Crusoe's Island* a century before. Such mismatches between fiction and fact had continued throughout the intervening century and a half. The odd rock formation at Puerto Inglese is still troubled by Americans looking for something that cannot be there. In such situations the locals have always been willing to fill the void. When the first excursion steamers arrived from Valparaiso early in the twentieth century they encountered islanders dressed as Crusoe and Friday, paddling about the bay in log boats to earn some cash.

The downside for any modern traveller, as Dana noted in the 1830s, was the indolent lassitude of the islanders. Their quiet, temperate paradise made only limited demands on their time and effort, offering no obvious occasion for great exertion of body or mind. While Clarke avoided explicitly concurring in that judgement, he did cite James and Mayme Bruce's highly censorious article in *The Explorer's Journal* of 1992. The article missed the point; if the locals evinced 'no curiosity or interest', living at an agonisingly slow pace, these were the very qualities that had endeared them to Joshua Slocum. Air travel denied modern tourists the opportunity to acclimatise, they arrive still thinking in the western clock time of flight schedules, an error that persists for at least a week, unaware of the deeper rhythms that dominate isolated fishing communities around the world. Clarke's local guide offered a telling insight, fearful that cruise liners might arrive, overwhelming the fragile way of life and the equally vulnerable ecosystem of a place ill-suited to modern tourism. At a deeper level the guide feared mass tourism would generate a cash economy, exacerbating divisions within the community. Clarke noted an extensive barter-based trading system at work, while locals 'feared development more than isolation' and were desperate not to leave. This was a constant trope of islander life. Such sentiments were reinforced by an eccentric bunch of incomers. Many were romantic dreamers, looking to drop out of the race. The island was a self-contained world, one where incomers could disappear after life-changing events. An Argentine couple reflected, 'this island slowly takes over the conscious mind, burying it in its soil'. Clarke concluded no one who had lived on Juan Fernández could ever truly escape. Some islanders reported that Selkirk haunted the famous Mirador, and they were taken very seriously. Richard Halliburton climbed the romantic viewpoint every day for a whole month, hoping to commune with the spirit of the monosyllabic Scot. Had the old man turned up Halliburton might have been surprised by a foul-mouthed rant, in a thick accent followed by an invitation to fisticuffs. Clarke concluded by describing Juan Fernández as a place 'where people come to find, or lose, themselves' where dreamers were often disappointed. Despite a sequence of island-hopping travels he found this one simply too remote to be attractive and, like most modern visitors, left with much the same sense of relief that islanders display when they return from the mainland.[7]

Clarke's enjoyable incomprehension reflected a deeply continental perspective. Describing the island as surrounded and cut off by the ocean, when in reality the ocean was the key to the island, itself a marginal space where land and sea interact in a strikingly unusual way, said more about him than it did about the location or character of Juan Fernández and its people. A community that lives by fishing can hardly be 'cut off' by the ocean.

Another recent visitor, author Diana Souhami, arrived in December 1999, high summer on Juan Fernández, to research the Selkirk story. Soon 'The Island' became a critical character in her story, a mysterious, volcanic place forever being invaded, abandoned, reinvented and reimagined. Here the islanders lived in a curious mix of ancient and modern, including cash payment and intermittent access to the worldwide web. They had a school, a doctor, a dentist and a midwife, but no pharmacy, hospital or vet. Secondary schooling involved leaving the island for the year, after which more boys than girls came home. Despite strict rules, including a ban on tethering livestock to the goalposts on the football pitch by the harbour, the 'gendarmes' had little to do. Local taxes funded the water supply and maintained the jetty. The dirt strip airfield provided an intermittent service to Santiago, exchanging live crayfish for medical cases and the odd tourist. The main link to 'the Continent' was the monthly supply ship *Navarino*, curiously named for a famous naval battle in a Greek bay. Supplies of fuel, building materials, tools, toys and trinkets shared space with vegetables and fruit. The island remained fertile, but rarely has anyone worked the land with serious intent. De Rodt's cattle-ranching ambitions created a gaucho culture of herding and pastoralism, wrecking the fragile soils to produce a little stringy beef. Several islanders confessed that anyone growing vegetables was sure to have them stolen, or trodden into the earth before they were ripe. They wait for tired vegetables to arrive by boat, and serve them with the freshest of fish.

The way to the island had changed in the 1970s, when an airstrip was laid out at El Puente at the far end of the island, linked to Bahía del Padre (Horseshoe Bay) by dirt road. The bay has a fine jetty, and massive herds of seals and sea lions that have lost their fear of humans since they acquired protected status in 1978. They bask, play and feed, filling the air with the same snorts, shouts and cries, night and day, that once startled Selkirk and Shelvocke. Then visitors make the ninety-minute trip to San Juan Bautista in a local fishing boat, running along the coast, much as Dampier, Selkirk, Shelvocke and Anson had, bewitched by the sudden strangeness of waterfalls cascading into the ocean, verdant valleys and scorched uplands, weird rock formations and rough beaches. For those able to take their eyes off the scenery a rich parade of marine life offers an alternative spectacle, dolphins and whales supported by flocks of seabirds, quick to exploit the fishy panic caused by hunting cetaceans. These are rich waters, where the Humboldt Current flowing up from the Antarctic meets warmer air.

Down on the beach at San Juan Bautista, Souhami found an assorted aggregation of shacks, together with the odd new guest house, providing all the accommodation, entertainment and souvenirs required at the end of the world. Alongside the local community, travellers, eccentrics and dreamers could experience the island life, indulge curiously ahistorical visions of hybrid Selkirk/Crusoe figures living on an island that had changed a great deal since 1704, listen to improbably tall tales, enjoy stiff climbs and boats trips laced with sea spray and startling sights. The airstrip may have eased access, but it did nothing to reduce the cost. Tourism remained exotic, and no one comes to Juan Fernández without some thought and a good deal of cash.

One of the more promising lines of business was ecological, visitors coming to sample the unique and strange flora and fauna. Early visitors only bothered to identify strange plants and creatures if they could eat them, or harvest them for profit. Most of the native sandalwood ended up in China, along with the pelts of the fur seals; the crayfish still travel to their doom in the best Santiago restaurants. Pioneering naturalists and botanists quickly identified many species as unique, and more recently the entire ecosystem has been understood, the remnants of a totally unique pre-human island. Carl Skottsberg's great book put the island ecosystem on the map. Unique and irreplaceable it may be, but the island is also home to around 500 people, who use it in much the same way that people around the world use their land. They cut down trees for timber and fuel, introduce non-native plants and graze their livestock. The results have been predictable. Without vegetation the soil erodes, blackberry bushes choke the native species, and cattle compound the ecological problems by exposing the soil and damaging natural drainage. The introduction of rabbits and Uruguayan coati deepened the devastation.

A belated counter-attack was launched in 1969 when a Chilean biologist with the suitably resolute name of Pizzaro demanded boundaries on the National Park, banning any construction or motor vehicles, exterminating the cattle, rabbits, coati, rats and even cats, along with the invasive blackberry. Four years later the Chilean forestry commission, CONAF (Corporación Nacional Forestal), acquired responsibility for the island, with a mandate to preserve and restore indigenous species. The park boundaries were marked, the exploitation of resources inside the park banned. After decades of living without rule or restraint local people found themselves restricted by a nature reserve, without any say in the way it was run. Predictably they ignored the rules. This led to confrontation, abuse and even violence. While the global attempt to end ecological degradation has many supporters it would appear remarkably few of them live on Juan Fernández. Local opposition did not stop UNESCO declaring the island a Worldwide Reserve of the Biosphere in 1977, a suitably grand title that meant little to people banned from cutting trees and grazing cattle on their own small speck of land.

Instead the project attracted foreign support. Dutch descendants of Schouten and Roggeveen provided $2.5 million, while
Communist Czechoslovakia offered equipment to begin the
revival of indigenous species, and chemicals to clear the invasive
maquis. Chile would pay the CONAF staff. Boundaries were
set: the villagers had 1,000 acres to call their own, along with
a section around the airstrip. The state claimed the remaining
24,000 acres and the outlying island of Santa Clara as a reserve.
Work on the restoration was always going to be slow; it began
with the high forest on the slopes of El Yunque, where some
indigenous plants survived. Working slowly downhill the invasive
species have been eradicated, replaced with newly germinated
indigenes. To reduce losses among new plants the rabbits had
a price put on their tails, encouraging the locals to shoot them.
Planting fast-growing eucalyptus and cypress trees on the lower
slopes helped to stabilise the soil, while providing timber and
firewood, reducing the temptation to cut rare species.

CONAF's garden and research centre in San Juan provides
work for locals and education for visitors, with regular crops of
cabbage palms, flowering shrubs, chonta pine, myrtle, orchids,
campanula and even sandalwood. The nursery also attracts the
indigenous hummingbirds. Reviving the island's native species
holds out the prospect of ecotourism, but the economics of travel
suggest that progress on this front will be limited. Things become
more complicated when it is understood that some invasive
species have become staples of the ecosystem, buzzards feed on
rabbits, blackberry is a major source of fruit and the roots helped
bind the soil. Other invasive species, right down to the amaryllis,
poppies and nasturtiums that bloom brightly along the shores of
Cumberland Bay, will be hard to remove. While CONAF wants
to decide how the island will be, taking life and death decisions,
species by species, 'like Crusoe's God', the pursuit of a perfect
restored island has run head first into a simple fact. The presence
of people on the island, and the frequent arrival of visitors is the
main barrier to ecological reconstruction.[8]

Yet there are positive signs. The restoration of adjacent Santa Clara was completed in 2010. Once known as Goat Island, it is now free of goats, blackberries and rabbits, while native species are growing with great success (both CONAF's seedlings and naturally regenerated plants). On Alejandro Selkirk Island a Dutch-funded goat-clearing programme had to be restrained when the lack of goats allowed the maquis to explode; the task here is on a far grander scale, and will tax the ingenuity of all concerned, unless some way can be found to make the island into a tourist destination. That might require a little imagination.

Islands, Nations and Continents

—◦◦◦◦—

With luck, Robinson Crusoe's island will survive, but what of the English world view that created it? What of Defoe's half-German, upwardly mobile, middle-class hero, and the vast blue ocean he wanted to rule? Will oceanic Englishness endure amid the stultifying mendacity of the new order, where Europe is the present and the future, a world where curiosity is compressed, and everything can be measured and judged in tabular form? Defoe did not advise his countrymen to follow a core curriculum; his island, real or imagined, emerged from free play of the intellect, opportunity and the human ability to be different. In our conformist culture there are no marginal spaces for the wilder flights of fancy. As we read Defoe's book we are losing touch with the essentials of his world, a world that consciously turned away from the Universal Monarchies of Europe, secular and religious, and the static societies they sustained. Crusoe was tolerant, progressive and enlightened, he saved Catholic castaways, converted heathens and defeated cannibals; he made the land fruitful, and did so without setting foot on the continent. He exemplified the 'British' identity of a newly united kingdom, and the dynamic culture that transformed German George I into 'Farmer' George III, the royal agriculturalist improver who helped his island bloom. George III followed Crusoe; he never visited Europe.

The high days of Crusoe's Empire, the seapower empire conceived by More, Raleigh, Bacon and Defoe, lasted two centuries. It was brought to ruin by the ignorance and folly that stumbled into a massive European war in 1914, and waged it in with such continental intensity that it bled the country dry, emptied the exchequer and pulled the empire asunder. Ironically Britain had won the First World War by December 1914: the remaining years were spent fighting to get the German Army out of France, a task beyond Britain's means, and eccentric to its interests.

The rot set in half a century before, when British statesmen compared their empire with that of Imperial Rome, bragging about its size and ubiquity. This Victorian boast should not detain us long. It was at once a delusion and snare. Not all empires are the same, and Britain's followed the seapower model of Athens, Carthage and Venice, not the militarised continental dominion of Rome. The great swathes of red empire that decorated the British world map of 1900 were mostly empty, uneconomic or assumed. Neither central Australia, nor the frozen North of Canada added as much to Britain's imperial power as Hong Kong, Gibraltar, Malta or Bermuda, fragmentary insular outcrops that, even taken together did not register as territorial assets. Instead they contained the dry docks, communication hubs, coal supplies and machine shops that enabled the Royal Navy to control the world ocean, and the trade that flowed over it. These tiny islands were the key to British imperium, microscopic dots linked by sea routes and submarine telegraph cables that enabled Britain to exert control without a major land footprint.

This approach was essential because Britain never had the manpower to rule a continent by force, as the crushing defeat suffered in 1782 demonstrated. The loss of America had more to do with the limited supply of sailors than soldiers; Britain simply could not keep the supply lines open. Having learned a painful lesson in the realities of global power the British rebuilt their empire on the original maritime lines. 'The sea, the one commodity apart from coal and sheep they had around them in abundance, allowed the British to compensate for sparsity of numbers by mobility and ubiquity.'[1] Critically, Britain prospered because none of its rivals had the luxury of such strategic single-mindedness.

The British experience of Empire was dominated by salt water. After 1782 Britain recognised that colonies of settlement would quickly develop into rooted communities with distinct, local views. Australia, New Zealand, Canada and South Africa were always going to spin off, while colonised peoples only became British by moving to Britain. Only small uninhabited islands like Juan Fernández or the Falklands could become truly British. By forming a link in the imperial chain, they escaped their own limits, much as the British Isles had escaped the limits of Europe, within a larger collective consciousness that tied the state to the sea. And so it is that in the twenty-first century we find the deepest lines of British imperial ambition remain indelibly scored onto the Falklands, tiny windswept outcrops at the end of the earth. The brief conflict of 1982 and the simmering stand-off of the 2010s were, at heart, a question of Britishness. That Britain was prepared to recapture and then defend the Falklands suggests the insular oceanic identity that began with the Tudors has not been entirely overwhelmed by European agendas.

The obverse of that image proved equally potent. Tiny, remote islands came to occupy a remarkably prominent place in the national consciousness, and they still do. They acquired British histories, British maps, British scientific studies and British economic significance. The island mattered because in the vast web of British power, trade and influence they were so few in number, and the individual threads by which they were connected were so terribly slight. Despite its significance, Juan Fernández remained a dream because it was not necessary. Ultimately the British Empire was different:

It was Britain's very smallness that helped to drive – as well as constrain, – its overseas enterprises, for without other peoples' land and resources it could not be powerful. Small can be aggressive, large can be confident and inward looking. However, there is another side. Because its core was so constrained, and because it depended on maritime power, Britain's empire was always overstretched, often superficial, and likely to be limited in duration.[2]

Tracing the origin of such thoughts is easy. Every commentator on English/British power since the fifteenth century to the

Edwardian age recognised the vital choice between land and sea, and understood that if the British lost sight of seapower, as they did when they built a sub-continental Raj and took a major share in the land combat of the First World War, they would be reduced to tourist attractions by the Continental superpowers.[3]

The British Empire may be largely a thing of the past; more often the occasion for fatuous apologies that reflect twenty-first century values than coherent reassessment, but is has suffered another, more insidious fate. Modern Britons are profoundly ignorant of their imperial past, having been systematically fed a very different identity, one of Continental origin. The search for a European future has distorted the past. Whether this is conscious, and thereby mendacious, or unconscious, and thereby careless, is of less moment than the impact such a profound shift in national intellectual engagement with the origins of identity will have on future generations. It is hardly surprising that people whose ancestors arrived in Britain as a legacy of Empire, from places as disparate as Hong Kong and Jamaica, India and Africa, are at a loss to comprehend their place in an artificial 'Britishness' that is entirely European in construction and regulation. Nor are they alone in this. My Australian relatives face significant barriers to entry into the United Kingdom, while vast populations with whom I share nothing in blood, language, history or culture are free to enter at will. As John Pocock has observed:

A point has unhappily been reached, however, at which the ideology of European union demands, or commands, that this kingdom's involvement in France be recognised as more important, because more truly European, than its involvement in the maritime frontier of the Atlantic archipelago.[4]

While this is patently absurd it is not a singular example. The British understanding of the First World War is dominated by the appalling tragedy of the Western Front, when this truly global war could only be won with the support of the entire British Empire, formal and informal, made possible by control of the world ocean. Today the British are being force-fed a Eurocentric past, one that denies the centrality of the sea and empire in the construction of all post-medieval English/British identities, reversing centuries of sustained intellectual effort that shifted the focus away from Europe after 1421. Little wonder some in Scotland consider their relationship with Europe more important than their membership of the United Kingdom.

This 'European' past has replaced the 'imperial' version because it serves present political needs. The maritime course set after the death of Henry V has been reversed in exactly the same way that it was created. A new past invented to support current agendas is repeated *ad nauseam* until all connection with other pasts has been lost, at which point it becomes the new orthodoxy. The process will be complete when Trafalgar Square is bulldozed, the *Victory* recycled, and the mortal remains of Lord Nelson cast out of St Paul's. This may seem far-fetched, but anyone familiar with the systematic, widespread and deliberate destruction of rejected pasts that followed the French Revolution or Irish Independence, to name but two cases, will recognise that contemporary change requires radical historical recreation on a grand scale. Ultimately, as Friedrich Nietzsche declared in 1873, 'You can explain the past only by what is most powerful in the present.'[5]

A century ago the oceanic, imperial vision of British history was dominant; historians described the Tudors as aspirational Victorians, turning Raleigh from a gold-crazed nationalist zealot into the architect of their world empire. This version worked because the imperial project had been a success story. In 1913 the Empire was strikingly successful. Insular, isolated Britain had become a world empire without Europe. It could never be a Continental Roman empire; instead it evolved, like all seapower empires, into a looser political model, better suited to the maritime imperium of islands linked by oceans and controlled by fleets rather than armies. This was a conscious choice. Between 1688 and 1914 British statesmen consistently avoided the continental delusion, turning back to the oceans and economic expansion as soon as possible. They recognised that European engagement led to spiralling national debt and standing armies, giving overbearing influence to the political leadership. Naval power, colonies and commerce enabled Britain to influence Europe without being drawn into binding alliances, or military commitments. It was in this context that Juan Fernández became 'British'. Naval power, economy and the absence of standing armies were rightly popular in a democratic nation.[6] This approach enabled Britain to survive and prosper in the total wars of the French Revolution and Empire, and shape the peace that followed.

Policy-makers, statesmen and opinion-formers must recognise that the English/British world view, dating back to the fifteenth and sixteenth centuries, and hastily dismantled in the last four decades of the twentieth, remains potent. Any culture that sees itself in tiny islands on the other side of the world is not ready to join the continental project. Much of this can be read in British responses to the Argentine grandstanding over the Falkland Islands. The curiously old-fashioned combination of economic opportunity, honour and common heritage provide visceral evidence of an enduring global vision, built on common values. The British are not going to abandon these islands. What is more, they retain close ties with other islands that were once part of the Empire. It seems the British are not ready to give up on the ocean, or the tiny specks of land that punctuate it. This sensibility may be the product of large scale global activity over many centuries, but it is best understood by taking a very specific focus, using a single exemplary island to follow the evolution of a unique global vision. That the island in question was neither British nor economically attractive sharpens the focus. Juan Fernández, a tiny, volcanic outcrop in the South Pacific, became British in the imaginations of sickly men and visionary writers because it added something vital to the structure of Englishness – something that was never real, but astonishingly powerful for all that.

Another Tragedy

—◦◦◦—

Juan Fernández entered the twenty-first century in flux. A mix of fishing and visitors provided an income of sorts, while the contentious issue of land use was never far from the surface. Yet behind the slow rhythms of island life there were deeper concerns. The other island history – of mutiny and disorder, of British sailors running to the hills, of Spaniards and Chileans desperate to get to the mainland – evolved into darker forms of small island life. At the same time the islands are threatened by another, more all-embracing danger. They have a dynamic history of seismological activity, including three major tsunami events in the past 250 years. Such tourism as there was led the bars and hostels of San Juan to creep down onto the beach, right alongside the jetty, the very area devastated by Sutcliffe's tidal wave. Fortunately there was an international warning system in place for earthquakes and other tectonic activity. But the warning never came.

On 27 February 2010 a 15-foot-high tsunami hit Cumberland Bay. It struck before the village received any warning, killing 16 people and destroying the waterfront area of San Juan Bautista. The vital lobster fishery in the bay was left cluttered with wreckage from shattered buildings, fishing boats and even an old Land Rover; this wreckage will take years to remove. The graveyard at the point has a new set of markers, memorials for young and old alike, close by the wrecked commemoration of the *Dresden* dead. The victims were familiar to all on an island which gets by with so few surnames: they join a select group of buccaneers, naval ratings, convicts and settlers who will call this place home for all eternity. They rest in peace with British, Spanish and Chilean histories.

The island has slowly recovered, supported by the Chilean Navy, which brings out building materials and takes away the wreckage. The village has been rebuilt higher up the slopes of the mountain. The loss of almost all the hotels, the museum and reliable telecommunications has been a handicap to recovery, while the latest tragedy – the loss of a Chilean Air Force transport plane which crashed into the sea while attempting to land, killing all 21 people on board in September 2011 – only increased the sense of isolation and danger. The weather deteriorated while the plane was en route, and it did not have the range to return to the mainland. After two or three failed attempts, the last proved fatal. On the mainland the political ramifications of the disaster rumble on, while the island slowly returns to the nearest equivalent to normality that can be found at the end of the world.

This tiny island on the opposite side of the earth will always be Robinson Crusoe's abode, a magical mixing of Selkirk's very real residence, Defoe's imaginary evocation, and persistent patterns of English/British visits from 1680 to the 1930s, as buccaneers, privateers, warriors, ocean harvesters and scientists sought a chance to refit, recover and reprovision on an island that promised to cure scurvy, healing the damaged minds of sickly mariners, while generations of hydrographers sounded and recorded the realities of finding and using tiny specks of land in the Great South Sea.

The British made other people's islands their own, burying their dead and naming the key features, and they kept coming back. That Juan Fernández was never taken under formal British rule is less important than the many layers of ownership that built up over time, layers that left the precise, legalistic Foreign Office in no doubt that a good title could be created. The British maritime perspective made the world into a series of islands and sea passages; they avoided the continental land masses favoured by other great powers, to build an oceanic identity, an identity crowned with tiny specks of pure strategic gold, inhabitable islands with good anchorages that commanded key trade routes. Juan Fernández is not so much an island as an opportunity. For three centuries it was the key to the South Pacific; now it is home to modern hopes and dreams inspired by ancient mariners, and Robinson Kreutzenaer, that quintessential English hero.

Although every island story has been retold and reworked, in a seemingly endless cycle, the scurvied madness of the seafarer, dreaming of the mines of Peru and the fresh green fields of home, retain their power. Immersion in the life of the island enabled me to see English identity from a very different perspective. Crusoe's island may be a very small mirror, but it can show us who we are. Today there are great holes in the ground at Puerto Inglese, where a lot of money has been spent looking for a treasure that never existed. Sometimes the truth is inconvenient.

Notes

INTRODUCTION

1 W.A. Rogers, *A Cruising Voyage Round the World; First to the South-Seas, thence to the East-Indies, and Homewards by the Cape of Good Hope. Begun in 1708, and Finish'd in 1711*, London, 1712, p. 122.

CHAPTER 1: OF ISLANDS AND ENGLISHMEN

1 T. More, *Utopia*, tr. & ed. P. Turner, Penguin, London, 2003; R.B. Wernham, *Before the Armada: The Growth of English Foreign Policy, 1485–1588*, Jonathan Cape, London, 1966, pp. 1–98.

2 F. Fernández-Armesto, *Amerigo: The Man Who Gave His Name to America*, Weidenfeld & Nicholson, London, 2006, pp. 95, 109, 133 discusses explorer's tales and the confusion that follows them into print.

3 More, *Utopia*, p. 81.

4 More, *Utopia*, pp. 50, 71, 82.

5 P. Salzman, 'Narrative Contexts for Bacon's *New Atlantis*', in B. Price (ed.), *Francis Bacon's New Atlantis: New Interdisciplinary Essays*, Manchester University Press, Manchester, 2003, pp. 30, 32–3, 36; F. Bacon, 'New Atlantis', in *The Essays: The Wisdom of the Ancients and the New Atlantis*, Odhams, London, n.d., p. 316. First published in 1627, the essay is considered incomplete.

6 Bacon, 'New Atlantis', pp. 329, 310.

7 L. Colley, *Captives: Britain, Empire and the World 1600–1850*, Jonathan Cape, London, 2002.

8 M. Lowry, *The World of Aldus Manutius*, Oxford, 1979, p. 144. Herodotus and Thucydides were published in England in 1502.

9 Bacon speech, 17 February 1607 in J. Spedding, R.L. Ellis & D.D. Heath (eds), *The Works of Francis Bacon*, Longman, London, 14 vols, 1867–74, vol. 13, pp. 221–3.

10 This concept, brilliantly developed in the opening section of Jakob Burckhardt's *Civilisation of Italy in the Renaissance* (tr. S.G.C. Middlemore, London, 1878), is applicable elsewhere, especially in the constructed spaces of seapower empires.

CHAPTER 2: SPANISH LAKES AND ENGLISH DREAMS

1 I am indebted to the panellists and discussants at the 2011 United
States Naval Academy Naval History Conference, chaired by Dr Larrie
Ferreiro, for the discussion of Imperial Spain's Pacific naval defence.
Also C. Rahn Phillips, *Six Galleons for the King of Spain: Imperial
Defense in the Early Seventeenth Century*, Johns Hopkins University
Press, Baltimore, MD, 1986, pp. 3–19.
2 O.H.K. Spate, *The Pacific since Magellan, Volume I: The Spanish Lake*,
Australian National University, Canberra, 1979, pp. 213–20.
3 Spate, *The Pacific since Magellan*, vol. I, pp. 117–18.
4 Spate, *The Pacific since Magellan*, vol. I, pp. 140–41; R.L. Woodward,
Robinson Crusoe's Island, University of North Carolina Press, Chapel
Hill, NC, 1969, pp. 9–12; G. Williams, *The Great South Sea: English
Voyages and Encounters 1570–1750*, Yale University Press, New Haven,
CT, 1997, pp. 55–7.
5 Spate, *The Pacific since Magellan*, vol. I, pp. 233–64.
6 J.A. Williamson (ed.), *The Observations of Sir Richard Hawkins*,
Argonaut Press, London, 1933, pp. lxxxii & 100 (first edition London
1622). The 1878 edition was edited by Clements Markham, who had
visited the island. P. Bradley & D. Cahill, *Habsburg Peru: Images,
Imagination and Memory*, Liverpool University Press, Liverpool, 2000,
p. 23; W. Edmundson, *A History of the British Presence in Chile: From
Bloody Mary to Charles Darwin and the Decline of British Influence*,
Palgrave, Basingstoke, 2011, p. 16.
7 Spate, *The Pacific since Magellan*, vol. I, pp. 265–79.
8 On Raleigh and his voyaging see M. Nicholls & P. Williams, *Sir Walter
Raleigh: In Life and Legend*, Continuum, London, 2011; V.T. Harlow
(ed.), *Raleigh's Last Voyage*, Argonaut Press, London, 1932; J. Lorimer
(ed.), *Sir Walter Ralegh's Discoverie of Guiana (1596)*, Hakluyt Society,
London, 2006.
9 Spate, *The Pacific since Magellan*, vol. I, p. 119.
10 O.H.K. Spate, *The Pacific since Magellan, Volume III: Paradise Found
and Lost*, Routledge, London, 1988, p. 33.
11 C. Skottsberg, *The Natural History of Juan Fernández and Easter Island*,
3 vols, Almqvist & Wiskell, Uppsala, 1956. The best source on the
geological, biological and ecological history of the island.
12 William Cornelison Schouten in P. Samuel (ed.), *Haklutus Posthumous
or Purchas his Pilgrimes*, vol. II, MacLehose, Glasgow, 1905, pp. 246–8.
Schouten appeared in the third edition of 1625.
13 Woodward, *Robinson Crusoe's Island*, p. 17.
14 O.H.K. Spate, *The Pacific since Magellan, Volume II: Monopolists and
Freebooters*, Australian National University, Canberra, 1983, p. 23.
15 P. Bradley, *The Lure of Peru: Maritime Intrusion into the South Sea,
1598–1701*, St Martin's Press, London, 1989, pp. 60–4.
16 Bradley & Cahill, *Habsburg Peru*, p. 31, from W. Schouten, *Journal afte
beschrijvinghe van der wonderlicke reyse*, Amsterdam, 1618.

17 Woodward, *Robinson Crusoe's Island*, p. 18 uses a later version from J.
    Campbell (ed.), *Navigantium; or A Complete Collection of Voyages and
    Travels*, London, 1744, vol. I, pp. 6–130.
18 Bradley, *The Lure of Peru*, pp. 52–3, 60–4.
19 Woodward, *Robinson Crusoe's Island*, pp. 20–21.
20 S. Schama, *The Embarrassment of Riches*, Collins, London, 1987;
    L. Jardine, *Going Dutch: How England Plundered Holland's Glory*,
    HarperCollins, London, 2008 manages to ignore the ocean.
21 Williams, *The Great South Sea*, pp. 72–5.
22 Charles II to Henrietta Maria (his sister), 20 January 1669: J.D. Davies,
    'Chatham to Erith via Dover: Charles II's Secret Foreign Policy and
    the Project for new Royal Dockyards, 1667–1672', in R. Riley (ed.),
    *Pepys and Chips: Dockyards Naval Administration and Warfare in the
    Seventeenth Century*, Naval Dockyards Society, Southsea, 2012, p. 116.
23 Reproduced in Williams, *The Great South Sea*, p. 69.
24 J. Seller, *Atlas Maritimus, or the Sea Atlas*, London, 1675, preface &
    pp. 8–9.

CHAPTER 3: PIRATES AND FREEBOOTERS

 1 P.J. Marshall & G. Williams, *The Great Map of Mankind: British
    Perceptions of the World in the Age of Enlightenment*, Dent & Sons,
    London, 1982, pp. 37–8. Today Potosi is in Bolivia.
 2 J. Esquemelin, *The Buccaneers of America*, Routledge, London, n.d.,
    pp. 395–401.
 3 D. Cordingly, *Spanish Gold: Captain Woodes Rogers and the Pirates of
    the Caribbean*, Bloomsbury, London, 2011, pp. 3–16.
 4 Williams, *The Great South Sea*, p. 86; G. Norris (ed.), *Buccaneer
    Explorer: William Dampier's Voyages*, Boydell Press, Woodbridge, 2005,
    p. xx suggests George Ridpath, who worked with Woodes Rogers,
    both published with James Knapton. R.H. Grove, *Green Imperialism:
    Colonial Expansion, Tropical Island Edens and the Origins of
    Environmentalism, 1600–1860*, Cambridge University Press, Cambridge,
    1995, p. 354 notes Coleridge was taught by William Wales, astronomer
    on Cook's second Pacific voyage, who may have inspired Coleridge's
    remark. Esquemelin, *The Buccaneers of America*, pp. 393, 397; Norris,
    Buccaneer Explorer, p. 33.
 5 Bradley, *The Lure of Peru*, pp. 115–17; T. Severin, *Seeking Robinson
    Crusoe*, Macmillan, Basingstoke, 2002, pp. 97–177.
 6 Sharp's journal in D. Howse & N. Thrower, *A Buccaneer's Atlas: Basil
    Ringrose's South Sea Waggoner*, University of California Press, Berkeley,
    CA, 1992, pp. 22, 257.
 7 Waggoner is English slang for a book of charts, corrupted version of the
    Dutch author Lucas Janszon Waghenaer; Williams, *The Great South Sea*,
    p. 88; Howse & Thrower, *A Buccaneer's Atlas*, introduction, p. 33.
 8 Norris, *Buccaneer Explorer*, p. 54; L.E.E. Joyce (ed.), *A New Voyage
    & Description of the Isthmus of America by Lionel Wafer, Surgeon on
    Buccaneering Expeditions in Darien, the West Indies, and the Pacific

from 1680 to 1688; with Wafer's Secret Report (1698) and Davis's Expedition to the Gold Mines (1704), Hakluyt Society, London, 1934, p. 127; Cordingly, *Spanish Gold*, p. 13.

9 Spate, *The Pacific since Magellan*, vol. II, p. 150–5; Bradley, *The Lure of Peru*, pp. 191–3.

10 Bradley, *The Lure of Peru*, pp. 154–69, 171–5; Williams, *The Great South Sea*, pp. 102–5; Joyce, *A New Voyage & Description of the Isthmus of America by Lionel Wafer*, p. 126.

11 W. Dampier, *A New Voyage Round the World: Describing Particularly The Isthmus of America, feveral Coafts and Iflands in the Weft Indies, the Ifles of Cape Ver, the Paffage by Tierra del Fuego, the South Sea Coafts of Chili, Peru, and Mexico, the Ifle of Guma, one of the Ladrones, Mindanao, and other Philippine and Eaft India Iflands near Cambodia, China, Formofa, Luconia, Celebes &c, New Holland, Sumatra, Nicobar Ifles, the Cape of Good Hope, and Santa Helena, Their Soil, Rivers, Harbours, Plants, Fruits, Animals, and Inhabitants, Their Customs, Religion, Government, Trade &c. Illustrated with Particular Maps and Draughts*, James Knapton, London, 2 vols, 1697 (see vol. I, pp. 83–93 for Juan Fernández).

12 Joyce, *A New Voyage & Description of the Isthmus of America by Lionel Wafer*, p. 144.

13 Williams, *The Great South Sea*, p. 115. Halifax and Sloane subscribed to Churchill's 1728 *Navigiantium*.

14 Cordingly, *Spanish Gold*, p. 15.

15 D. Souhami, *Selkirk's Island*, Weidenfeld & Nicholson, London, 2001, pp. 33, 45–6.

16 Spate, *The Pacific since Magellan*, vol. II, pp. 181–94.

17 Souhami, *Selkirk's Island*, pp. 70–80; W. Funnell, *A Voyage Round the World*, London, 1707.

CHAPTER 4: 'THE ABSOLUTE MONARCH OF THE ISLAND'

1 Souhami, *Selkirk's Island*, p. 107.

2 Notably in the case of Captain William Kidd.

3 Cordingly, *Spanish Gold*, pp. 16–24.

4 Rogers, *A Cruising Voyage Round the World*, p. 122.

5 Rogers, *A Cruising Voyage Round the World*, p. 122.

6 I. James, *Providence Displayed: or, The Remarkable Adventures of Alexander Selkirk, of Largo, in Scotland; Who Lived Four Years and Four Months by Himself, on the Island of Juan Fernandez; from whence He Returned with Capt. Woodes Rogers, of Bristol, and on whose Adventures was Founded the Celebrated Novel of Robinson Crusoe*, London, 1800, pp. 6, 9.

7 Rogers, *A Cruising Voyage Round the World*, p. 122.

8 Cordingly, *Spanish Gold*, pp. 51, 253.

9 Rogers, *A Cruising Voyage Round the World*, pp. 123–31; James, *Providence Displayed*, p. 6. I am indebted to local expert Felipe for a

discussion of goat hunting techniques and goat habits. In addition to his expertise he has the most formidable goat's head tattooed across his belly, at a level where not all of the beast's features are discernible in polite company.

10 D. Takahashi, D.H. Caldwell, I. Càceres, M. Calderón, A.D. Morrison, M.A. Saavedra & J. Tate, 'Excavation at Aguas Buenas, Robinson Crusoe Island, Chile, of a Gunpowder Magazine and the Supposed Campsite of Alexander Selkirk, together with an Account of Early Navigational Dividers', *Post-Medieval Archaeology* 41(2) (2007), pp. 27–304, here p. 300.

11 Bradley, *The Lure of Peru*, p. 189; D. Reinhartz, *The Cartographer and the Literati: Herman Moll and his Intellectual Circle*, Edwin Mellen Press, Lewiston, NY, 1997, pp. 75–97, 113–30; Williams, *The Great South Sea*, pp. 160–67.

12 Spate, *The Pacific since Magellan*, vol. II, pp. 156–8.

13 Cordingly, *Spanish Gold*, p. 27.

14 Spate, *The Pacific since Magellan*, vol. II, p. 195; Cordingly, *Spanish Gold*, pp. 92–3; Souhami, *Selkirk's Island*, pp. 171–2.

15 Williams, *The Great South Sea*, p. 148, from Rogers *Cruising Voyage*, p. 137; Cordingly, *Spanish Gold*, pp. 93–5, 253, fn 6.

16 Souhami, *Selkirk's Island*, p. 173

17 Marshall & Williams, *The Great Map of Mankind*, p. 40.

18 Williams, *The Great South Sea*, pp. 170–4, Woodward, *Robinson Crusoe's Island*, pp. 51–2; Welbe, 27 May 1715, cited by J.A. Williamson in introduction to W. Dampier, *A Voyage to New Holland, &c. in the year 1699*, Argonaut Press, London, 1939, pp. lx–lxii.

19 J. Carswell, *The South Sea Bubble*, Sutton Publishing, Gloucester, 1993 remains the standard account.

20 See Reinhartz, *The Cartographer and the Literati*, pp. 113–30 for the South Sea Company.

21 A. Churchill & J. Churchill, *Navigantium atque Itinerantium Bibliotheca: A Collection of Voyages and Travels*, London, vols I–IV, 1704, vols V–VI, 1732, vol. III, p. 46.

22 Churchill & Churchill, *Navigantium atque Itinerantium Bibliotheca*, vol. III, p. 46.

23 Marshall & Williams, *The Great Map of Mankind*, pp. 48–51, 54–7; G.A. Crone & R.A. Skelton, 'English Collections of Voyages and Travels, 1625–1846', in E. Lynam (ed.), *Richard Hakluyt and his Successors*, Hakluyt Society, London, 1946, p. 87; Dampier, *A New Voyage Round the World*, pp. lii–lvii.

CHAPTER 5: THE MAGICAL ISLAND OF DANIEL DEFOE

1 Williams, *The Great South Sea*, p. 175.

2 H. Heidenreich (ed.), *The Libraries of Daniel Defoe and Phillips Farewell: Olive Payne's Catalogue (1731)*, Berlin, 1970, pp. viii–xvi, xii fn 11, with p. xxii quoting Defoe's *Compleat English Gentleman*.

3 M.E. Novak, *Daniel Defoe, Master of Fictions: His Life and Ideas*, Oxford University Press, Oxford, 2001, p. 591. Tim Severin travelled to the relevant locations for several buccaneer tales, and to engage with the reality. Cordingly, *Spanish Gold*, pp. 90, 98–9; Souhami, *Selkirk's Island*, pp. 176–8; J. Entick, *A New Naval History, or a Compleat View of the British Marine*, London, 1757, p. 671.

4 Novak, *Daniel Defoe, Master of Fictions*, pp. 539–40, 687. However, Nicholls & Williams, in *Sir Walter Raleigh*, ignore this connection.

5 Fernández-Armesto, *Amerigo*, p. 137.

6 Skottsberg, *The Natural History of Juan Fernández and Easter Island*, vol. I, p. 122 offers the best assessment: 'the famous Robinson's cave, a favourite goal for visiting tourists. It is hardly probable that the cave, described in some detail by Guzman, served the recluse as his permanent abode.' Of course Skottsberg, a scientist, actually means Selkirk.

7 Novak, *Daniel Defoe, Master of Fictions*, pp. 546–7, 567–9, 571, 575, 582, 597.

8 Novak, *Daniel Defoe, Master of Fictions*, pp. 637–40, 646, 669–71.

9 D. Defoe, *A Plan of the English Commerce*, Oxford, 1927, p. 276.

10 D. Defoe, *Atlas Maritimus and Commercialis*, London, 1728, p. 239; Novak, *Daniel Defoe, Master of Fictions*, pp. 687–8, 691–2; P. Rahe, *Montesquieu and the Logic of Liberty: War, Religion, Commerce, Climate, Terrain, Technology, Uneasiness of Mind, the Spirit of Political Vigilance, and the Foundations of the Modern Republic*, Yale University Press, New Haven, CT, 2009, pp. 3–61, esp. p. 59. The influence on Bolingbroke must also be acknowledged.

11 C. Flynn, 'Nationalism, Commerce, and Imperial Authority in Defoe's Later Works', *Rocky Mountain Review* (Fall 2000), pp. 11–24, here p. 13.

12 Souhami, *Selkirk's Island*, p. 196; J. Brewer, *The Pleasures of the Imagination: English Culture in the Eighteenth Century*, HarperCollins, London 1997, pp. 173–4 is remarkably thin on the oceanic dimension, ignoring Crusoe, Selkirk, Anson and Cook, while Sir Joseph Banks appears as a London figure, not a world traveller.

CHAPTER 6: SHELVOCKE'S SOJOURN

1 Belgium, then the Austrian Netherlands, was ruled by the Habsburg Empire then at war with Spain.

2 Hatley, unlike Shelvocke, was a South Seas veteran. R. Fowke, *The Real Ancient Mariner: Pirates and Poesy on the South Sea*, Travelbrief, Shropshire, 2010.

3 G. Shelvocke, *A Voyage Round the World by Way of the Great South Sea Performed in the Years 1719, 20, 21, 22, in the Speedwell of London, of 24 Guns and 100 Men, (under His Majesty's Commission to Cruise on the Spaniards in the Late War with the Spanish Crown) till She was Cast Away on the Island of Juan Fernández, in May 1720; and was afterwards Continued in the Recovery, the Jesus Maria and Sacra*

Familia &c., Sennen, Innys, Osborn & Longman, London, 1726, pp. 115–20 (spellings modernised).

4 Shelvocke, *A Voyage Round the World*, pp. 205, 210, 208; Skottsberg, *The Natural History of Juan Fernández and Easter Island*, vol. I, p. 111 noted Bahía Pangal was named after the *Gunnera peltata* (giant pangues) that grew there with trees and ferns. He also noted the waterfall that Shelvocke used.

5 Williams, *The Great South Sea*, pp. 197–204; W. Betagh, *A Voyage Round the World: Being an Account of a Remarkable Enterprise Begun in 1719, Chiefly to Cruise on the Spaniards in the Great South Ocean*, London, 1728: T. Beattie, '"Entirely the Most Absurd and False Narrative that was ever Deliver'd to the Publick": An Inquiry into What Really Happened on George Shelvocke's Privateering Voyage', *The Mariner's Mirror* 97(3) (2011), pp. 163–76.

6 Shelvocke, *A Voyage Round the World*, p. 215.

7 Shelvocke, *A Voyage Round the World*, pp. 219, 221, 232–3, 238–41, 244.

8 T. Sutcliffe, *Crusoiana; or Truth versus Fiction elucidated in a History of the Islands of Juan Fernández*, Manchester, 1843, pp. 55–6.

9 Shelvocke, *A Voyage Round the World*, pp. 259–62.

10 Shelvocke, *A Voyage Round the World*, pp. 246–7.

11 Shelvocke, *A Voyage Round the World*, pp. 248–51.

12 Shelvocke, *A Voyage Round the World*, pp. 257–8, with a picture of the two creatures at the western end of Windy Bay, pp. 252–3.

13 Spate, *The Pacific since Magellan*, vol. II, pp. 213–14; Campbell, *Navigantium*, vol. I, p. 239; D. Starkey, *British Privateering Enterprise in the Eighteenth Century*, University of Exeter Press, Exeter, 1990, pp. 46–8, 95–6, 112–15.

14 A. Sharp (ed.), *The Journal of Jacob Roggeveen*, Oxford University Press, Oxford, 1974; Campbell, *Navigantium*, vol. I, pp. 184–320.

15 Sharp, *The Journal of Jacob Roggeveen*, pp. 81–2.

16 A. Frost, 'Shaking Off the Spanish Yoke: British Schemes to Revolutionise America, 1739–1807', in M. Lincoln (ed.), *Science and Exploration in the Pacific: European Voyages to the Southern Oceans in the Eighteenth Century*, Boydell Press, Woodbridge, 1998, pp. 19–37, here pp. 19–20.

CHAPTER 7: GEORGE ANSON'S VOYAGE

1 Williams, *The Great South Sea*, p. 215; Tassell and Hutchinson to Sir Robert Walpole, 11 September 1739, in G. Williams (ed.), *Documents Relating to Anson's Voyage Round the World*, Navy Records Society, London, 1967, pp. 18–26.

2 G. Williams, *The Prize of All the Oceans: The Triumph and Tragedy of Anson's Voyage Round the World*, HarperCollins, London, 1999, p. 54. Captain William Douglas, HMS *Worcester*, to the Admiralty, 29 June 1740, in Williams, *Documents Relating to Anson's Voyage Round the World*, p. 52.

3 R. Walter & B. Robins, *Lord Anson's Voyage Round the World*, London, 1748; page numbers herein are all from the more accessible 1911 Everyman edition, edited by John Masefield (here pp. 104–5).

4 Walter & Robins, *Lord Anson's Voyage Round the World*, p. 106.

5 P. Thomas, *A True and Impartial Journal of a Voyage to the South Seas and Round the Globe in his Majesty's Ship the Centurion*, London, 1745, p. 29; Walter & Robins, *Lord Anson's Voyage Round the World*, pp. 108–10.

6 L. Heaps (ed.), *Log of the Centurion: Based on the Original Papers of Captain Philip Saumarez on Board HMS Centurion, Lord Anson's Flagship During his Circumnavigation 1740–44*, Hart Davies, London, 1973, pp. 109–12 (hereafter 'Saumarez').

7 Thomas, *A True and Impartial Journal*, pp. 30, 35, 42.

8 Thomas, *A True and Impartial Journal*, p. 31; Walter & Robins, *Lord Anson's Voyage Round the World*, p. 125.

9 Walter & Robins, *Lord Anson's Voyage Round the World*, pp. 127–8.

10 Saumarez, p. 114.

11 Walter & Robins, *Lord Anson's Voyage Round the World*, p. 125.

12 Walter & Robins, *Lord Anson's Voyage Round the World*, p. 149.

13 Woodward, *Robinson Crusoe's Island*, p. 71.

CHAPTER 8: THE MAGICAL ISLAND

1 Saumarez, pp. 119–21.

2 Thomas, *A True and Impartial Journal*, p. 31, 36–37.

3 Thomas, *A True and Impartial Journal*, pp. 36–37.

4 Anon., *Authentic Account of Commodore Anson's Expedition*, London, 1744, p. 43; Thomas, *A True and Impartial Journal*, p. 39; Saumarez, p. 118.

5 Walter & Robins, *Lord Anson's Voyage Round the World*, pp. 114–18; Saumarez, pp. 118–20.

6 Walter & Robins, *Lord Anson's Voyage Round the World*, pp. 114–15; Thomas, *A True and Impartial Journal*, p. 40.

7 Walter & Robins, *Lord Anson's Voyage Round the World*, pp. 120–1; Saumarez, p. 120; Thomas, *A True and Impartial Journal*, p. 30. They remain a culinary highlight.

8 Thomas, *A True and Impartial Journal*, p. 41.

9 Walter & Robins, *Lord Anson's Voyage Round the World*, pp. 111–14.

10 Saumarez, pp. 120–1.

CHAPTER 9: MAKING JUAN FERNÁNDEZ ENGLISH

1 Thomas, *A True and Impartial Journal*, p. 42.

2 Thomas, *A True and Impartial Journal*, p. 42; Walter & Robins, *Lord Anson's Voyage Round the World*, p. 116 (text and engraving are at p. 120).

3 Thomas, *A True and Impartial Journal*, pp. 35–6; quote from *Paradise Lost*, book IV, verse 245; Williams, *The Great South Sea*, p. 233.

4 Thomas, *A True and Impartial Journal*, pp. 38, 42; Saumarez, pp. 120–1.

5 Saumarez; Denis to his brother, 1 December 1742, and Millechamp's narrative in Williams, *Documents Relating to Anson's Voyage Round the World*, pp. 166, 176–9, 66–82.

6 Saumarez, p. 116; Thomas, *A True and Impartial Journal*, p. 42, & appendix, p. 29.

7 Williams, *Documents Relating to Anson's Voyage Round the World*, p. 82; Walter & Robins, *Lord Anson's Voyage Round the World*, pp. 128–9.

8 Saumarez, p. 121; Thomas, *A True and Impartial Journal*, p. 33; Walter & Robins, *Lord Anson's Voyage Round the World*, pp. 113, 148–9, 156–7.

9 Saumarez; Williams, *Documents Relating to Anson's Voyage Round the World*, p. 166.

10 Thomas, *A True and Impartial Journal*, pp. 43–4, 49.

11 *London Gazette* (April 1743), pp. 202–3; Williams, *Documents Relating to Anson's Voyage Round the World*, pp. 170–6.

CHAPTER 10: MAKING BOOKS

1 Williams, *The Prize of All the Oceans*, p. 63.

2 Campbell, *Navigantium*, vol. I, pp. xv–xvi.

3 J.S. Corbett, *England in the Mediterranean: A Study of the Rise and Influence of British Power within the Straits, 1603–1713*, Longman, London, 1904, pp. 525–58. On the rapid Anglicisation of Gibraltar, see S. Conn, *Gibraltar in British Diplomacy in the Eighteenth Century*, Yale University Press, New Haven, CT, 1942.

4 Campbell, *Navigantium*, vol. I, pp. 325, 328; Frost, 'Shaking Off the Spanish Yoke', pp. 20–1.

5 A.D. Lambert, *Admirals: The Men Who Made Britain Great*, Faber & Faber, London, 2007, ch. 4.

6 Marshall & Williams, *The Great Map of Mankind*, p. 260.

7 Williams, *The Great South Sea*, pp. 254–6; Williams, *The Prize of All the Oceans*, pp. 237–41.

8 Walter & Robins, *Lord Anson's Voyage Round the World*, pp. 2–3.

9 J. Barrow, *The Life of George, Lord Anson*, John Murray, London, 1839, pp. 41–2.

10 Walter & Robins, *Lord Anson's Voyage Round the World*, pp. 4, 380. The authorship of this section cannot be in doubt; it was composed by an engineer, and improved by a navigator. Williams, *The Prize of All the Oceans*, p. 224.

11 J. Brown, *Lancelot 'Capability' Brown, 1716–1784: The Omnipotent Magician*, Chatto & Windus, London, 2011. Anson spent at least £6,000 on the Moor Park garden (see pp. 97–8). D. Stroud, *Capability Brown*, Country Life, London, 1950, pp. 31–2 (Greek temple by James 'Athenian' Stuart, an Anson client). M. Pedrick, *Moor Park: The Grosvenor Legacy*, Riverside Books, Rickmansworth, 1989, pp. 22–5.

12 Legge to Anson, 4 September 1748 & n.d., in Barrow, *The Life of George, Lord Anson*, pp. 409–10; Williams, *The Prize of All the Oceans*, p. 237.

13 Translated by E. Joncourt, published in Leipzig and Amsterdam in 1749. Grove, *Green Imperialism*, p. 233; C. Thacker, '"O Tininan! O Juan-Fernández!" Rousseau's "Elysée" and Anson's Desert Islands', *Garden History* 5 (1977), pp. 41–7.

14 Both engraved in 1751 by Jacobus Houbraken (National Maritime Museum, PAF 3415 and 3416).

15 Skottsberg, *The Natural History of Juan Fernández and Easter Island*, vol. I, p. 174.

CHAPTER 11: CLOSING THE STABLE DOOR

1 Walter & Robins, *Lord Anson's Voyage Round the World*, p. 92.

2 Williams, *The Great South Sea*, pp. 258–63.

3 L.D. Ferreiro, *Measure of the Earth: The Enlightenment Expedition that Reshaped Our World*, Basic Books, New York, 2011, pp. 190–6 for the impact of Anson's voyage.

4 J. Juan and A. de Ulloa, *A Voyage to South America*, London, 1758, vol. II, extracts in Williams, *Documents Relating to Anson's Voyage Round the World*, pp. 138–44, quote at p. 143. Originally published in Madrid, 1748.

5 I am indebted to Catherine Scheybeler for information on these texts.

6 R. Navarro Mallebrera and A.M. Navarro Escolano (eds), *Inventario de bienes de Jorge Juan y Santacilia*, Instituto de Estudios Juan Gil Albert-Caja de Ahorros del Mediterráneo, Alicante, 1988.

7 Ferreiro, *Measure of the Earth*, pp. 238–41; Woodward, *Robinson Crusoe's Island*, p. 82. Juan wrote on 16 June 1749 after visiting the ship at Deptford (information from Catherine Scheybeler). R. Winfield, *British Warships in the Age of Sail, 1714–1792: Design, Construction, Careers and Fates*, Seaforth Publishing, Barnsley, p. 273.

8 Frost, 'Shaking Off the Spanish Yoke'; Bedford to Keene, 24 April 1749, SP 94/135 ff. 177–8; Keene to Bedford, 21 May 1749; Bedford to Keene, 5 June 1749, SP 94/135 ff. 177–8, 265–8, 271–3; Woodward, *Robinson Crusoe's Island*, p. 78.

9 Spate, *The Pacific since Magellan*, vol. III, p. 71.

10 C. de Brosses, *Histoire des Navigations aux Terres Australes*, Paris, 1756; Marshall & Williams, *The Great Map of Mankind*, p. 260.

11 Woodward, *Robinson Crusoe's Island*, pp. 82–5.

12 Edmundson, *A History of the British Presence in Chile*, p. 24.

CHAPTER 12: MASTERING THE PACIFIC

1 V.T. Harlow, *The Founding of the Second British Empire 1763–1793, Volume II: New Continents and Changing Values*, Longman, London, 1964, pp. 633–4.

2 H.T. Fry, *Alexander Dalrymple and the Expansion of British Trade*, Toronto University Press, Toronto, 1970, pp. 100–2.

3 R.E. Gallagher (ed.), *Byron's Journal*, Hakluyt Society, Cambridge, 1964, p. xxxi.

4 Gallagher, *Byron's Journal*, pp. 84–8.

5 Más Afuera: ADM 344/2255, admiralty records, The National Archives, Kew.

6 Williams, *The Prize of All the Oceans*, pp. 234–5; Woodward, *Robinson Crusoe's Island*, pp. 88–9.

7 H. Wallis (ed.), *Carteret's Voyage Round the World: 1766–1769*, Hakluyt Society, Cambridge, 1965, vol. I, p. 50.

8 Wallis, *Carteret's Voyage Round the World*, vol. I, pp. 128–41.

9 Spate, *The Pacific since Magellan*, vol. III, p. 196.

10 B. Smith, *European Vision and the South Pacific, 1768–1850*, Clarendon Press, Oxford, 1960, pp. 3–13, 37–41.

11 J. Dunmore (ed.), *The Journal of Jean François de Galaup de la Pérouse, 1785–1788*, 2 vols, Hakluyt Society, Cambridge, 1994–5, pp. 36–40, 472–4.

CHAPTER 13: SCURVY RESOLVED

1 Cheap later alleged indiscipline, but he had no authority to inflict summary capital punishment.

2 Much of what follows is based on the outstanding seminar 'The Natural History of Scurvy' held at the National Maritime Museum, Greenwich on 26–7 March 2012. I am indebted to the convenor, Professor Jonathan Lamb, and all those who took part. Proceedings of the seminar are in the *International Journal of Maritime History* for June 2013. See also J. Lamb, *Preserving the Self in the South Seas, 1680–1840*, University of Chicago Press, Chicago, IL, 2001, pp. 116–31.

3 Walter & Robins, *Lord Anson's Voyage Round the World*, p. 81.

CHAPTER 14: DISTANT DESPAIR

1 W. Cowper, *The Task and Other Poems*, ed. J. Sambrook, Longman, London, 1994, pp. 12, 18, 272–5. Of Anson he writes: 'No braver chief could Albion boast' (p. 317).

2 Cowper letter of 6 October 1783, in Cowper, *The Task and Other Poems*, p. 12; 'The Task', pp. 144–5.

3 Cowper, *The Task and Other Poems*, p. 14

4 Cowper, *The Task and Other Poems*, pp. 78, 71–2.

5 Cowper, *The Task and Other Poems*, pp. 78, 319, 45–6.

CHAPTER 15: WHALING AND THE SOUTH PACIFIC

1 Harlow, *The Founding of the Second British Empire 1763–1793*, vol. II, pp. 638–9.

2 Dalrymple, 1 March 1780; Frost, 'Shaking Off the Spanish Yoke', pp. 30–1.

3 Harlow, *The Founding of the Second British Empire 1763–1793*, vol. II, p. 1.

4 J. Ehrman, *The Younger Pitt: The Years of Acclaim*, Constable, London, 1969, p. 346. Palliser to Jenkinson, 23 November 1785, BT 6/93, quoted in Harlow, *The Founding of the Second British Empire 1763–1793*, vol. II, pp. 302–3.

5 E.A. Stackpole, *Whales and Destiny: The Rivalry between America, France, and Britain for Control of the Southern Whale Fishery, 1785–1825*, University of Massachusetts Press, Amherst, MA, 1972, p. 76.

6 Ehrman, *The Younger Pitt*, pp. 350–1; Harlow, *The Founding of the Second British Empire 1763–1793*, vol. II, pp. 301–7.

7 Harlow, *The Founding of the Second British Empire 1763–1793*, vol. II, p. 317; M.E. Thurman, *The Naval Department of San Blas: New Spain's Bastion for Alta California and Nootka 1767 to 1798*, Clark, Glendale, CA, 1967, pp. 309–18.

8 Sir J. Dalrymple, *Memoirs of Great Britain*, London, 1789, appendix I, part II.

9 *The Times* (12 November 1790), p. 2, col. C; Anglo-Spanish Convention, 1790: Harlow, *The Founding of the Second British Empire 1763–1793*, vol. II, pp. 318, 645.

10 Harlow, *The Founding of the Second British Empire 1763–1793*, vol. II, pp. 322, 326.

11 Enderby to Banks, 26 August 1788, in N. Chambers (ed.), *The Indian and Pacific Correspondence of Sir Joseph Banks, 1768–1820*, Pickering & Chatto, London, 2008, vol. II, p. 329. Enderby to Banks, 16 February 1793, for scientific specimens in W.R. Dawson (ed.), *The Banks Letters*, British Museum, London, 1958, p. 309.

12 Mulgrave to Banks, 19 October 1790, in Dawson, *The Banks Letters*, p. 669.

13 J. Moss, *Naval Chronicle* 18 (1807), pp. 32–6.

14 M. Harris, 'Commander John Ralph Moss, RN (1759–1799)', *Naval Review* 100 (February 2012), pp. 60–5.

15 W. Kaye Lamb (ed.), *The Voyage of George Vancouver, 1791–1795*, Hakluyt Society, Cambridge, 1984, vol. I, pp. 20–4; Spate, *The Pacific since Magellan*, vol. III, p. 184.

16 B.M. Gough, *Distant Dominion: Britain and the North-West Coast of North America, 1579–1809*, British Columbia University Press, Vancouver, 1980, p. 133; Kaye Lamb, *Vancouver*, vol. I, pp. 196–7, & vol. IV, pp. 1468–74; Archibald Menzies to Banks, 26 March 1795, in N. Chambers (ed.), *The Indian and Pacific Correspondence of Sir Joseph Banks*, vol. IV, Pickering & Chatto, London, 2011, p. 272–4.

17 J. Beaglehole, *The Exploration of the Pacific*, London, 1960, pp. 185–6; Churchill & Churchill, *Navigantium atque Itinerantium Bibliotheca*; J. Harris, *Navigantium atque Itinerantium Biblotheca*, 2 vols, London, 1705; new edition by Campbell, 'carefully revised with large additions', London, 1744.

18 Stackpole, *Whales and Destiny*, pp. 155–7 focuses too closely on whaling to see the deeper import.

19 J. Colnett, *A Voyage to the South Atlantic and Round Cape Horn into the Pacific Ocean for the Purpose of Extending the Spermacetti Whale Fisheries and Other Objects of Commerce by Ascertaining the Ports, Bays, Harbours, and Anchoring Births in Certain Islands and Coasts in Those Seas at which the Ships of the British Merchants Might be Refitted*, London, 1798, pp. 24–7. The Gale Outline Edition has Banks's signature.

20 Spanish Chart of Northern Chile, Peru and San Felix: ADM 352/350/2.

21 Colnett, *A Voyage to the South Atlantic*, pp. 20, 28–9, 32.

22 Colnett, *A Voyage to the South Atlantic*, pp. 35–7. This idea may have come from Banks, who made similar observations on St Helena and Ascension Island; Grove, *Green Imperialism*, pp. 325–6.

23 Colnett, *A Voyage to the South Atlantic*, pp. 46–63 (quote at p. 63), 69–75.

24 Colnett, *A Voyage to the South Atlantic*, pp. 137, 145, 158–9.

25 Thurman, *The Naval Department of San Blas*, p. 359; T.W. Keeble, *Commercial Relations between British Overseas Territories and South America, 1806–1914*, London, Athlone Press, 1970, pp. 1–3, 7–9, 28.

26 A. David, F. Fernández-Armesto, C. Novi & G. Williams (eds), *The Malaspina Expedition, 1789–1794*, vol. I, Hakluyt Society, Cambridge, 2001, pp. 165–7.

27 Jenkinson to Sir Joseph Banks, 24 February 1802, cited in Harlow, *The Founding of the Second British Empire 1763–1793*, vol. II, p. 327.

CHAPTER 16: THE END OF AN ERA

1 S. Clissold, *Bernardo O'Higgins and the Independence of Chile*, London, 1968, p. 48; Woodward, *Robinson Crusoe's Island*, pp. 92–9.

2 Frost, 'Shaking Off the Spanish Yoke', pp. 34–6.

3 *The Times* (9 January 1808); Harlow, *The Founding of the Second British Empire 1763–1793*, vol. II, p. 660.

4 M. Ellery, 'William Campbell and the *Harrington*: Privateering in Chilean Waters in 1804', *The Mariner's Mirror* 97(4) (2011), pp. 315–40, esp. p. 319.

5 Spate, *The Pacific since Magellan*, vol. II, pp. 285–6, 318–19; J. Lynch, *The Spanish–American Revolutions, 1808–1826*, W.W. Norton, New York, 1973 (see pp. 127–56 for the Chilean Revolution).

6 A.D. Lambert, *The Challenge: Britain versus America in the Naval War of 1812*, Faber & Faber, London, 2012, pp. 270–304 for Pacific operations in the War of 1812. B.M. Gough, *The Royal Navy and the Northwest Coast of North America 1810–1914: A Study of British Maritime Ascendancy*, University of British Columbia Press, Vancouver, 1971, pp. 15–17.

7 Log of HMS *Phoebe*, 11–19 September 1813, 5 February 1814: ADM 51/2675. Coastal views of Juan Fernández and Más Afuera from Byron's voyage, *Phoebe*, *Tagus* and *Beagle*: ADM 344/2255.

8 Admiral Dixon to Admiralty, 24 December 1814: ADM 1/22. Also in
   G.S. Graham & R.A. Humphreys (eds), *The Navy in South America,
   1807–1823*, Navy Records Society, London, 1962, p. 149.
9 J. Shillibeer, *A Narrative of the Briton's Voyage to Pitcairn's Island*,
   Taunton, 1817, pp. 152–8.
10 View of the Island of Juan Fernández from the anchorage: HMS *Tagus*,
   Captain Pipon, rec'd 23 November 1816, ADM 344/2255. One of
   these may be the battered MS ADM 352/350/2 showing San Felix. I am
   indebted to Captain Michael Barritt RN for his advice on this subject.
11 Woodward, *Robinson Crusoe's Island*, p. 133–4; Clissold, *Bernardo
   O'Higgins and the Independence of Chile*, p. 178.
12 M. Graham, *Journal of a Residence in Chile During the year 1822, and
   a Voyage from Chile to Brazil in 1823*, ed. T. Hayward, University of
   Virginia Press, Charlottesville, VA, 2003, p. 180.
13 E.B. Billingsley, *In Defence of Neutral Rights: United States Navy
   and the Wars of Independence in Chile and Peru*, University of North
   Carolina Press, Chapel Hill, NC, 1968, pp. 142–3 records that the USS
   Constellation took Chilean Troops to restore order in 1821.
14 Graham, *Journal of a Residence in Chile*, pp. 180–5.
15 A.L. Mitchell & S. House, *David Douglas: Explorer and Botanist*,
   Aurum Press, London, 1999, pp. 43–5; D. Douglas, *Journal Kept by
   David Douglas during His Travels in North America 1823–1827*, Wesley
   & Sons, London, 1914 (reprinted by Cambridge University Press), see
   pp. 53–4, 93–9 for Juan Fernández.
16 Douglas, *Journal*, p. 54.
17 Douglas, *Journal*, p. 54. They were London fire bricks.
18 Douglas, *Journal*, pp. 94–9; Skottsberg, *The Natural History of Juan
   Fernández and Easter Island*, vol. II, p. 797; Mitchell & House, *David
   Douglas*, p. 45.
19 P.J. Cain & A.G. Hopkins, *British Imperialism: Innovation and
   Expansion 1688–1914*, Longman, London, 1993, pp. 306–11; Keeble,
   *Commercial Relations between British Overseas Territories and South
   America*, pp. 6–9; R.A. Humphreys, *British Merchants and South
   American Independence*, Oxford University Press, Oxford, 1967.
20 John White to Lord Aberdeen (foreign secretary), 14 January 1830,
   in C.K. Webster (ed.), *Britain and the Independence of Latin America
   1812–1830: Select Documents from the Foreign Office Archives*,
   Oxford University Press, Oxford, 1938, vol. I, pp. 369–70 (taken from
   FO 16/12a).
21 Consular Correspondence is dominated by humdrum economic issues,
   presidential speeches and long-running financial disputes, some dating
   back to the War of Independence. See FO 16/4-70 for the 1840s. Nugent
   to George Canning 24 June 1824 & 5 July 1825, in Webster, *Britain and
   the Independence of Latin America*, vol. I, pp. 353–4, 359–60.
22 John White to Lord Aberdeen 4 & 14 January 1830, 30 June 1830, and
   John Bidwell (FO) to White, 21 June 1830, in Webster, *Britain and the
   Independence of Latin America*, vol. I, pp. 368–71.

CHAPTER 17: IMAGINARY VOYAGES

1 P.A. Longley, *Virtual Voyages: Travel Writing and the Antipodes 1605–1837*, Anthem Press, London, 2010, pp. xvii–xxiii, 4, citing an unpublished 1996 lecture by Jonathan Lamb.

2 Longley, *Virtual Voyages*, p. 133; J. Cameron, 'John Barrow, the *Quarterly Review*'s Imperial Reviewer', in J. Cutmore (ed.), *Conservatism and the Quarterly Review: A Critical Analysis*, Pickering & Chatto, London, 2007, pp. 133–50.

3 R. Dampier, *To the Sandwich Islands on HMS Blonde*, ed. P.K. Joerger, University of Hawaii Press, Honolulu, HI, 1971, p. 13, quote at p. 79.

4 B. Gough (ed.), *To the Pacific and Arctic with Beechey: The Journal of Lieutenant George Peard of HMS Blossom*, Hakluyt Society, Cambridge, 1973, p. 69.

5 P.P. King, *Narrative of the Surveying Voyages of His Majesty's Ships Adventure and Beagle between the Years 1826 and 1836: The First Expedition, 1826–1830*, London, 1839, preface, & pp. 298–308.

6 King, *Narrative of the Surveying Voyages of His Majesty's Ships*, pp. 298–308.

7 King, *Narrative of the Surveying Voyages of His Majesty's Ships*, pp. 298–308.

8 L. Dawson, *Memoirs of Hydrography*, vol. II, pp. 26–8. HMS *Beagle*, Juan Fernández: ADM 344/2255.

9 Charles Darwin to Captain Robert Fitzroy, HMS *Beagle*, 28 August 1834, in F. Burkhardt & S. Smith (eds), *The Correspondence of Charles Darwin, Volume 1: 1821–1836*, Cambridge University Press, Cambridge, 1985, pp. 406–7. The editors of the volume did not uncover Sutcliffe's suitably fabulous history.

10 'A Modern Crusoe', *The Times* (9 May 1835), p. 7, col. B.

11 T. Sutcliffe, *The Earthquake of Juan Fernández as it Occurred in the Year 1835*, Advertiser Office, Manchester, 1839, pp. 6, 9. Severely wounded at Waterloo, Sutcliffe joined the Columbian revolutionaries, but was detained by the Spanish at Havana. He was released in 1821 and joined the Chilean army the following year.

12 Robert Winthrop Simpson (1799–1877), British-born Chilean naval officer, arrived in Chile with Lord Cochrane and became rear-admiral of the Chilean navy.

13 Sutcliffe, *The Earthquake of Juan Fernández*, p. 9, col 2.

14 *The Times* (1 February 1836), p. 3 col. A; Woodward, *Robinson Crusoe's Island*, pp. 155–67.

15 Sutcliffe, *Crusoiana*, preface.

16 Sutcliffe, *Crusoiana*, pp. 112–92 on Anson and the *Wager*, p. 194 for Moss.

17 For more about Thomas Sutcliffe (1790?–1849) see www.oxforddnb.com/view/printable/26793.

18 *The Times* (20 October 1837), p. 3, col. B; Skottsberg, *The Natural History of Juan Fernández and Easter Island*, vol. II, p. 798; J.S.-C.D.

D'Urville, *An Account of Two Voyages to the South Seas, Volume II: The Astrolabe and Zélée 1837–1840*, tr. & ed. H. Rosenman, Melbourne University Press, Carlton, 1987.

CHAPTER 18: AN AMERICAN SOUTH PACIFIC

1 F.W. Howay (ed.), *Voyages of the Columbia to the North-West Coast 1787–1790 and 1790–1793*, Oregon Historical Society, Portland, OR, 1990, pp. 23–4. The reference is to page 322 of volume I.

2 Howay, *Voyages of the Columbia to the North-West Coast*, pp. 22–6 (quote at p. 24).

3 Howay, *Voyages of the Columbia to the North-West Coast*, pp. 162–3.

4 A. Delano, *Narrative of Voyages and Travels in the Northern and Southern Hemispheres: Comprising Three Voyages Round the World; Together with a Voyage of Survey and Discovery in the Pacific Ocean and the Oriental Islands*, Boston, 1817, reprinted ed. E.R. Segroves, Stockingbridge, MA, 1994, pp. 234–44.

5 H. Melville, *Billy Budd and Other Stories*, ed. H. Beaver, London, 1967, pp. 215–309, 443–50; Woodward, *Robinson Crusoe's Island*, pp. 107–9.

6 Keeble, *Commercial Relations between British Overseas Territories and South America*, pp. 1–3; Delano, *Narrative of Voyages and Travels*, pp. 239–43. For the *Bounty* chronometer, see W. Hayes, *The Captain from Nantucket and the Mutiny on the Bounty*, William L. Clements Library, Ann Arbor, MI, 1996, p. 86 (see also pp. 30–6, 42–7, 79).

CHAPTER 19: A LITERATURE OF DEFEAT: RECONSTRUCTING THE LOSS OF THE USS *ESSEX*

1 D. Porter, *Journal of a Cruise to the Pacific Ocean by Captain David Porter in the United States Frigate Essex, in the years 1812, 1813, and 1814, Containing descriptions of the Cape de Verde Islands, Coasts of Brazil, Patagonia, Chile and of the Galapagos Islands*, 2 vols, Bradford and Inskip, Philadelphia, PA, 1815, p. 180, citing Colnett, *A Voyage to the South Atlantic*. Porter had planned an expedition into the Pacific before the war.

2 D.F. Long, *Nothing Too Daring: A Biography of Commodore David Porter 1783–1843*, US Naval Institute Press, Annapolis, MD, 1970, p. 170.

3 The second edition, 'to which is now added an introduction, in which the charges contained in the *Quarterly Review*, of the first edition of this Journal and examined', appeared in 1822 from Wiley and Halstead, New York. See Long, *Nothing Too Daring*, pp. 71–2, 331–2. The *Cambridge History of American Literature*, p. 763 lists Porter as an 'important text on or concerning the New World', the only naval work so noted for this period. G.S. Hellman, *Washington Irving*, London, 1924, p. 82.

4 See S.E. Morison, *'Old Bruin': Commodore Matthew C. Perry, 1794–1858*, Little, Brown, Boston, MA, 1967, pp. 270–409 for the expedition.

Critically, Perry's squadron entered the Pacific via the Cape of Good Hope.

5 Long, *Nothing Too Daring*, pp. 124–6.

6 H. Blum, *The View from the Masthead: Maritime Imagination and Antebellum American Sea Narratives*, University of North Carolina Press, Chapel Hill, NC, 2008, pp. 119, 30–8, 204–5.

7 Blum, *The View from the Masthead*, pp. 9, 14, 72–3, 128–9.

8 O. Chase, *The Wreck of the Whaleship Essex: A Narrative by Owen Chase, First Mate*, 1821, new edition ed. I. Haverstick & B. Shepard, Harcourt Brace & Co., London, 1997, p. 6.

9 Chase, *The Wreck of the Whaleship Essex*, p. 67.

10 Chase, *The Wreck of the Whaleship Essex*, pp. 86–7

11 Billingsley, *In Defence of Neutral Rights*, p. 126.

12 C. Wilkes, *Autobiography of Rear Admiral Charles Wilkes US Navy 1798–1877*, Naval Historical Centre, Washington, DC, 1978, pp. 141–5, 168; C. Berube & J. Rodgaard, *A Call to the Sea: Captain Charles Stewart of the USS Constitution*, Potomac Books, Washington, DC, 2005, pp. 146–88.

13 R.E. Johnson, *Thence Round Cape Horn: The Story of United States Naval Forces on the Pacific Station, 1818–1923*, US Naval Institute Press, Annapolis, MD, 1963, pp. 30–31; Berube & Rodgaard, *A Call to the Sea*, pp. 166–8; Billingsley, *In Defence of Neutral Rights*, pp. 151–7, 170–7.

CHAPTER 20: SEA STORIES

1 R.H. Dana Jr., *Two Years Before the Mast: A Personal Narrative of Life at Sea*, Boston, 1840 (all quotes taken from the 1911 London Macmillan edition), pp. 44–51.

2 Dana, *Two Years Before the Mast*, pp. 44–51.

3 Blum, *The View from the Masthead*, pp. 72–3.

4 D. Loveman, *No Higher Law: American Foreign Policy and the Western Hemisphere since 1776*, University of North Carolina Press, Chapel Hill, NC, 2010, pp. 107–10.

5 J.R. Browne, *Crusoe's Island: A Ramble in the Footsteps of Alexander Selkirk, with Sketches of Adventure in California and Washoe*, New York, 1868, p. 24.

6 Woodward, *Robinson Crusoe's Island*, pp. 184–91 quoting Browne.

7 *The Times* (12 July 1859), p. 9, col. F (my insertions in brackets).

CHAPTER 21: POET OF THE PACIFIC

1 H. Parker, *Herman Melville: A Biography, Volume I: 1819–1851*, Johns Hopkins University Press, Baltimore, MD, 1996, pp. 689, 724–6; Blum, *The View from the Masthead*, pp. 109, 115–16, 128–9.

2 C.S. Stewart, *A Visit to the South Seas, in the US Ship Vincennes, During the Years 1829 and 1830*, Fisher, Son, & Jackson, London, 1832; Parker, *Herman Melville*, vol. I, p. 75; Blum, *The View from the Masthead*, p. 10.

3 Chase, *The Wreck of the Whaleship Essex*, p. 100; Parker, *Herman Melville*, vol. I, pp. 194–8.

4 Parker, *Herman Melville*, vol. I, pp. 220–12 quotes from the novel *Typee*.

5 Parker, *Herman Melville*, vol. I, p. 233. 265, 385–6.

6 Parker, *Herman Melville*, vol. I, p. 267.

7 Woodward, *Robinson Crusoe's Island*, pp. 180–1.

8 Parker, *Herman Melville*, vol. I, pp. 273–7.

9 Melville thought sending the manuscript of *Moby Dick* to Dana 'the best publication'; see Parker, *Herman Melville*, vol. I, p. 715.

10 Murray to Melville, 5 December 1847, in L. Hoth (ed.), *Correspondence of Herman Melville*, Chicago, 1960, p. 591.

11 Reviews cited in Parker, *Herman Melville*, vol. I, pp. 709–14.

12 Review cited in Parker, *Herman Melville*, vol. I, p. 715.

13 Parker, *Herman Melville*, vol. I, pp. 832, 835.

14 Parker, *Herman Melville*, vol. I, pp. 843, 694. Melville gathered whale and whaling books; few texts were so useful as Colnett's *A Voyage to the South Atlantic*, which he may have encountered in Porter's *Journal*.

15 Parker, *Herman Melville*, vol. I, pp. 476–7.

16 Blum, *The View from the Masthead*, pp. 131–57. H. Melville, 'Islands of the Pacific', *Putnam's Monthly Magazine* (August 1856), p. 156, quoted in Blum, *The View from the Masthead*, p. 157. Text in Melville, *Billy Budd and Other Stories*, pp. 129–94.

17 H. Parker, *Herman Melville: A Biography, Volume II: 1851–1891*, Johns Hopkins University Press, Baltimore, MD, 2002, pp. 374–8.

18 Loveman, *No Higher Law*, pp. 143–9. M.R. Shulman, *Navalism and the Emergence of American Sea Power, 1882–1893*, US Naval Institute Press, Annapolis, MD, 1995 examines a later clash between old and new views of the Pacific.

19 Blum, *The View from the Masthead*, p. 194; H. Springer (ed.), *America and the Sea: A Literary History*, Georgia University Press, Athens, GA, 1995, p. ix.

CHAPTER 22: A BRITISH BASE IN THE PACIFIC

1 Barrow, *The Life of George, Lord Anson*, pp. 393, 418–19.

2 Thomas to Admiralty, Valparaiso, 16 April 1842, rec'd 28 July 1842: ADM 1/5512.

3 Admiralty to Seymour, 25 July 1844: ADM 172/4.

4 F. Merk, *The Oregon Question: Essays in Anglo-American Diplomacy and Politics*, Harvard University Press, Cambridge, MA, 1967, esp. pp. 2116–394; Gough, *The Royal Navy and the Northwest Coast of North America*, pp. 70–2. Thomas to Admiralty, 23 April 1842, Callao rec. 28 July 1842: ADM 1/5512 on steam ships. Foreign Office to Admiralty, 1 November 1847: ADM 12/477, cut 51 25.

CHAPTER 23: THE ADMIRAL'S PICNIC

1   D. Crane, *Men of War: Courage under Fire in the 19th Century Navy*, Harper Press, London, 2009, p. 327

2   *The Times* (9 March 1848). Log book 6-17-12.1847, HMS *Collingwood*: ADM 53/2281. Admiral Sir George Seymour's Journal: ADM 50/213, p. 489.

3   A.H. Markham, *A Brief Memoir of Commodore J.G. Goodenough*, Portsmouth, 1877.

4   Crane, *Men of War*, pp. 327–32. Markham added the shrieks of non-existent owls to an overnight ordeal he did not share! For a different perspective on Goodenough, see J. Samson, *Imperial Benevolence: Making British Authority in the Pacific Islands*, University of Hawaii Press, Honolulu, HI, 1998, pp. 147–75.

5   Seymour diary of places visited, 6 December 1847: CR114A/421, Warwick Record Office. F. Walpole, *Four Years in the Pacific in Her Majesty's Ship Collingwood, from 1844 to 1848*, second edition, 2 vols, Richard Bentley, London, 1850, p. 378.

6   Crane, *Men of War*, pp. 319–422; J. Samson, 'Hero, Fool or Martyr? The Many Deaths of Commodore Goodenough', *Journal for Maritime Research* 10(1) (February 2008), pp. 1–22.

7   H.A. Kay (ed.), *HMS Collingwood, 1844–48: From the Journals of Philip Horatio Townsend Somerville*, Pentland Press, Edinburgh, 1986, pp. 244–6.

8   Walpole sat as Conservative MP for North Norfolk from 1868 until his death in 1876. His decision to leave the sea may have followed a near-death experience: Walpole fell overboard and was lucky to be rescued. See *Naval and Military Gazette* (26 October 1844). Admiralty to Seymour, 22 November 1844: ADM 172/4 27.

9   Journal entries 30 March 1845 & 5 March 1846 in Kay, *HMS Collingwood*, pp. 49, 175.

10 Journal entry 13 June 1846 in Kay, *HMS Collingwood*, p. 196.

11 Walpole, *Four Years in the Pacific*, ch. 14 (quote at p. 362).

12 Anyone who has suffered the irritation of clothes washed in salt water will understand this reference.

13 Woodward identifies one man as Pedro Maurelio.

14 Walpole, *Four Years in the Pacific*, pp. 359–60.

15 Walpole, *Four Years in the Pacific*, pp. 367–8.

16 Walpole, *Four Years in the Pacific*, pp. 370–6.

17 Walpole, *Four Years in the Pacific*, pp. 379–81.

18 Seymour to Walpole, 27 September 1849: CR 114A 414/4 f281. Seymour to Lord Auckland (first lord of the admiralty), 28 November 1846: CR114A 418/3, p. 54. Journal for 10 December 1847: CR114A /421. Seymour to hydrographer Francis Beaufort, 29 December 1847: CR114A 414/4 ff.61–3.

19 Walpole, *Four Years in the Pacific*, pp. 354–5, 361, 365, 373.

CHAPTER 24: OCCUPATION, POSSESSION, OWNERSHIP AND TITLE

1 Blum, *The View from the Masthead*, p. 167. Woodward, *Robinson Crusoe's Island*, pp. 181–3; 'Naval Intelligence', *The Times* (9 January 1849).

2 'Burning of the Ship *Townsend*', *The Times* (26 August 1854), p. 5, col. E. In 1855 a damaged British ship put into Cumberland Bay: 'Ship News', *The Times* (2 January 1855), p. 10, col. B.

3 'Shipping Intelligence: The Ship *Horsburgh*, Laden with Guanao', *The Times* (29 October 1860), p. 9, col. B.

4 G. Bennett, *Charlie B: A Biography of Admiral Lord Beresford*, London, 1968, p. 32.

5 Woodward, *Robinson Crusoe's Island*, p. 47; 'Alexander Selkirk, the Original of Robinson Crusoe', *The Times* (21 December 1868), p. 6. Selkirk actually died in 1721.

6 'The Earthquake in Peru', *The Times* (23 October 1868), p. 10, col. D.

7 W. Kennedy, *Hurrah for the Life of a Sailor!*, William Blackwood, Edinburgh, 1900, p. 173; 'Naval and Military Intelligence', *The Times* (16 April 1873), p. 3, col. E; Woodward, *Robinson Crusoe's Island*, pp. 206–7.

8 M. Deacon, *Scientists and the Sea: A Study of Marine Science*, Academic Press, London, 1971, pp. 306–66; H. Rozwadowski, *Fathoming the Ocean: The Discovery of the Deep Sea*, Belknap Press, Cambridge, MA, 2005, p. 28; E. Linklater, *The Voyage of the Challenger*, John Murray, London, 1972, pp. 243–9.

9 J.Y. Buchanan, H.N. Moseley, J. Murray & T.H. Tizard, *The Report of the Scientific Results of the Exploring Voyage of HMS Challenger during the Years 1873–1876*. 50 volumes were published between 1885 and 1895. The 'Narrative' formed volume one, and even that came in two parts.

10 Linklater, *The Voyage of the Challenger*, p. 243; *The Times* (31 March 1877), p. 7, col. A.

11 Lord G. Campbell, *Log Letters from the Challenger*, Macmillan, London, 1877, p. 392.

12 H.N. Moseley, *Notes by a Naturalist on HMS Challenger*, John Murray, London, 1892, pp. 466–71.

13 Moseley, *Notes by a Naturalist on HMS Challenger*, p. 466. Friday was a Miskito Indian based on Will.

14 Moseley, *Notes by a Naturalist on HMS Challenger*, p. 467.

15 Campbell, *Log Letters from the Challenger*, pp. 392–4.

16 Moseley, *Notes by a Naturalist on HMS Challenger*, pp. 469–70; *Report of HMS Challenger*, part II, p. 51.

17 Moseley, *Notes by a Naturalist on HMS Challenger*, p. 517.

18 G. Douglas, *Autobiography and Memoirs*, London, 1906, vol. II, p. 513.

CHAPTER 25: SETTLERS

1 Souhami, *Selkirk's Island*, p. 215.

2 D.W. Williams & J. Armstrong, 'An Appraisal of the Progress of the Steamship in the Nineteenth Century', in G. Harlaftis, S. Tenold & J. Valadiso (eds), *The World's Key Industry: History and Economics of International Shipping*, Macmillan, Basingstoke, 2012, pp. 49–55.

3 Ship's log, Maritime Museum, Bath, ME. Material supplied by Pedro Niada.

4 Johnson, *Thence Round Cape Horn*, pp. 144–52.

5 'Disasters at Sea', *The Times* (31 December 1891), p. 6, col. C. Hotham to Admiralty, 27 January 1892, no. 27: ADM 1/7111 (the report is missing). *Melpomene* log book, 30 December 1891 to 1 January 1892: ADM 53/14524.

6 Nova Scotian born Slocum (1844–1909) became a naturalised American citizen, serving as a seaman and master mariner before turning to literature. J. Slocum, *Sailing Alone*, London, 1900, pp. 122–9.

7 Slocum, *Sailing Alone*, p. 135.

8 'Naval and Military Intelligence', *The Times* (21 February 1902), p. 9, col. B. Armoured cruiser, 8,500 tons, completed 1886, Captain Colin Keppel. Rear Admiral A.K. Bickford to Admiralty, 7 March 1902, no.56: ADM 1/7592. *Warspite* log book 21–22 February 1902: ADM 53/16567. Admiral Bickford's journal: ADM 50/360.

9 H. Blakemore, *British Nitrates and Chilean Politics 1886–1896: Balmaceda and North*, University of London Press, London, 1974, pp. 12–14; J. Mayo, *British Merchants and Chilean Development, 1851–1886*, Westview, London, 1987, pp. 6, 66–7, 71–3, 83, 229–33; H. Barty-King, *Girdle Round the Earth: The Story of Cable & Wireless*, Heinemann, London, 1979, pp. 47, 51, 96, 152.

10 *The Times* (20 June 1912), p. 4. *Atrato* sold to Viking Cruising Company later that year, renamed *Viking*, and was lost with all hands off Northern Ireland on 13 January 1915 while serving as armed merchant cruiser *Viknor*. See R. Osborne, H. Spong, & T. Grover, *Armed Merchant Cruisers 1878–1945*, World Ship Society, Windsor, 2007, pp. 56, 134.

CHAPTER 26: THE BATTLE OF CUMBERLAND BAY

1 J.S. Corbett, *Naval Operations, Volume I*, Longmans, Green & Co., London, 1920, pp. 344–5, 355, 406; N. Lambert, *Planning Armageddon*, Harvard University Press, Cambridge, MA, 2012, p. 248.

2 *The Times* (23 & 25 November 1914).

3 Corbett, *Naval Operations*, vol. I, pp. 365–6, 409, 435; J.S. Corbett, *Naval Operations, Volume II*, Longmans, Green & Co., London, 1921, p. 240.

4 A.W. Jose, *The Royal Australian Navy 1914–1918, volume IX*, Sydney, 1928, pp. 124–8, 135, 262–3; D. Stevens, *The Royal Australian Navy*, Oxford University Press, Melbourne, 2001, pp. 36–7; Corbett, *Naval Operations*, vol. II, pp. 243–5.

5 *Orama*, 13,000 tons, 18 knots, Oriental Steam Navigation Company ship, built 1911, armed with eight 6-inch guns. Sunk by a U-boat on 10 October 1917. Osborne, Spong & Grover, *Armed Merchant Cruisers 1878–1945*, pp. 45–6, 125; Corbett, *Naval Operations*, vol. II, pp. 248–51.

CHAPTER 27: FROM THE *CHALLENGER* TO THE ADMIRALTY HANDBOOK

1 T.W. Freeman, *A History of Modern British Geography*, Longman, London, 1980, pp. 19–20.
2 Freeman, *A History of Modern British Geography*, pp. 56, 67, 186.
3 H. Clout & C. Gosme, 'The Naval Intelligence Handbooks: A Monument in Geographical Writing', *Progress in Human Geography* 27(2) (2003), pp. 153–73, here p. 155.
4 FO Handbook 'prepared for the Peace Conference', no 141b, June 1919: FO 373/7/14 editorial note.
5 FO 373/7/14 no.141b.
6 FO 373/7/14 no.141b, pp. 20–2 (a critical passage missing from the 1920 publication) & p. 23.
7 *Juan Fernández no. 143*, 1920, pp. 33–60, bibliography at pp. 59–60. 1,000 printed, September 1920.
8 Skottsberg's article from the American *Geographical Review* (May 1918), pp. 363–83.
9 FO 373/7/14 no.141b, pp. 22–4.
10 1920 published handbook, p. 56.
11 *The Times* (9 November 1926), p. 2. The *Orduna* survived both World Wars. *Pacific Islands: Volume II Eastern Pacific*, B.R. 519 B (Restricted) Geographical Handbook Series, November 1943, p. 46.
12 Edmundson, *A History of the British Presence in Chile*, pp. 229–31.
13 Anon., *With HMS 'Caradoc' round South America*, produced by the ship's officers, foreword by Captain H. Moore, privately printed by Flood of Lowestoft, n.d. (but *c.*1930). I am indebted to my friend Ann Savours for this text.
14 Skottsberg, *The Natural History of Juan Fernández and Easter Island*, vol. I, p. 190.
15 Clout & Gosme, 'The Naval Intelligence Handbooks', is the best modern source; see ADM 223/444 for the typescript history of the project. See also *Pacific Islands* vol. II, p. 3, & vol. 1, p. 531.
16 *Esmeralda* paid off in the 1930s. I am indebted to Captain Carlos Tromben Corbalen, Chilean Navy for this information.

CHAPTER 28: MAKING ROBINSON'S ISLAND

1 Skottsberg, *The Natural History of Juan Fernández and Easter Island*, vol. I, pp. 180–90.
2 K. Rushby, *Paradise: A History of the Idea that Rules the World*, Basic Books, New York, 2007, pp. 32, 111–14, 146.

3 Grove, *Green Imperialism*, p. 54, citing Marshall & Williams, *The Great Map of Mankind*, pp. 8, 54–9.
4 Grove, *Green Imperialism*, pp. 63, 222–37, 325–6, 454.
5 Grove, *Green Imperialism*, pp. 222–5.
6 Woodward, *Robinson Crusoe's Island*, pp. xiii–xxiv.
7 T. Clarke, *Islomania: A Journey among the Last Real Islands*, Abacus, New York, 2002, pp. 28–39.
8 Souhami, *Selkirk's Island*, pp. 220–2.

CHAPTER 29: ISLANDS, NATIONS AND CONTINENTS

1 Colley, *Captives*, p. 11.
2 Colley, *Captives*, p. 378.
3 J. Ruskin, *The Stones of Venice: The Foundations*, London, 1851, p. 1; D. Wormell, *Sir John Seeley and the Uses of History*, Cambridge University Press, Cambridge, 1980, p. 41–2; J.R. Seeley, *The Expansion of England*, London, 1883, p. 1.
4 J.G.A. Pocock, *The Discovery of Islands: Essays in British History*, Cambridge University Press, Cambridge, 2005, p. 49. New Zealander Pocock takes a radically different view of British history to the current 'European' phase of historiography. The founding father of British naval history made the same argument a century ago; see A.D. Lambert (ed.), *Letters and Papers of Sir John Knox Laughton*, Navy Records Society, London, 2002, pp. 263–97.
5 F. Nietzsche, *The Use and Abuse of History*, 1873, tr. A. Collins, Bobbs-Merrill, Indianapolis, IN, 1949, p. 40.
6 Pocock, *The Discovery of Islands*, pp. 109–10, 146–8.

Bibliography

━━◈◈◈━━

Anon., *Authentic Account of Commodore Anson's Expedition*, London, 1744.

Anon., *With HMS 'Caradoc' Round South America*, produced by the ship's officers, foreword by Captain H. Moore, privately printed by Flood of Lowestoft, n.d.

Bacon, F., *The Essays: The Wisdom of the Ancients and the New Atlantis*, Odhams, London, n.d.

Barrow, J., *The Life of George, Lord Anson*, John Murray, London, 1839, pp. 41–2.

Barty-King, H., *Girdle Round the Earth: The Story of Cable & Wireless*, Heinemann, London, 1979.

Beaglehole, J., *The Exploration of the Pacific*, London, 1960.

Beattie, T., '"Entirely the Most Absurd and False Narrative that was ever Deliver'd to the Publick": An Inquiry into What Really Happened on George Shelvocke's Privateering Voyage', *The Mariner's Mirror* 97(3) (2011), pp. 163–76.

Bennett, G., *Charlie B: A Biography of Admiral Lord Beresford*, London, 1968.

Berube, C. & J. Rodgaard, *A Call to the Sea: Captain Charles Stewart of the USS Constitution*, Potomac Books, Washington, DC, 2005, pp. 146–88.

Betagh, W., *A Voyage Round the World: Being an Account of a Remarkable Enterprise Begun in 1719, Chiefly to Cruise on the Spaniards in the Great South Ocean*, London, 1728.

Billingsley, B., *In Defence of Neutral Rights: United States Navy and the Wars of Independence in Chile and Peru*, University of North Carolina Press, Chapel Hill, NC, 1968.

Blakemore, H., *British Nitrates and Chilean Politics 1886–1896: Balmaceda and North*, University of London Press, London, 1974.

Blum, H., *The View from the Masthead: Maritime Imagination and Antebellum American Sea Narratives*, University of North Carolina Press, Chapel Hill, NC, 2008.

Bradley, P., *The Lure of Peru: Maritime Intrusion into the South Sea, 1598–1701*, St Martin's Press, London, 1989.

————— & D. Cahill, *Habsburg Peru: Images, Imagination and Memory*, Liverpool University Press, Liverpool, 2000.

Brewer, J., *The Pleasures of the Imagination: English Culture in the Eighteenth Century*, HarperCollins, London 1997.

Brown, J., *Lancelot 'Capability' Brown, 1716–1784: The Omnipotent Magician*, Chatto & Windus London, 2011.

Browne, J.R., *Crusoe's Island: A Ramble in the Footsteps of Alexander Selkirk, with Sketches of Adventure in California and Washoe*, New York, 1868.

Buchanan, J.Y., H.N. Moseley, J. Murray & T.H. Tizard, *The Report of the Scientific Results of the Exploring Voyage of HMS Challenger during the Years 1873–1876*, 50 vols, 1885–95.

Burckhardt, J., *Civilisation of Italy in the Renaissance*, tr. S.G.C. Middlemore, London, 1878.

Burkhardt, F. & S. Smith (eds), *The Correspondence of Charles Darwin, Volume 1: 1821–1836*, Cambridge University Press, Cambridge, 1985.

Cain, P.J. & A.G. Hopkins, *British Imperialism: Innovation and Expansion 1688–1914*, Longman, London, 1993.

Cameron, J., 'John Barrow, the Quarterly Review's Imperial Reviewer', in J. Cutmore (ed.), *Conservatism and the Quarterly Review: A Critical Analysis*, Pickering & Chatto, London, 2007, pp. 133–50.

Campbell, J. (ed.), *Navigantium; or A Complete Collection of Voyages and Travels*, London, 1744.

Campbell, G., *Log Letters from the Challenger*, Macmillan, London, 1877.

Carswell, J., *The South Sea Bubble*, Sutton Publishing, Gloucester, 1993.

Chambers, N. (ed.), *The Indian and Pacific Correspondence of Sir Joseph Banks, 1768–1820*, 6 vols, Pickering & Chatto, London, 2008–14.

Chase, O., *The Wreck of the Whaleship Essex: A Narrative by Owen Chase, First Mate, 1821*, new edition ed. I. Haverstick & B. Shepard, Harcourt Brace & Co., London, 1997.

Churchill, A.& J. Churchill, *Navigantium atque Itinerantium Bibliotheca: A Collection of Voyages and Travels*, London, vols I–IV, 1704, vols V–VI, 1732, vol. III, p. 46.

Clarke, T., *Islomania: A Journey among the Last Real Islands*, Abacus, New York, 2002.

Clissold, S., *Bernardo O'Higgins and the Independence of Chile*, London, 1968.

Clout, H. & C. Gosme, 'The Naval Intelligence Handbooks: A Monument in Geographical Writing', *Progress in Human Geography* 27(2) (2003), pp. 153–73.

Colley, L., *Captives: Britain, Empire and the World 1600–1850*, Jonathan Cape, London, 2002.

Colnett, J., *A Voyage to the South Atlantic and Round Cape Horn into the Pacific Ocean for the Purpose of Extending the Spermacetti Whale Fisheries and Other Objects of Commerce by Ascertaining the Ports, Bays, Harbours, and Anchoring Births in Certain Islands and Coasts in Those Seas at which the Ships of the British Merchants Might be Refitted*, London, 1798.

Conn, S., *Gibraltar in British Diplomacy in the Eighteenth Century*, Yale University Press, New Haven, CT, 1942.

Corbett, J.S., *England in the Mediterranean: A Study of the Rise and Influence of British Power within the Straits, 1603–1713*, Longman, London, 1904.

————, *Naval Operations, Volume I*, Longmans, Green & Co., London, 1920.

————, *Naval Operations, Volume II*, Longmans, Green & Co., London, 1921.

Cordingly, D., *Spanish Gold: Captain Woodes Rogers and the Pirates of the Caribbean*, Bloomsbury, London, 2011.

Cowper, W., *The Task and Other Poems*, ed. J. Sambrook, Longman, London, 1994.

Crane, D., *Men of War: Courage under Fire in the 19th Century Navy*, Harper Press, London, 2009.

Crone, G.A. & R.A. Skelton, 'English Collections of Voyages and Travels, 1625–1846', in E. Lynam (ed.), *Richard Hakluyt and his Successors*, Hakluyt Society, London, 1946.

Dalrymple, J., *Memoirs of Great Britain*, London, 1789.

Dampier, W., *A New Voyage Round the World: Describing Particularly The Isthmus of America, feveral Coafts and Iflands in the Weft Indies, the Ifles of Cape Ver, the Paffage by Tierra del Fuego, the South Sea Coafts of Chili, Peru, and Mexico, the Ifle of Guma, one of the Ladrones, Mindanao, and other Philippine and Eaft India Iflands near Cambodia, China, Formofa, Luconia, Celebes &c, New Holland, Sumatra, Nicobar Ifles, the Cape of Good Hope, and Santa Helena, Their Soil, Rivers, Harbours, Plants, Fruits, Animals, and Inhabitants, Their Customs, Religion, Government, Trade &c. Illustrated with Particular Maps and Draughts*, James Knapton, London, 2 vols, 1697.

————, *A Voyage to New Holland, &c. in the year 1699*, Argonaut Press, London, 1939.

Dampier, R., *To the Sandwich Islands on HMS Blonde*, ed. P.K. Joerger, University of Hawaii Press, Honolulu, HI, 1971.

Dana Jr., R.H., *Two Years Before the Mast: A Personal Narrative of Life at Sea*, Boston, 1840.

David, A., F. Fernández-Armesto, C. Novi & G. Williams (eds), *The Malaspina Expedition, 1789–1794*, vol. I, Hakluyt Society, Cambridge, 2001.

Davies, J.D., 'Chatham to Erith via Dover: Charles II's Secret Foreign Policy and the Project for new Royal Dockyards, 1667–1672', in R. Riley (ed.), *Pepys and Chips: Dockyards Naval Administration and Warfare in the Seventeenth Century*, Naval Dockyards Society, Southsea, 2012.

Dawson, L., *Memoirs of Hydrography*, vol. II, pp. 26–8

Dawson, W.R. (ed.), *The Banks Letters*, British Museum, London, 1958.

Deacon, M., *Scientists and the Sea: A Study of Marine Science*, Academic Press, London, 1971.

De Brosses, C., *Histoire des Navigations aux Terres Australes*, Paris, 1756.

Defoe, D., *The Life and Strange Surprizing Adventures of Robinson Crusoe, of York, Mariner: Who Lived Eight and Twenty Years, All Alone in an Un-inhabited Island on the Coast of America, Near the Mouth of the Great River of Oroonoque; Having Been Cast on Shore by Shipwreck, wherein All the Men Perished but Himself; with an Account How He Was at Last as Strangely Deliver'd by Pyrates*, W. Taylor, London, 1719.

————, *A Plan of the English Commerce: Being a Compleat Prospect of the Trade of This Nation, as Well the Home Trade as the Foreign*, London, 1728.

————, *Atlas Maritimus and Commercialis*, London, 1728.

Delano, A., *Narrative of Voyages and Travels in the Northern and Southern Hemispheres: Comprising Three Voyages Round the World; Together with a Voyage of Survey and Discovery in the Pacific Ocean and the Oriental Islands*, Boston, 1817, reprinted ed. E.R. Segroves, Stockingbridge, MA, 1994.

Douglas, D., *Journal Kept by David Douglas during His Travels in North America 1823–1827*, Wesley & Sons, London, 1914.

Douglas, G., *Autobiography and Memoirs*, London, 1906, vol. II, p. 513.

Dunmore, J. (ed.), *The Journal of Jean François de Galaup de la Pérouse, 1785–1788*, 2 vols, Hakluyt Society, Cambridge, 1994–5.

D'Urville, J.S.-C.D., *An Account of Two Voyages to the South Seas, Volume II: The Astrolabe and Zélée 1837–1840*, tr. & ed. H. Rosenman, Melbourne University Press, Carlton, 1987.

Edmundson, W., *A History of the British Presence in Chile: From Bloody Mary to Charles Darwin and the Decline of British Influence*, Palgrave, Basingstoke, 2011.

Ehrman, J., *The Younger Pitt: The Years of Acclaim*, Constable, London, 1969.

Ellery, M., 'William Campbell and the Harrington: Privateering in Chilean Waters in 1804', *The Mariner's Mirror* 97(4) (2011), pp. 315–40.

Entick, J., *A New Naval History, or a Compleat View of the British Marine*, London, 1757.

Esquemelin, J., *The Buccaneers of America*, Routledge, London, n.d.

Fernández-Armesto, F., *Amerigo: The Man Who Gave His Name to America*, Weidenfeld & Nicholson, London, 2006.

Ferreiro, L.D., *Measure of the Earth: The Enlightenment Expedition that Reshaped Our World*, Basic Books, New York, 2011.

Flynn, C., 'Nationalism, Commerce, and Imperial Authority in Defoe's Later Works', *Rocky Mountain Review* (Fall 2000), pp. 11–24.

Fowke, R., *The Real Ancient Mariner: Pirates and Poesy on the South Sea*, Travelbrief, Shropshire, 2010.

Freeman, T.W., *A History of Modern British Geography*, Longman, London, 1980.

Frost, A., 'Shaking Off the Spanish Yoke: British Schemes to Revolutionise America, 1739–1807', in M. Lincoln (ed.), *Science and Exploration in the Pacific: European Voyages to the Southern Oceans in the Eighteenth Century*, Boydell Press, Woodbridge, 1998, pp. 19–37.

Fry, H.T., *Alexander Dalrymple and the Expansion of British Trade*, Toronto University Press, Toronto, 1970.

Funnell, W., *A Voyage Round the World*, London, 1707.

Gallagher, R.E. (ed.), *Byron's Journal*, Hakluyt Society, Cambridge, 1964.

Gough, B.M., *The Royal Navy and the Northwest Coast of North America 1810–1914: A Study of British Maritime Ascendancy*, University of British Columbia Press, Vancouver, 1971.

—— (ed.), *To the Pacific and Arctic with Beechey: The Journal of Lieutenant George Peard of HMS Blossom*, Hakluyt Society, Cambridge, 1973.

——, *Distant Dominion: Britain and the North-West Coast of North America, 1579–1809*, British Columbia University Press, Vancouver, 1980.

Graham, G.S. & R.A. Humphreys (eds), *The Navy in South America, 1807–1823*, Navy Records Society, London, 1962.

Graham, M., *Journal of a Residence in Chile During the year 1822, and a Voyage from Chile to Brazil in 1823*, ed. T. Hayward, University of Virginia Press, Charlottesville, VA, 2003.

Grove, R.H., *Green Imperialism: Colonial Expansion, Tropical Island Edens and the Origins of Environmentalism, 1600–1860*, Cambridge University Press, Cambridge, 1995.

Harlow, V.T. (ed.), *Raleigh's Last Voyage*, Argonaut Press, London, 1932.

——, *The Founding of the Second British Empire 1763–1793, Volume II: New Continents and Changing Values*, Longman, London, 1964.

Harris, M., 'Commander John Ralph Moss, RN (1759–1799)', *Naval Review* 100 (February 2012), pp. 60–5.

Harris, J., *Navigantium atque Itinerantium Biblotheca*, 2 vols, London, 1705.

Hayes, W., *The Captain from Nantucket and the Mutiny on the Bounty*, William L. Clements Library, Ann Arbor, MI, 1996.

Heaps, L. (ed.), *Log of the Centurion: Based on the Original Papers of Captain Philip Saumarez on Board HMS Centurion, Lord Anson's Flagship During his Circumnavigation 1740–44*, Hart Davies, London, 1973.

Heidenreich, H. (ed.), *The Libraries of Daniel Defoe and Phillips Farewell: Olive Payne's catalogue (1731)*, Berlin, 1970.

Hellman, G.S., *Washington Irving*, London, 1924.

Hoth, L. (ed.), *Correspondence of Herman Melville*, Chicago, 1960.

Howay, F.W. (ed.), *Voyages of the Columbia to the North-West Coast 1787–1790 and 1790–1793*, Oregon Historical Society, Portland, OR, 1990.

Howse, D. & N. Thrower, *A Buccaneer's Atlas: Basil Ringrose's South Sea Waggoner*, University of California Press, Berkeley, CA, 1992.

Humphreys, R.A., *British Merchants and South American Independence*, Oxford University Press, Oxford, 1967.

James, I., *Providence Displayed: or, The Remarkable Adventures of Alexander Selkirk, of Largo, in Scotland; Who Lived Four Years and Four Months by Himself, on the Island of Juan Fernandez; from whence He Returned with Capt. Woodes Rogers, of Bristol, and on whose Adventures was Founded the Celebrated Novel of Robinson Crusoe*, London, 1800.

Jardine, L., *Going Dutch: How England Plundered Holland's Glory*, HarperCollins, London, 2008.

Johnson, R.E., *Thence Round Cape Horn: The Story of United States Naval Forces on the Pacific Station, 1818–1923*, US Naval Institute Press, Annapolis, MD, 1963, pp. 30–31;

Jose, A.W., *The Royal Australian Navy 1914–1918*, volume IX, Sydney, 1928.

Joyce, L.E.E. (ed.), *A New Voyage & Description of the Isthmus of America by Lionel Wafer, Surgeon on Buccaneering Expeditions in Darien, the*

West Indies, and the Pacific from 1680 to 1688; with Wafer's Secret Report (1698) and Davis's Expedition to the Gold Mines (1704), Hakluyt Society, London, 1934.

Juan, J. & A. de Ulloa, *A Voyage to South America*, London, 1758.

Kay, H.A. (ed.), *HMS Collingwood, 1844–48: From the Journals of Philip Horatio Townsend Somerville*, Pentland Press, Edinburgh, 1986.

Kaye Lamb, W. (ed.), *The Voyage of George Vancouver, 1791–1795*, Hakluyt Society, Cambridge, 1984.

Keeble, T.W., *Commercial Relations between British Overseas Territories and South America, 1806–1914*, London, Athlone Press, 1970.

Kennedy, W., *Hurrah for the Life of a Sailor!*, William Blackwood, Edinburgh, 1900.

King, P.P., *Narrative of the Surveying Voyages of His Majesty's Ships Adventure and Beagle between the Years 1826 and 1836: The First Expedition, 1826–1830*, London, 1839.

Lamb, J., *Preserving the Self in the South Seas, 1680–1840*, University of Chicago Press, Chicago, IL, 2001.

Lambert, A.D. (ed.), *Letters and Papers of Sir John Knox Laughton*, Navy Records Society, London, 2002.

———, *Admirals: The Men Who Made Britain Great*, Faber & Faber, London, 2007.

———, *The Challenge: Britain versus America in the Naval War of 1812*, Faber & Faber, London, 2012.

———, '"Now is Come a Darker Day": Britain, Venice and the Meaning of Seapower', in M. Taylor (ed.), *The Victorian Empire and Britain's Maritime World, 1837–1901: The Sea and Global History*, Palgrave Macmillan, Basingstoke, 2013, pp. 19–42.

Lambert, N., *Planning Armageddon*, Harvard University Press, Cambridge, MA, 2012.

Linklater, E., *The Voyage of the Challenger*, John Murray, London, 1972.

Long, D.F., *Nothing Too Daring: A Biography of Commodore David Porter 1783–1843*, US Naval Institute Press, Annapolis, MD, 1970.

Longley, P.A., *Virtual Voyages: Travel Writing and the Antipodes 1605–1837*, Anthem Press, London, 2010.

Lorimer, J. (ed.), *Sir Walter Ralegh's Discoverie of Guiana (1596)*, Hakluyt Society, London, 2006.

Loveman, D., *No Higher Law: American Foreign Policy and the Western Hemisphere since 1776*, University of North Carolina Press, Chapel Hill, NC, 2010.

Lowry, M., *The World of Aldus Manutius*, Oxford, 1979.

Lynch, J., *The Spanish–American Revolutions, 1808–1826*, W.W. Norton, New York, 1973.

Markham, A.H., *A Brief Memoir of Commodore J.G. Goodenough*, Portsmouth, 1877.

Marshall, P.J. & G. Williams, *The Great Map of Mankind: British Perceptions of the World in the Age of Enlightenment*, Dent & Sons, London, 1982.

Mayo, J., *British Merchants and Chilean Development, 1851–1886*, Westview, London, 1987.

Melville, H., 'Islands of the Pacific', *Putnam's Monthly Magazine* (August 1856), p. 156.
———, *Billy Budd and Other Stories*, ed. H. Beaver, London, 1967.
Merk, F., *The Oregon Question: Essays in Anglo-American Diplomacy and Politics*, Harvard University Press, Cambridge, MA, 1967.
Mitchell, A.L. & S. House, *David Douglas: Explorer and Botanist*, Aurum Press, London, 1999.
More, T., *Utopia*, tr. & ed. P. Turner, Penguin, London, 2003.
Morison, S.E., *'Old Bruin': Commodore Matthew C. Perry, 1794–1858*, Little, Brown, Boston, MA, 1967.
Moseley, H.N., *Notes by a Naturalist on HMS Challenger*, John Murray, London, 1892.
Navarro Mallebrera, R. & A.M. Navarro Escolano (eds), *Inventario de bienes de Jorge Juan y Santacilia*, Instituto de Estudios Juan Gil Albert-Caja de Ahorros del Mediterráneo, Alicante, 1988.
Nicholls, M. & P. Williams, *Sir Walter Raleigh: In Life and Legend*, Continuum, London, 2011.
Nietzsche, F., *The Use and Abuse of History*, tr. A. Collins, Bobbs-Merrill, Indianapolis, IN, 1949.
Norris, G. (ed.), *Buccaneer Explorer: William Dampier's Voyages*, Boydell Press, Woodbridge, 2005.
Novak, M.E., *Daniel Defoe, Master of Fictions: His Life and Ideas*, Oxford University Press, Oxford, 2001.
Osborne, R., H. Spong & T. Grover, *Armed Merchant Cruisers 1878–1945*, World Ship Society, Windsor, 2007.
Parker, H., *Herman Melville: A Biography, Volume I: 1819–1851*, Johns Hopkins University Press, Baltimore, MD, 1996.
———, *Herman Melville: A Biography, Volume II: 1851–1891*, Johns Hopkins University Press, Baltimore, MD, 2002.
Pedrick, M., *Moor Park: The Grosvenor Legacy*, Riverside Books, Rickmansworth, 1989.
Pocock, J.G.A., *The Discovery of Islands: Essays in British History*, Cambridge University Press, Cambridge, 2005.
Porter, D., *Journal of a Cruise to the Pacific Ocean by Captain David Porter in the United States Frigate Essex, in the years 1812, 1813, and 1814, Containing descriptions of the Cape de Verde Islands, Coasts of Brazil, Patagonia, Chile and of the Galapagos Islands*, 2 vols, Bradford and Inskip, Philadelphia, PA, 1815.
Rahe, P., *Montesquieu and the Logic of Liberty: War, Religion, Commerce, Climate, Terrain, Technology, Uneasiness of Mind, the Spirit of Political Vigilance, and the Foundations of the Modern Republic*, Yale University Press, New Haven, CT, 2009.
Rahn Phillips, C., *Six Galleons for the King of Spain: Imperial Defense in the Early Seventeenth Century*, Johns Hopkins University Press, Baltimore, MD, 1986.
Reinhartz, D., *The Cartographer and the Literati: Herman Moll and his Intellectual Circle*, Edwin Mellen Press, Lewiston, NY, 1997.

Rogers, W.A., *A Cruising Voyage Round the World; First to the South-Seas, thence to the East-Indies, and Homewards by the Cape of Good Hope. Begun in 1708, and Finish'd in 1711*, London, 1712.

Rozwadowski, H., *Fathoming the Ocean: The Discovery of the Deep Sea*, Belknap Press, Cambridge, MA, 2005.

Rushby, K., *Paradise: A History of the Idea that Rules the World*, Basic Books, New York, 2007.

Ruskin, J., *The Stones of Venice: The Foundations*, London, 1851.

Salzman, P., 'Narrative Contexts for Bacon's New Atlantis', in B. Price (ed.), *Francis Bacon's New Atlantis: New Interdisciplinary Essays*, Manchester University Press, Manchester, 2003.

Samson, J., *Imperial Benevolence: Making British Authority in the Pacific Islands*, University of Hawaii Press, Honolulu, HI, 1998.

———, 'Hero, Fool or Martyr? The Many Deaths of Commodore Goodenough', *Journal for Maritime Research* 10(1) (February 2008), pp. 1–22.

Samuel, P. (ed.), *Haklutus Posthumous or Purchas his Pilgrimes*, vol. II, MacLehose, Glasgow, 1905.

Schama, S., *The Embarrassment of Riches*, Collins, London, 1987.

Schouten, W., *Journal afte beschrijvinghe van der wonderlicke reyse*, Amsterdam, 1618.

Seeley, J.R., *The Expansion of England*, London, 1883.

Seller, J., *Atlas Maritimus, or the Sea Atlas*, London, 1675.

Severin, T., *Seeking Robinson Crusoe*, Macmillan, Basingstoke, 2002.

Sharp (ed.), A., *The Journal of Jacob Roggeveen*, Oxford University Press, Oxford, 1974.

Shelvocke, G., *A Voyage Round the World by Way of the Great South Sea Performed in the Years 1719, 20, 21, 22, in the Speedwell of London, of 24 Guns and 100 Men, (under His Majesty's Commission to Cruise on the Spaniards in the Late War with the Spanish Crown) till She was Cast Away on the Island of Juan Fernández, in May 1720; and was afterwards Continued in the Recovery, the Jesus Maria and Sacra Familia &c.*, Sennen, Innys, Osborn & Longman, London, 1726.

Shillibeer, J., *A Narrative of the Briton's Voyage to Pitcairn's Island*, Taunton, 1817.

Shulman, M.R., *Navalism and the Emergence of American Sea Power, 1882–1893*, US Naval Institute Press, Annapolis, MD, 1995.

Skottsberg, C., *The Natural History of Juan Fernández and Easter Island*, 3 vols, Almqvist & Wiskell, Uppsala, 1956.

Slocum, J., *Sailing Alone*, London, 1900.

Smith, B., *European Vision and the South Pacific, 1768–1850*, Clarendon Press, Oxford, 1960.

Souhami, D., *Selkirk's Island*, Weidenfeld & Nicholson, London, 2001.

Spate, O.H.K., *The Pacific since Magellan, Volume I: The Spanish Lake*, Australian National University, Canberra, 1979.

———, *The Pacific since Magellan, Volume II: Monopolists and Freebooters*, Australian National University, Canberra, 1983.

————, *The Pacific since Magellan, Volume III: Paradise Found and Lost*, Routledge, London, 1988.

Spedding, J., R.L. Ellis & D.D. Heath (eds), *The Works of Francis Bacon*, Longman, London, 14 vols, 1867–74.

Springer, H. (ed.), *America and the Sea: A Literary History*, Georgia University Press, Athens, GA, 1995.

Stackpole, E.A., *Whales and Destiny: The Rivalry between America, France, and Britain for Control of the Southern Whale Fishery, 1785–1825*, University of Massachusetts Press, Amherst, MA, 1972.

Starkey, D., *British Privateering Enterprise in the Eighteenth Century*, University of Exeter Press, Exeter, 1990.

Stevens, D., *The Royal Australian Navy*, Oxford University Press, Melbourne, 2001.

Stewart, C.S., *A Visit to the South Seas, in the US Ship Vincennes, During the Years 1829 and 1830*, Fisher, Son, & Jackson, London, 1832.

Stroud, D., *Capability Brown*, Country Life, London, 1950.

Sutcliffe, T., *Crusoiana; or Truth versus Fiction Elucidated in a History of the Islands of Juan Fernández*, Manchester, 1843.

————, *The Earthquake of Juan Fernández as it Occurred in the Year 1835*, Advertiser Office, Manchester, 1839.

Takahashi, D., D.H. Caldwell, I. Càceres, M. Calderón, A.D. Morrison, M.A. Saavedra & J. Tate, 'Excavation at Aguas Buenas, Robinson Crusoe Island, Chile, of a Gunpowder Magazine and the Supposed Campsite of Alexander Selkirk, together with an Account of Early Navigational Dividers', *Post-Medieval Archaeology* 41(2) (2007), pp. 27–304.

Thacker, C., '"O Tininan! O Juan-Fernández!" Rousseau's "Elysée" and Anson's Desert Islands', *Garden History* 5 (1977), pp. 41–7.

Thomas, P., *A True and Impartial Journal of a Voyage to the South Seas and Round the Globe in his Majesty's Ship the Centurion*, London, 1745.

Thurman, M.E., *The Naval Department of San Blas: New Spain's Bastion for Alta California and Nootka 1767 to 1798*, Clark, Glendale, CA, 1967.

Wallis, H. (ed.), *Carteret's Voyage Round the World: 1766–1769*, Hakluyt Society, Cambridge, 1965.

Walpole, F., *Four Years in the Pacific in Her Majesty's Ship Collingwood, from 1844 to 1848*, second edition, 2 vols, Richard Bentley, London, 1850.

Walter, R. & B. Robins, *Lord Anson's Voyage Round the World*, London, 1748.

Webster, C.K. (ed.), *Britain and the Independence of Latin America 1812–1830: Select Documents from the Foreign Office Archives*, Oxford University Press, Oxford, 1938.

Wernham, R.B., *Before the Armada: The Growth of English Foreign Policy, 1485–1588*, Jonathan Cape, London, 1966.

Wilkes, C., *Autobiography of Rear Admiral Charles Wilkes US Navy 1798–1877*, Naval Historical Centre, Washington, DC, 1978.

Williams, D.W. & J. Armstrong, 'An Appraisal of the Progress of the Steamship in the Nineteenth Century', in G. Harlaftis, S. Tenold &

J. Valadiso (eds), *The World's Key Industry: History and Economics of International Shipping*, Macmillan, Basingstoke, 2012, pp. 49–55.

Williams, G. (ed.), *Documents Relating to Anson's Voyage Round the World*, Navy Records Society, London, 1967.

——, *The Great South Sea: English Voyages and Encounters 1570–1750*, Yale University Press, New Haven, CT, 1997.

——, *The Prize of All the Oceans: The Triumph and Tragedy of Anson's Voyage Round the World*, HarperCollins, London, 1999.

Williamson, J.A. (ed.), *The Observations of Sir Richard Hawkins*, Argonaut Press, London, 1933.

Winfield, R., *British Warships in the Age of Sail, 1714–1792: Design, Construction, Careers and Fates*, Seaforth Publishing, Barnsley.

Woodward, R.L., *Robinson Crusoe's Island*, University of North Carolina Press, Chapel Hill, NC, 1969.

Wormell, D., *Sir John Seeley and the Uses of History*, Cambridge University Press, Cambridge, 1980.

Index

≈∞∞≈

Note: numbers in brackets preceded by *n* are endnote numbers.